MYSTERY OF THE NEW BABYLON

I can say with confidence that Troy Black has written a prophetic book for this hour. What struck me most is the way Troy weaves together biblical history, prophetic vision, and his own deeply personal journey into the voice of God. From the opening chapters, where he uncovers the hidden spiritual roots of Babylon in both Scripture and ancient culture, to the later sections where he shares vivid visions and words from the Holy Spirit concerning our own age, the book carries both urgency and authenticity.

Troy does not shy away from weighty themes—the influence of demonic systems, the lure of "secret knowledge," and even the internet as a modern expression of Babylon. Yet his aim is never fear-mongering. Instead, he consistently points the reader back to Christ, to the Word of God, and to the hope of Heaven's antidote. I especially appreciated the way he humbly submits every prophetic word to the test of Scripture and the discernment of the church. That posture alone sets him apart in a time when so many voices are clamoring for attention.

What makes this book powerful is not only its prophetic insights but also Troy's vulnerability. He shares about the wilderness seasons of his life, the humbling of his own ambitions, and the surprising way the Spirit drew him into visions, dreams, and prophetic evangelism. Because of this, the book doesn't just read like a commentary on Babylon; it reads like an invitation into intimacy with the Lord, even in the midst of cultural captivity.

I wholeheartedly recommend Mystery of the New Babylon. It is a sobering yet hope-filled guide for discerning the times, resisting deception, and anchoring our lives in the only One who can overcome Babylon—the Lord Jesus Christ.

Chris Garcia
Founder & President, Father's Glory International

Troy Black's new book offers a compelling exploration of the history and spirituality of Babylon and the Babylonian Empire, connecting ancient events to their profound significance in the book of Revelation. With clarity and insight from his own personal prophetic journey, Troy uncovers the deep symbolism behind Babylon, inviting readers to reflect on its relevance for today's world. This book is a must-read for anyone seeking a deeper understanding of biblical prophecy and the enduring spiritual lessons found in Scripture. It's a reminder of how we are meant to be a witness, proclaiming the truth of the gospel to the world, allowing His light to shine through us everywhere we go. By proclaiming the finished work of Jesus Christ, believers can, and will, see Babylon invaded by the Kingdom of God.

Rob Sanchez
LIVG Ministries

MYSTERY OF THE NEW BABYLON

DECODING THE END-TIMES AGENDA THREATENING YOUR WORLD

TROY BLACK

© Copyright 2026– Troy Black

All rights reserved. This book is protected by the copyright laws of the United States of America. This book may not be copied or reprinted for commercial gain or profit. The use of short quotations or occasional page copying for personal or group study is permitted and encouraged. Permission will be granted upon request. Scripture quotations marked ESV are taken from The Holy Bible, English Standard Version® (ESV®), copyright © 2001 by Crossway, a publishing ministry of Good News Publishers. Used by permission. All rights reserved. Scripture quotations marked KJV are taken from the King James Version. Scripture quotations marked NASB are taken from the NEW AMERICAN STANDARD BIBLE®, Copyright © 1960, 1962, 1963, 1968, 1971, 1972, 1973, 1975, 1977, 1995, 2020 by The Lockman Foundation. Used by permission. Scripture quotations marked CSB are taken from the Christian Standard Bible. Copyright © 2017 by Holman Bible Publishers. Used by permission. Christian Standard Bible®, and CSB® are federally registered trademarks of Holman Bible Publishers, all rights reserved. All emphasis within Scripture quotations is the author's own. Take note that the name satan and related names are not capitalized. We choose not to acknowledge him, even to the point of violating grammatical rules.

DESTINY IMAGE® PUBLISHERS, INC.
P.O. Box 310, Shippensburg, PA 17257-0310
"Publishing cutting-edge prophetic resources to supernaturally empower the body of Christ"

This book and all other Destiny Image and Destiny Image Fiction books are available at Christian bookstores and distributors worldwide.

For more information on foreign distributors, call 717-532-3040.
Reach us on the Internet: www.destinyimage.com.

ISBN 13 TP: 979-8-8815-0549-3
ISBN 13 eBook: 979-8-8815-0550-9

For Worldwide Distribution, Printed in the U.S.A.
2 3 4 5 6 7 8 / 30 29 28 27 26

CONTENTS

FOREWORD BY JOSEPH Z

In a time when the world is increasingly captivated by fleeting ideologies and shifting cultural narratives, it is vital for believers to anchor themselves in the unchanging truth of God's Word. As a prophetic voice, my lens for evaluating any work is simple: Does it align with Scripture, and does it magnify Jesus Christ? These are the benchmarks by which I measure the value of a book, and I am very pleased to say that Troy Black's *Mystery of the New Babylon* meets these standards with clarity and deep conviction.

Troy Black is not only a friend but a fellow laborer in the Kingdom of God. His heart for obedience to the Holy Spirit and his passion for sharing the gospel are evident in every page of this book. Troy's exploration and painstaking research are evident in the insights he lays out in this book, which prove to be timely and necessary, offering readers a biblical perspective on the spiritual forces at work in our world today. He does not shy away from addressing complex topics. Yet, he consistently points readers back to the ultimate truth: Jesus Christ is the answer to every question, the antidote to every deception, and the hope for every heart.

This book is more than an analysis of end-times prophecy; it is a call to action for the Church to rise, walk in the Spirit, and shine the light of Christ in the midst of darkness. Troy's insights are rooted in Scripture and guided by the Holy Spirit, making this work a valuable resource for anyone seeking to understand the times in which we live and how to navigate them as followers of Jesus.

Troy carries a humble approach to prophecy, as well as insightful views on the Word of God. His love for Jesus and his desire to reach the lost are only enhanced by his passion to share relevant prophetic insights about what is happening in the world around us. I am very impressed by his character and love for the truth. This book is packed with detailed insights and shocking information that will inform both casual readers and in-depth students.

As you read Mystery of the New Babylon, I encourage you to approach it in faith. Troy often says on his broadcast to take what is shared to the Lord in prayer, allowing the Holy Spirit to speak to your heart, and that is what should be applied here. What Troy delivers is not meant to scare you, but to prepare you, causing you to take your position in this last days prophetic army.

May this book inspire you to draw closer to Jesus, deepen your understanding of His Word, and step boldly into the purpose He has for your life!

Joseph Z
Author, Broadcaster, Prophetic Voice
JosephZ.Com

INTRODUCTION

There exists a dark mystery in the book of Revelation being uncovered before us today. I'm referring to the mystery of the new Babylon. An angelic warning of this shrouded city is revealed in Revelation 18:

> After this I saw another angel coming down from heaven, having great authority, and the earth was made bright with his glory. And he called out with a mighty voice, "Fallen, fallen is Babylon the great! She has become a dwelling place for demons, a haunt for every unclean spirit, a haunt for every unclean bird, a haunt for every unclean and detestable beast" (Revelation 18:1-2 ESV).

What is this place called Babylon? Is the angel in this Scripture passage referring to a physical city or location on earth? Does the Babylonian Empire many of us studied in history class somehow rise again in the last days? Or is there another mystery behind this warning? Could it be that Babylon returns in another form entirely—a new Babylon? More significantly, could it be that we are already living in the midst of this great empire?

On these pages, not only will we be searching out the truth behind this new Babylon being re-established in the earth today, but we will also uncover the dark, *secret knowledge* that made Babylon great.

> By wisdom a house is built, and by understanding it is established; and by knowledge the rooms are filled with all precious and pleasant riches (Proverbs 24:3-4 NASB).

The same principles used to construct a house and fill it with wealth can be used in a broader scale to build an empire. We see this aspect of Babylon in Revelation 18:3 (ESV) when it tells us: *"…the merchants of the earth have grown rich from the power of her luxurious living."*

As it was historically, the new Babylon is a nation of wealth, and there is a secret knowledge behind its treasures. I use the word *secret* because this knowledge is not obvious, but rather purposefully hidden from the world. It's a form of code. The knowledge (and wisdom) behind the building of this great nation actually feeds itself off of the fact that it is hidden. It relies on stealth in order to maintain its power.

To understand the secret knowledge behind the new Babylon, we must trace it back to its source, journeying to the beginnings of the ancient world. The same knowledge assembling the new Babylon was also behind the old, historical Babylon.

Is there really a secret knowledge (or code) that we can trace back to the origins of ancient Babylon? And if so, what is it? Could it even be that this secret knowledge has now infiltrated the modern church? Could it also be that God has given His church a spiritual antidote to this secret knowledge?

If this coded knowledge really does exist, is it possibly linked to the mark of the beast and the rise of the antichrist? Could all of this also be linked to the advancement of artificial intelligence and a one world government?

In this book, we explore answers to these questions. I will also share some of my own story of beginning to prophesy and my personal journey of discovering Heaven's antidote.

What does prophecy have to do with the new Babylon and the secret knowledge of our time? Everything. In fact, God's response to the many manifestations of Babylon found throughout Scripture nearly always involved the activation of His prophets. Nearly every time you see Babylon, you see prophets in its midst.

Could it be through prophetic revelation that God is bringing answers to the major questions in today's culture? Could it be that the answers are being entrusted to the church through the gift of prophecy?

In this book, I share segments of my journey into prophetic ministry. I will also release several prophetic words, so I want to be straightforward. If you need to, please take this as a type of disclaimer. The prophetic words I share are utterances from the Holy Spirit that I have heard during times of prayer and worship. I don't share prophecy under the guise of being a "mouth" of God. Instead, every word I share I am humbly submitting to the church under the guidelines of 1 Corinthians 14:29 (NASB) and 1 Thessalonians 5:19-22 (NASB):

> Have two or three prophets speak, and have the others pass judgment.

> Do not quench the Spirit, do not utterly reject prophecies, but examine everything; hold firmly to that which is good, abstain from every form of evil.

All true prophecy must be supported by or in agreement with Scripture, and so I submit the prophetic words in this book to you, the reader, to judge in accordance with the written Word and the voice of the Holy Spirit.

If prophecy counteracts the Bible, discard it. The same goes for any prophecies in this book. My heart is not to impress you but rather to simply be obedient. With that said, I also deeply understand my humanity. As the saying goes, "to err is human." However, when the Holy Spirit is involved, He can bypass our humanity and speak through us divine words of wisdom and knowledge. I do believe that is what I am sharing here.

However, prophecy still must be tested, and I encourage you to do just that. If something doesn't sit right with you, pray about it. The Holy Spirit may ask you to believe it. He may ask you to reject it. He may say it's not for you at this moment. That's okay. Be based in the Word, led by the Spirit, and encouraged and built up by prophecy—in that order.

The Days of Dreams and Visions

Ten years ago, I would never have written a book like this, but the Lord has been in many ways culling my ministry down to prophecy. He has been demonstrating to me the need for the prophetic utterances of the Holy Spirit and the impact prophecy can have on the church and the world.

I believe we are living in the days of dreams and visions. We are living in the days of the revelation of the deep things of God—the secret knowledge of Heaven. In this book, I not only share my personal experience of these things, but I also give you the opportunity to step into the stream of revelation for yourself.

Many thoughts may come to your mind when I say, "These are the days of dreams and visions and the deep things of God." You might balk, asking, "Really? What does the Bible say about that?" You might experience doubt, wondering if I can be trusted as an authority on this issue or not. You might leap for joy, getting ready for the experience of glory that potentially follows such a premise. Or, you might feel a weight on your shoulders, thinking that such things are meant for other, more spiritual people.

Whichever perspective you come with, I believe this book is for you. I believe you will experience the glory of God as you read it. His glory may appear differently to different people, and it will absolutely come with various purposes depending on where you are in your spiritual walk. Nonetheless, if you read this with the expectation, "If God is in this, He will do something," then His glory will come.

A Journey Into the Prophetic

It was July 2019 when it all started. For nearly eight years, I had struggled to build an online evangelistic ministry, focusing my time mostly on writing scripts for YouTube videos, filming videos, and also writing books on the side. I would also answer personal emails from people looking for hope or seeking answers. Every so often, I would speak at a small live event.

During those years, I learned what it meant to hear the voice of the Lord. I focused much of my time and energy toward just being with Jesus on a daily basis. Taking walks around our neighborhood, I prayed, sought the Lord, and sang songs of worship to my King. I wanted to be *with* Jesus, not just working for Him. I had lived through enough of those days when I felt no glory, no presence, and no power. I needed Him. I needed His presence, and I kept seeking Him with every moment I could.

As I spent time with the Lord, He began to drop ideas into my mind about new ways I could minister. He would give me sermon topics, insights into Scripture, and creative ways to illustrate spiritual truths. It was almost as if, while I sought Him, He did the work of the ministry for me.

I never wanted this way of life to change, or at least that's what I thought. What I didn't realize at the time was that deep down I felt like something was missing, and this longing within me would ultimately become the very thing fighting against my purpose. The desire I'm talking about is this: I wanted my ministry to grow. I wanted to reach more people for Jesus's sake, yes, but I also wanted it to grow to satisfy an unhealthy need within me—a need for people's approval and acceptance.

Looking back, I can now describe my feelings and thoughts much better than I could then. I wanted people to see that I had grown a ministry all on my own. I wanted people to think I had succeeded at something "great." Inside, I battled feelings of rejection, loneliness, and discontentment. I thought that a successful ministry would somehow fix these feelings of lack in my heart. It didn't.

In the summer of 2019, these feelings came to a head. I had poured my time, energy, and heart into the ministry, yet somehow it wasn't growing. It was actually shrinking. Every time I uploaded a video, I reached less and less people. Readers had once regularly bought my testimony book, but not anymore. I felt like God had somehow let me down. It was as if I had done my part, but He had failed on His end. I couldn't see then what He was planning.

I kept thinking back to the first two years of YouTube ministry. One of my videos, "Stop Worrying," had taken off—gone viral—and had reached more than a million people. This one video boosted the views across my entire channel. However, as that video fell out of the algorithm, my channel stopped growing. My ministry success waned, or so I thought. It was in the summer of 2019 when I believe I learned what success really is.

I had had enough. I was angry at God, furious that He would essentially let me fail. "If I've been listening to *Your* voice this whole time, doing what You asked me to do, why isn't this working?" Silence. Yet, when the Lord is silent, it's not that He isn't speaking. We often have something plugging up our ears. So, in my frustration, I kept waiting upon the Lord. Finally, He began to lay out a path I dreaded.

I remember where I was when He said it. It was July of 2019, and I was desperate for some good news. As I pulled up to a stoplight in my minivan, He began to speak. This is what He said, *If I asked you to run this ministry into the ground, would you do it?* I could not believe what I was hearing. My normal response would have been, "Yes, Lord," but this time I felt paralyzed with confusion.

"If I asked you to run this ministry into the ground...?" *What? Why would You ever want me to do that?* I couldn't understand it. What would the purpose be? Why would God give me a ministry just so I could run it into the ground and watch it utterly fail?

Looking back, I now have answers to my spiraling thoughts. I'm standing on the mountain and looking back into the valley. I'm not on the mountain because everything is perfect or because I'm claiming maturity. I'm on the mountain in the sense that now I can see the reasons for God's delay. I can see why He did what He did, and now I agree with Him that it was the best possible path for Him to lead me down. I can see the motives behind His actions.

The Holy Spirit desired to bring me into a season of dreams, visions, and the deep things of God, but first He had to address the Babylonian ways that had crept into my heart. I didn't know it, but I had swallowed the *secret knowledge* of the world and let it take root inside me. Before God could move me forward in His plan, He first had to set me free from spiritual captivity to the ways of the new Babylon.

For us to understand what the new Babylon is, we first must understand the history of Babylon and what Babylon represents in Scripture. The keys to unlocking the Babylonian code running today's world are found in the ancient texts.

1

WHO IS BABYLON?

I would ask the question *what* is Babylon, but Revelation 17 refers to Babylon as a female, a great prostitute, a wayward woman. So, we must ask an alternative question, *who* is Babylon? The Scripture personifies Babylon for a few reasons. First, it allows us to more easily recognize her when we see her. If we understand the characteristics of Babylon in a personal way, we can spot the effects of Babylon upon a culture. Second, the personification of Babylon helps us to clearly identify her ways within ourselves and warns us of the dangers of becoming like her.

So, what is she like? Revelation 17:3-5 (NASB) begins to reveal her personality:

> And he carried me away in the Spirit into a wilderness; and I saw a woman sitting on a scarlet beast, full of blasphemous names, having seven heads and ten horns. The woman was clothed in purple and scarlet, and adorned with gold, precious stones, and pearls, holding in her hand a gold cup full of abominations

> and of the unclean things of her sexual immorality, and on her forehead a name was written, a mystery: "BABYLON THE GREAT, THE MOTHER OF PROSTITUTES AND OF THE ABOMINATIONS OF THE EARTH."

Immediately, we see a prostitute beautifully clothed, but she herself is not necessarily beautiful. She flaunts the latest fashions and the big diamonds. She is also full of abominations—atrocities and obscenities, and she celebrates doing sexually immoral things. On top of this, she behaves like a mother, teaching her children to act just like her.

So if Babylon is a mysterious woman of the night, she must have at one point been born. To reason through why Babylon is the way she is, let us glance back in time to her conception. To discover the secrets of the new Babylon, we must dig into the historical and cultural accounts of this infamous empire.

The Great Whore

Babylon was not just another city. It was at one time the greatest city in the world, being the capital city in Babylonia, a city-state and cultural region in ancient Mesopotamia. This cultural region, located in the modern-day area between Baghdad in Southern Iraq and the Persian Gulf, has a rich history of being settled, conquered, and ruled by many different people groups.

When telling the story of a great person's life, legends are often mixed in, such as the widely spread myth of young George Washington and the cherry tree. The same could be said about Babylon. In her younger years, around 2650 BC, what would later be known as Babylonia was then the Sumerian Empire.

Perhaps the most famous writing about this time is the stone tablet-inscribed *Epic of Gilgamesh.* History knows Gilgamesh as the fifth king of Uruk, a city in southern Mesopotamia. Legends that would develop over the next several centuries after his death paint him as a super-human, almost god-like figure of a man.[1]

During the second half of the epic, Gilgamesh embarks on a journey to discover the secret to immortality. The answer to his quest is cleverly stated as: "Life, which you look for, you will never find. For when the gods created man, they let death be his share, and life withheld in their own hands."[2]

The latter of the two main versions of the epic, known as The Standard Babylonian version, opens by giving Gilgamesh the title: "He who saw the deep." The "deep" at least partially refers to the information or mysteries of life that Gilgamesh received from the immortal Utnapishtim.[3]

Although Utnapishtim[4] cannot grant Gilgamesh the secret to eternal life, he attempts to provide a workaround to the problem. First, he tells Gilgamesh to attempt to overcome the need for sleep. Second, he gives Gilgamesh the task of retrieving a plant from the bottom of the ocean that can supposedly reverse aging. Gilgamesh fails the first test and has the prize of the second test stolen away by a serpent. In the tale, he returns to Uruk, a wiser man.[5]

The mysteries, or "secret knowledge," Gilgamesh returned with include information about how to worship the gods, how to explain death, how to be a good ruler, and how to have a good life.

Stepping back into our time period for a moment, it sounds like Gilgamesh—or at least the people who wrote the stories about him after his death—was looking for answers to the same questions people continue to ask today. What happens after you die? Is there a higher being or a higher frame of existence? What does true success look like, and how do I get there? How do I achieve happiness?

One interesting fact about Utnapishtim is that his story was a multicultural counterpart to the biblical story of the flood. He was essentially a Noah character. Unlike Noah, who was tasked by God to create an ark, Utnapishtim is supposedly warned about the gods' plan to flood the earth by the Akkadian god Enki, also known in the Sumerian culture as Ea, the god of wisdom.[6] In Sumerian mythology, this Ea also happens to be the father of Marduk, the national god of Babylonia.[7]

So, a secret knowledge or "divine wisdom" actually predated the Babylonian Empire, and the "deity" of Babylon during the time of its height was the seed of wisdom itself. Another way of saying it: Babylon was built upon a "secret knowledge" handed down by the gods.[8]

Sumerian Rule

This is more true than most know, and we will get into that later. For now though, another example of the information-based progression that began to dominate the culture of Babylonia is the series of inventions that began to unfold.

There is no recorded mention of Babylon itself until around 2300 BC, but it existed prior to that as a settlement in Sumeria, a collection of city-states. The Sumerian people are credited by historians as having invented the potter's wheel, the sailboat, water-control systems, the seed plow, and bronze. They also made their contribution to the intellectual side of life, being known for having created prototype forms of writing, schools, legal codes, court systems, mathematical systems, and libraries. Literary work, music, and architectural advancements also blossomed, shaping the cultures that followed. With claims like that, it's no wonder ancient Mesopotamia is called the "cradle of civilization."[9]

Even though Babylon as a city had not yet risen to greatness, because of the importance and prominence it would one day hold—standing at a sort of peak in time among many of the world's cultures—all of the pre-Babylon, Sumerian culture and history are now nestled neatly under the title of *Babylonia* in many of today's history books. How nice would that be…to be so famous you were able to take credit for the accomplishments that came before you?

It was in the city-states of Sumeria where the great whore Babylon was first conceived. She grew up out of the Sumerian culture, adopting its technology, cultural heritage, and even gods.

Akkadian Rule

If Sumeria birthed Babylon, the Akkadian Empire could be considered her "adolescent years." Sargon the Great conquered the Sumerian people, setting himself up as ruler over the world's first true empire, which included all of Mesopotamia and much of the Middle East. Sargon constructed roads in his empire, implemented a postal system, and further developed irrigation. Despite these improvements however, he dealt with constant revolts by the Sumerian people. These revolts continued during the reign of Sargon's two sons and grandson.

Sargon's grandson, Naram-Sin proclaimed himself to be a god and all of Mesopotamia soon plunged into a dark age. During his successor's reign, the Akkadian Empire collapsed, a doom brought on by the combination of severe droughts, rebellions, and invasions.[10]

The thread weaving together Babylon's conception with her adolescence is the adoption of the culture. The Akkadians had mainly inhabited northern Mesopotamia, the Sumerians resided in the south, and their cultures were somewhat intermixed. When the Akkadians rose to power, instead of dominating the Sumerian culture, they appropriated and adapted it for their own. The cultural progression of the Sumerians continued to thrive throughout the Akkadian rule.[11] The same occurred in the next stage of young Babylon's life. Instead of the culture being erased, it morphed and grew, almost as if it were leading up to some climactic pinnacle.

Amorite Rule

Babylon fell under Amorite rule, and in 1792 BC, the famous Hammurabi became king. Thus began the combining of the city-states of Mesopotamia into one cohesive kingdom, which would officially become Babylonia.[12] At the center of it all sat the great whore, Babylon. As Hammurabi conquered people, he also greatly improved their way of life, ensuring less rebellions than his predecessors faced in the Akkadian Empire.

A Time of Various Rulings

After Hammurabi's death, the Babylonian empire declined. The Assyrian Empire began to grow separately and simultaneously, and Babylonia was conquered by the Kassites. Assyria, fighting for power with the Arameans and Chaldeans, gained and lost control of Babylonia a few times over the following several centuries. It was during this time period that Nebuchadnezzar I reigned (1119–1098 BC).[13]

Chaldean Rule

A few kings later, Babylon was finally officially established as the capital of Babylonia by the Chaldean leader Nabopolassar.

Nebuchadnezzar II, who is known in Scripture for demolishing Jerusalem and taking many Israelites into exile, was Nabopolassar's son.[14]

Persian Rule

In 539 BC, Cyrus the Great gained power over Babylonia, and Darius I ruled after him.[15] Both of these men play critical roles in the biblical narrative.

You may be asking, is there a point to this history lesson? The answer is yes. The historical and mythological accounts of Babylon both point to the same origin story: special knowledge. Babylon was able to grow into the greatest city on earth because of what she knew. But where did her knowledge first come from? For that answer, we must now look at the spiritual.

2

THE SPIRIT OF BABYLON

Let's rewind time for a minute. To fully understand who this woman Babylon is, we have briefly looked at her origin story, but now we need to go even further back. To truly know someone, we must know those who came before the person. Why? Because the forging of someone's personality and character relies heavily on what aspects they choose to inherit or reject from their ancestors. Many times the sins of the fathers are passed down.

This principle involves natural cause and effect, but it also incorporates a spiritual element. That's why the Bible speaks of generational curses and blessings—there's a very real, spiritual effect transferred when one generation chooses to accept and claim the same tendencies as the former.

So what was Babylon's spiritual heritage? Babylon has its roots in the story of the Tower of Babel. In fact, the Babylonians historically boasted about having descended from a race of giants, those labeled by Genesis chapter 6 as Nephilim. Nimrod, who according to Jewish and Christian tradition, initiated the building process of the Tower of Babel and is also commonly associated with the same race of giants.

Nimrod and the builders of the Tower of Babel were raising their voices against the God of Heaven, attempting to make God unnecessary, irrelevant, or powerless. In their pride, they tried to reach Heaven apart from God. Genesis 11:4-9 (NASB) reveals God's response:

> And they said, "Come, let's build ourselves a city, and a tower whose top will reach into heaven, and let's make a name for ourselves; otherwise we will be scattered abroad over the face of all the earth." Now the Lord came down to see the city and the tower which the men had built. And the Lord said, "Behold, they are one people, and they all have the same language. And this is what they have started to do, and now nothing which they plan to do will be impossible for them. Come, let Us go down and there confuse their language, so that they will not understand one another's speech." So the Lord scattered them abroad from there over the face of all the earth; and they stopped building the city. Therefore it was named Babel....

In this passage, God scatters the workers across the face of the earth through confusing their languages. Yet, this was a temporary solution. The same pride still arose through the Babylonian culture later on, and it still rises today.

Could there be a spiritual connection point between the pride of the builders and the pride of Babylon who descended from those who stayed in that same area? It seems likely, especially based on the boasts of Babylon.

History shows that the culture of Babylon attempted to associate its own advancements with a "divine knowledge" that existed before the great flood. This "divine knowledge" was the secrets of the gods that had helped to build society before everything was wiped out. This connection point was a source of pride for the Babylonians. It's as if they were saying, *the gods favor us, which makes us the greatest people group on earth.*[16]

Some people argue that the Jewish telling of the story of the flood and the history of the giants loses credibility due to the other historical sources from various ancient cultures that contain similar stories. But I believe the opposite is true. When a tragic event occurs, you don't just see one news station reporting it. Everyone talks about it because it really happened. The same is true with the flood narrative and the Nephilim.

Babylonia's own account of the flood and the giants lined up closely with the Jewish version. Instead of *nephilim,* they used the word *apkallus*. They believed the Apkallus to be semi-divine giants descended from divine beings and humans. Though these beings were destroyed by a great flood, their secret knowledge was passed on after the flood by another generation of Apkallus who existed later.[17] This sounds eerily similar to the biblical story of the giants.

This book is not dedicated to the study of the giants, though I will often reference them. If you are interested in the topic, I recommend Dr. Michael S. Heiser's book, *The Unseen Realm,* which delves deeply into the subject.

Here is where we come to the hinge on which I believe the Babylonian boast rested. In immersing themselves wholly into the "superior being" framework of their culture, the Babylonian kings themselves professed to have been the direct line from the Apkallus—the giants.[18] They relied so heavily on the "secret knowledge" of their time that it seemed to become part of them—whether literally true or not.

Instead of renouncing and rejecting their supposed heritage, they embraced it and even took up a boast about it. They appreciated and even celebrated their heritage as descendants of the giants and as people who knew better than God. (We will cover the demonic nature of the cultural practices of Babylon in the next chapter.)

The Origin of the Giants

Scripture describes the origin of the "giants" in Genesis 6:1-5 (NASB):

> Now it came about, when mankind began to multiply on the face of the land, and daughters were born to them, that the sons of God saw that the daughters of mankind were beautiful; and they took wives for themselves, whomever they chose. Then the Lord said, "My Spirit will not remain with man forever, because he is also flesh; nevertheless his days shall be 120 years." The Nephilim were on the earth in those days, and also afterward, when the sons of God came in to the daughters of mankind, and they bore children to them. Those were the mighty men who were of old, men of renown. Then the Lord saw that the wickedness of mankind was great on the earth, and that every intent of the thoughts of their hearts was only evil continually.

We also see references to the origin of these beings in Jude 6:6 (NASB) and 2 Peter 2:4-5 (NASB):

> And angels who did not keep their own domain but abandoned their proper dwelling place, these He has kept in eternal restraints under darkness for the judgment of the great day.

> For if God did not spare angels when they sinned, but cast them into hell and committed them to pits of darkness, held for judgment; and did not spare the ancient world, but protected Noah, a preacher of righteousness, with seven others, when He brought a flood upon the world of the ungodly.

Scholars debate the possible meaning of Genesis 6, and many rely on the extra-biblical texts such as the book of Enoch to further explain the history of the Nephilim. However, based simply on these passages alone, it is not an unfounded premise to say that these "men of renown" or "giants" had their origin in a strange spiritual act of disobedience to God.

This act of disobedience (angels laying with human women), was a gross distortion of God's intended plan for both angelic beings and humanity. It was a perversion, out of which was seemingly birthed a supernaturally infused lineage of beings with a track record for rebellion.

The Holy Spirit spoke a direct word to me about the Nephilim in December 2022, which I share here. Along with all the prophetic words I relate in this book, I implore you to not accept this solely on the basis of it being written down in this book. Instead, I am submitting this as a prophetic word that needs to be tested. Please compare all prophecy to the Scriptures to make sure that it lines up with the message and truth of the written Word. Please also pray and ask the Holy Spirit for confirmation if you need it before accepting a word as true.

I also would like to note: prophecy given under the New Covenant does not carry the same weight as Scripture. It is a word from God, yes. True prophecy is a word from our perfect God delivered through an imperfect, human vessel. Just because a word was spoken by the Holy Spirit does not guarantee that the hearer related or interpreted it perfectly.

With that being said, the prophecies shared in this book have been tested against the Scripture, and I am only submitting them after much prayer and confirmation. I do believe these are all words God is speaking to the church today.

The Shortcut Prophecy

In December 2022, as I was waiting upon the Lord, I heard the Holy Spirit say, *The spirit of the Nephilim never left the earth. There's a shadow of their effects at work all over—in any work that is born out of demonic influence.*

I later heard, *The spirit of the Nephilim is the spirit of the shortcut mentality. It is a shortcut to freedom—a shortcut to God's promise.*

We see this same idea propitiated in extra-biblical texts, such as the book of Enoch. It describes the fallen angels who procreated the Nephilim as exchanging knowledge about technology and magic arts for relations with human women. Now, though I am referencing Enoch as a cultural or historical source, I am not relying on it as a spiritual source of truth. Instead, I would point back to Scripture for better examples of this perverted "shortcut" mentality at work. I allude to Nimrod and the Tower of Babel.

Genesis 6:4 (NASB) says about the giants, *"The Nephilim were on the earth in those days, and also afterward…."* Presuming the before and after here speaks of the pre-flood and post-flood days, it's not unlikely that the Nephilim, or some form of them, walked the earth after the great flood. Some scholars believe that Nimrod himself, who ruled the pre-Babylonian kingdom of Babel, was one of these giants.

Several factors point to Nimrod potentially being of Nephilim blood. First, both Nimrod and the Nephilim are described using the Hebrew word *gibborim,* meaning "mighty men." Second, Micah 5:6 associates "the land of Nimrod" with the land of Assyria, which later became a vassal state of Babylon. Third, the historian Josephus, an extra-biblical source, described Nimrod as desiring to get revenge on God for destroying his forefathers through the flood.[19]

Thus, the reasoning behind the Tower of Babel itself was not merely a power play against the mighty hand of God, but also possibly a form of protection against another flood. If they could build the tower high enough, the waters of judgment would not be able to penetrate their earthly kingdom. They were essentially saying, "We don't need to do this God's way. We can make our own way that circumvents God and His judgment." They were attempting to build a shortcut to paradise, but it was a perverted path they took.

After Nimrod's death, his memory was exalted by some to a god-like state. Sources even exist linking both the *Epic of Gilgamesh* and the story of Hercules to the man Nimrod.[20]

It is clear that even back to its ancient roots, at its very core Babylon possessed pride and rebellion against the God of Heaven.

Another biblical link between Nimrod and the Nephilim can be uncovered in Numbers 13 when the Israelite spies return from spying out the Promised Land after their first journey through the wilderness.

> So they reported to him and said, "We came into the land where you sent us, and it certainly does flow with milk and honey, and this is its fruit. Nevertheless, the people who live in the land are strong, and the cities are fortified and very large. And indeed, we saw the descendants of Anak there! Amalek is living in the land of the Negev, the Hittites, the Jebusites, and the Amorites are living in the hill country, and the Canaanites are living by the sea and by the side of the Jordan" (Numbers 13:27-29 NASB).

The Israelites observe the descendants of Anak living in the land of Canaan. The Canaanites came from Canaan, son of Ham. Ham was Nimrod's grandfather (see Genesis 10:8).

As we continue to read, we see the direct connection between the sons of Anak and the Nephilim.

> So they brought a bad report of the land which they had spied out to the sons of Israel, saying, "The land through which we have gone to spy out is a land that devours its inhabitants; and all the people whom we saw in it are people of great stature. We also saw the ***Nephilim there (the sons of Anak are part of the Nephilim)***; and we were like grasshoppers in our own sight, and so we were in their sight" (Numbers 13:32-33 NASB).

Not only were all the people inhabiting the promised land apparently large in stature, verse 33 directly relates the Anakim with the Nephilim. Whether this means they were directly descended from the Nephilim, or whether it means they had a similar origin story, it does not much matter. Either way, they were both giant and rebellious, following the same pattern as their physical, or possibly spiritual, ancestors.

Nimrod goes on to found many cities, including the beginnings of the great Babylon:

> And the beginning of his kingdom was Babel, Erech, Accad, and Calneh, in the land of Shinar. From that land he went to Assyria, and built Nineveh, Rehoboth-Ir, Calah, and Resen between Nineveh and Calah; that is the great city (Genesis 10:10-12 NASB).

What was the prophetic word I heard about the Nephilim?

> *The spirit of the Nephilim never left the earth. There's a shadow of their effects at work all over—in any work that is born out of demonic influence. The spirit of the Nephilim is the spirit of the shortcut mentality. It is a shortcut to freedom—a shortcut to God's promise.*

Spiritually infused strength and stature would fuel and catapult forward a people's ability to dominate the earth. Could it be that Nimrod was able to build many cities in a pre-colonized world because of his and his kin's great strength? Could his giant-like nature have been the shortcut to domination? I believe so. Beyond that, I believe the same shortcut mentality is still at work today, and it is still being infused with "strength" by spiritual beings—demons.

We see this same shortcut pattern displayed, not just in the life of Nimrod, but also throughout the story of Scripture. It started with Adam and Eve being tempted by the serpent in the Garden of Eden. The serpent convinced Eve that the forbidden fruit would provide deeper wisdom that God had hidden from her (Genesis 3:5). Yet eating the fruit resulted in the Fall of humankind.

God promised Abraham and Sarah a son and heir, yet they both attempted to cut short the waiting period, producing an heir not according to God's plan. This son, Ishmael, created many problems not just for Abraham and Sarah, but also later for the sons of Israel (Genesis 16:12).

The Israelites themselves complained in the desert, speaking about rising up against Moses and returning to Egypt (Numbers 14:4). They also whined about the food and water resources (Exodus 15:24, 16:3), not trusting that the same God who delivered them from Egypt could provide for their wilderness trek. Their lack of trust and impatience led them into a shortcut mentality, and they suffered for it.

The devil tried the same tricks with Jesus when He fasted in the wilderness. In exchange for worship, satan promised to give Jesus the kingdoms of the earth that He came to redeem (Matthew 4:9), yet Jesus overcame this temptation to cut short God's plan. He submitted Himself to the will of the Father in every way, and this submission ultimately led Him to His death.

The story of humankind's rebellion against God eventually wraps up with God judging the kingdoms of the earth in the book of Revelation. Babylon the Great, the mother of prostitutes becomes the symbol for God's judgment on the systems that have rebelled against Him throughout the history of humanity.

The name Babylon comes from the Akkadian word *babilu,* which literally means "gate of god."[21] From what we know of Babylon in Scripture, it's obvious that this city is not a gate to the true city of God but rather an imitation and impostor, presenting a false system of godlikeness to humanity. This system started in the Garden of Eden with the serpent telling Eve she would be like God. It expanded until it reached a pinnacle at the Tower of Babel, and even after God's judgment through the confusing of languages, this system has reestablished itself time and time again in different forms. You could say that Babylon has manifested itself throughout Scripture and throughout history in many different ways but always with the same purpose.

The same way that the literal Babylon acts as a kind of nemesis or adversary to the land of Israel in the Old Testament, metaphorically speaking, the idea of Babylon immortally acts as an adversary against God's system on earth.[22] In short, *Babylon* is used by God as a descriptive word for the spiritual force that utilizes the cultures of earth to raise itself up against Him. The same way that Nimrod began to build a tower to thwart God, humanity is constantly building "towers" of many different natures to fulfill the same purpose. Revelation tells us that when God wants to reference the climax of humankind's rebellion against Him, He uses the word *Babylon*.

From this, it is not injudicious to say that the same spirits that were acting behind the building of the original tower of Babel are still acting today to try to supersede and supplant God as the true Ruler of earth. These spirits are what I'm calling *the spirit of the Nephilim*.

Look at John's reaction to hearing about Babylon the Great, the Mother of Prostitutes in Revelation 17:6 (NASB):

> And I saw the woman drunk with the blood of the saints, and with the blood of the witnesses of Jesus. When I saw her, I wondered greatly.

The angel obviously notices John's bewilderment and proceeds to offer an explanation:

> And the angel said to me, "Why do you wonder? I will tell you the mystery of the woman and of the beast that carries her, which has the seven heads and the ten horns" (Revelation 17:7 NASB).

There is a mystery surrounding the great prostitute involving both a historical explanation and a spiritual one. In Revelation 17:9-10,15,18 (NASB) he says:

> Here is the mind which has wisdom. The seven heads are seven mountains upon which the woman sits, and they are seven kings.... The waters which you saw where the prostitute sits are peoples and multitudes, and nations and languages. ...The woman whom you saw is the great city, which reigns over the kings of the earth.

One of the major characteristics of the prostitute is her influence over humanity. She sits upon the seven mountains and the seven kings. She sits among the waters of the peoples of the earth. She is then identified as the great city which reigns over the kings of the earth. This city has already been labeled. It is Babylon.

Not only does she exist historically as a city of influence; she also exists as a system of influence. The seven kings can represent seven kingdoms that have risen to power throughout history; yet, the seven mountains can themselves be representative of seven different major spheres of society in general. We see further implications of this in verse 15. The waters are not limited to specific nations or people groups or times in history.

Instead, they include all peoples, all multitudes, and all nations and languages. She is a city that reigns over many nationalities despite their autonomy to each other. That's because she is a spiritual city that transcends time and location, and spiritual entities are governed and ruled in the spiritual world by spiritual beings.

The system God calls Babylon in Scripture is an evil system that has existed in the spiritual world since the fall of Lucifer. It is satan's system through which he is and always has been attempting to gain control of the kingdoms and peoples of the earth.

The Dominion Prerogative

When satan was cast out of Heaven, he was temporarily judged for his rebellion against God, and that judgment involved the loss of responsibility and authority. Lucifer was unsatisfied with his role as a guardian cherub (see Ezekiel 28:14), so he set his sights infinitely higher and began to covet God's own authority and dominion. Let us examine the description of Lucifer's fall in Isaiah 14:12-14 (NASB):

> How you have fallen from heaven, you star of the morning, son of the dawn! You have been cut down to the earth, you who defeated the nations! But you said in your heart, "I will ascend to heaven; I will raise my throne above the stars of God, and I will sit on the mount of assembly in the recesses of the north. I will ascend above the heights of the clouds; I will make myself like the Most High."

Lucifer desired ascension—to rise above God's own rule and establish his own heavenly kingdom. Every aspect of his thoughts here are reflected in the construction of the Tower of Babel. The builders said, "Let's build ourselves a city, and a tower whose top will reach into heaven, and let's make a name for ourselves." We also see Lucifer's plan reflected in the prostitute's influence in Revelation 17, *"The seven heads are seven mountains upon which the woman sits."* Lucifer sought to set himself upon the mount of assembly—the highest point. In ancient cultures, mountains were commonly believed to be the places where the "gods" lived and ruled from.[23] He meant to rise to the top of the mountain—the pinnacle of God's dwelling place—and exercise dominion like God.

Here's where Isaiah 14 gets interesting. This prophecy is not solely about satan. It simultaneously describes two beings—one spiritual and one physical. It metaphorically refers to Lucifer's ambitions while also literally referring to the ambitions of the then-current king of Babylon. Isaiah 14:4 says, *"you will take up this taunt against the king of Babylon...."*

So we see that this passage draws a direct parallel between the king of ancient Babylon and his historical dominion and the prince of the air, satan, and his desired spiritual dominion.[24]

This same Babylon—the spiritual system set up against God's dominion—is the one that reaches its pinnacle of influence in Revelation 17. No matter what form the New Babylon takes, which is a mystery we are still going to uncover, we can know that satan is the ultimate ruler of that New Babylon. His desire is the same as it always was: to rise above and take dominion. Since he was unable to exalt himself to the mountain of God in Heaven, he now attempts to use his spiritual systems of influence to exalt himself to rulership over the mountains of society.

Dominion by Force

Along with the continued desire for dominion comes a fight. Through the historical account of the Scripture, a constant struggle existed between two entities: those descended from the serpent and those descended from Eve. God declares this to the serpent in Genesis 3:15 (NASB), saying:

> And I will make enemies of you and the woman, and of your offspring and her Descendant; He shall bruise you on the head, and you shall bruise Him on the heel.

What seemingly started as a scuffle in the Garden was quickly unmasked to reveal its true nature as a cosmic battle between light and darkness—good and evil—those of the seed of God and those of the seed of satan. God promises Joshua in Joshua 1:3 (NASB):

> Every place on which the sole of your foot steps, I have given it to you, just as I spoke to Moses.

The "problem" or hurdle that comes with this promise is that some of the places Joshua went were already occupied, and he had to fight to get what was already his. The occupants in this case were of divine origin. We've already read in Numbers about the spies saying, *"We also saw the Nephilim there."* Joshua's fight to take the Promised Land was a continuation of the fight that started in the Garden between the woman and the serpent—a fight for dominion.

These occupants were not merely following the desires of their father (what Jesus points out about the Pharisees in John 8:44), but they were literally descended from corrupt spiritual beings who rebelled in like kind to Lucifer. The Nephilim were a physical force on earth, planted by the spiritual entities of darkness, bent on carrying out the will of the evil one.

This war between the "sons of God" and the true sons and daughters of God is perpetuated throughout the Bible (see Genesis 6:1-4). After the "sons of God" bore offspring, God sends a flood to wipe out all those who do evil on the earth, saving the one righteous family that remained. Under orders from God, Joshua leads the children of Israel into the Promised Land with the goal of destroying the pagan nations (and the race of giants) that resided there. Because the job was incomplete, God anoints a shepherd boy named David to be king over His people, and David rises to popularity by slaying a giant. He and his mighty men go on to slay many giants that remained in the land (see 2 Samuel 21).

Finally, when Jesus comes to earth, He begins to drive out the spiritual forces that occupied dominion over the people of Israel. While freeing a woman from a demon in Luke 13:16 (NASB), He describes her as, *"a daughter of Abraham...whom Satan has bound for eighteen long years."* In one sense, she was a daughter of God suffering under the dominion of darkness.

You might say, people aren't fighting giants today. But we've already read Revelation 17:6 (NASB), which says, *"And I saw the woman drunk with the blood of the saints, and with the blood of the witnesses of Jesus...."*

Just because the war for dominion is not always a physical one does not mean that it won't become physical again. In many places around the world, the persecution described in Revelation is already happening to the church. As the end draws nearer, the physical manifestations of this war will increase in many ways (as described in Revelation).

However, let us not lose sight of the fact that there is also a much greater fight occurring in the spiritual world, and this fight has been perpetuated throughout history and will be continued until the end of time when God's angel permanently throws satan into the pit of fire. The fight I'm referring to is the fight for dominion over people's lives—the fight for control over the will of humanity. The physical is tied to the spiritual.

However, the physical ramifications of this war are more easily seen in the stories of history. Looking strictly at the Old Testament, we see that God's people come out of Egypt with a mandate to follow the ways of God (spiritual) and to subsequently wipe out the remnants of the Nephilim upon the earth (physical).

In Deuteronomy, while preparing them to enter the Promised Land, God decrees a series of blessings upon His people if they follow His commands along with a series of curses upon the breaking of His commands. In Deuteronomy 28:15 (NASB), He declares:

> But it shall come about, if you do not obey the Lord your God, to be careful to follow all His commandments and His statutes which I am commanding you today, that all these curses will come upon you and overtake you.

In Deuteronomy 28 verses 25, 41, and 64 (NASB) we see one of the curses listed includes physical domination:

> The Lord will cause you to be defeated by your enemies; you will go out one way against them, but you will flee seven ways from their presence....
>
> You will father sons and daughters but they will not remain yours, because they will go into captivity.
>
> Furthermore, the Lord will scatter you among all the peoples, from one end of the earth to the other; and

> there you will serve other gods, made of wood and stone, which you and your fathers have not known.

Both Assyria and Babylon (along with other nations) take part in the fulfilling of this prophecy as the children of Israel reject God's truths and are led by their own unrighteous desires. Yet, Babylon remains one of the greatest examples of the prophetic fulfillment of Deuteronomy 28.

Nearly 1,000 years later, Jeremiah relates a more specific prophecy concerning the judgment of God through the nation of Babylon.[25]

Jeremiah tells us:

> Therefore this is what the Lord of armies says: "Because you have not obeyed My words, behold, I will send and take all the families of the north," declares the Lord, "and I will send to Nebuchadnezzar king of Babylon, My servant, and will bring them against this land and against its inhabitants and against all these surrounding nations; and I will completely destroy them and make them an object of horror and hissing, and an everlasting place of ruins. Moreover, I will eliminate from them the voice of jubilation and the voice of joy, the voice of the groom and the voice of the bride, the sound of the millstones and the light of the lamp. This entire land will be a place of ruins and an object of horror, and these nations will serve the king of Babylon for seventy years" (Jeremiah 25:8-11 NASB).

Fulfillment of this prophecy begins around 600 BC when King Nebuchadnezzar wages war against Jerusalem, taking captive Belteshazzar (Daniel), Shadrach, Meshach, and

Abednego along with a host of other young Israelites. This deportation to Babylon is followed by two others.[26]

Here is where the sovereign plan of the Lord comes into play. Babylon could have completely destroyed Jerusalem and removed God's people completely from the face of the earth, but God would not allow that to happen. Instead, He purposed that they would be taken into captivity for a time—70 years—until they cried out to the Lord and returned to Him in their hearts (see Daniel 9). Would the devil have loved to simply destroy the nation of Israel? Sure. But God's hand was upon this season of punishment and discipline. He only allowed their enemies to go so far.

Yet, we see that because of the physical dominion that took place, the opportunity for a spiritual dominion also occurred.

> In the third year of the reign of Jehoiakim king of Judah, Nebuchadnezzar king of Babylon came to Jerusalem and besieged it. And the Lord handed Jehoiakim king of Judah over to him, along with some of the vessels of the house of God; and he brought them to the land of Shinar, to the house of his god, and he brought the vessels into the treasury of his god (Daniel 1:1-2 NASB).

The vessels of God's house were brought to the land of Shinar, where the Tower of Babel had been constructed. These vessels were repurposed to no longer serve the God of Israel, but now to serve to gods of Babylon. Yet, we see that these were not the only vessels being repurposed.

Nebuchadnezzar knew what successfully displacing a people group involved. Instead of just placing the intelligent youth into service in his kingdom, he first had their brains rewired.

He forced them into a reeducation process, meant to do one thing: turn them into Babylonians.

> ...he ordered Ashpenaz to teach them the literature and language of the Chaldeans. The king also allotted for them a daily ration from the king's choice food and from the wine which he drank, and ordered that they be educated for three years, at the end of which they were to enter the king's personal service (Daniel 1:4-5 NASB).

Because of how well-known this story is, I'm not going to dive deeply into the details. You can read the full story for yourself in the book of Daniel. Instead, I want to simply point out the connection between the physical dominion and the spiritual one. Daniel and his friends (along with other youth) were physically taken into Babylon by force, and then they endured an attempted spiritual captivity, worked upon them through philosophy, education, and the pressures of culture.

The Secret Knowledge of Babylon

These same strategies are occurring today. The same spirit behind the cultural war waged against Daniel is also at work today, waging war against the youth (along with everyone) within the church. The specific strategies of this spiritual attack will become more clear as we begin to uncover the mystery of the New Babylon in the following chapters.

If the enemy can't take you out, he will take you captive through the philosophy of his kingdom—what I call the *secret knowledge of Babylon*.

This "secret knowledge" does not necessarily always look like a satanic agenda or a demonic ideology. Sometime it presents itself simply as an idea that goes against the nature or voice of God. For example, what knowledge was David presented with upon facing Goliath? First, he heard the shouting and mocking from the giant. This I would label the direct voice of the enemy.

Second, King Saul told David he needed to wear the king's armor to stand a chance against the enemy. This was a more subtle version of the secret knowledge I'm talking about, but it still falls into the same category. For David to wear that armor would not have been a shortcut to victory, it would have been a fast track to defeat. Setting aside the common sense, intelligent, and experience-based perspective, David instead held onto a deep-rooted trust in the nature and nearness of God. It was his knowing of the true God that gave David an uncommon, yet better perspective. He had Heaven's perspective, and it fueled him to take on a giant with little more than God Himself to help him.

It wasn't just the giant's taunts that tried to hinder David. It was also the king's suggestions. The kind of secret knowledge that Babylon offers can come in many forms.

Abram waiting for the promised son and heir is another good example. God spoke, essentially promising him a miracle, and yet the knowledge of how reproduction and the human body works came to tell Abraham that he would need to take matters into his own hands. So, when Sarah offered Abraham her maidservant as an alternate option through whom a son could come, Abraham may have tried connecting the dots in his mind, saying, "Perhaps this is what God meant." Yet, he knew deep down it's not what God said. Ishmael was birthed out of the shortcut mentality. It's the idea that says, "I know too much to believe God. Perhaps I need to help Him fulfill this promise." How often do we fight our battles from this perspective?

God begins to give us a framework for Heaven's secret knowledge in Isaiah 55:8-9 (NASB) when He says:

> For My thoughts are not your thoughts, nor are your ways My ways, declares the Lord. For as the heavens are higher than the earth, so are My ways higher than your ways and My thoughts than your thoughts.

What is the antithesis to God's perspective here? Our thoughts. Oftentimes, the battle is fought and won in the thoughts that drive us. There are times when we must choose between what we know and what God has said. Our natural way of doing things does not always line up with His. Receiving Heaven's secret knowledge starts with humility—with admitting that we need His help.

As I end this chapter, I share this brief prophetic word I heard while studying Abraham's story. Many people could ask a similar question to the one Abraham might have asked at one point, saying, "It's been 25 years and why am I still doing nothing in regard to the promise?"

I heard the Lord say: *You're not doing nothing. You're waiting, and waiting is something. Wait in faith and you will grow in faith.*

It's better to receive a slow fulfillment than a distorted one. The shortcut looks inviting at times, but it ends in deformity. Keep standing on the Word of Truth. Keep trusting in the One who spoke. He is faithful to fulfill His word to you.

3

THE CULTURE OF BABYLON

Looking into the book of Revelation, we have discussed the spiritual roots of this promiscuous lady called Babylon. The spirit behind the person helps to determine her origin and makeup. Yet, to more fully understand what the New Babylon is today, we must also study Babylon's culture. Personality and habits paint a fuller picture of who a person truly is—even more than their history. So, what was Babylon like? How does the culture of Babylon still manifest on earth today?

When spiritual forces of darkness infiltrate a society, they shape its culture to reflect their own. Could it be that the culture of Babylon is the culture of the demonic? And if so, could this be the key to the rebirth of this great empire in the modern world? We can assume that the literal ancient nation named Babylon will not rise again, yet Revelation warns us of a prostitute called Babylon who rules the kingdoms of the earth. This prostitute may rise, not so much in title, but in form. In many ways, she is already here, and it's through her personality—her culture—that she takes influence over the nations of the earth.

Am I saying that the Babylon of Revelation 17 is no more than a cultural movement? No. I believe Babylon will rise again in specific, identifiable ways—one of which we uncover through a prophetic vision later in this book. However, Babylon is never removed from its cultural markers. To recognize Babylon in her many forms, we must understand her culture. We will briefly examine Babylon's influences, gateways, walls, religion, intelligence, and philosophy.

Babylon's Influences

Long before Babylon existed, the land was divided between Sumer and Akkad. Studying the cultural aspects of the historical city of Babylon, you find a culmination of societal movements that had already been developing for centuries. Babylon eventually became the central commercial and political city in Mesopotamia, but Babylonia as a region predates the city itself. When many people talk about the culture of Babylon, they are really referring to the cultural impact of that entire area and time in history, reaching all the way back to 4000 BC.[27]

Instead of one people group developing over time, Babylonia became the merging of many peoples, many practices, and many religious beliefs. One good term that describes Babylon culture is the term *melting pot*. Just like ingredients mixed to form a famous recognizable soup, Babylonia is known by her many cultural influences just as much as her history.

Babylon's Gateway

To be introduced to Babylon means to be engulfed into her culture. Every relationship starts with an introduction. The kings of the earth in Revelation 17 had to at one point be introduced to the Great City. The historical Babylon also had a point of introduction—her gateway.

For a culture to shift, it must pass from one practice to another, from one way of thinking to another, or from one place to another. The critical point of passage is the gateway: the opening or frame through which access is gained. Port cities or major cities are often called the gateways to nations. Low-risk drugs are often called gateway drugs leading to more dangerous substances. Similarly, the ancient city of Babylon had gateways, and the New Babylon has her own gateways today.

The Ishtar Gate

German archaeologist Robert Koldewey undertook excavations in the location of ancient Babylon in the late 1800s and early 1900s. These archeological digs led to the discovery of what is possibly King Nebuchadnezzar II's most celebrated construction: The Ishtar Gate.[28]

To enter the inner city of ancient Babylon, one passed through this bright-blue, glazed gateway painted with the images of Ishtar, Adad, and Marduk.[29] The Processional Way was a half-mile walkway between the outer walls and the inner city, and it led up to the Ishtar Gate. Babylonians featured this beautiful, garnished walkway in a pagan ceremony at the start of the New Year.[30] During this celebratory parade, statues of the deities passed through the gate and were displayed along the path of the Processional Way.[31]

The Ishtar Gate itself, like many of the gates of ancient Babylon, was named after a deity. We will discuss the significance of this specific deity in a later chapter.

The Temple Gate

Every day in Babylon started with the same ritual. A "waking of the temple" would take place directly before the temple gate was opened. Then the sun would rise. Similarly, the temple gate would later be closed, signifying the end of the day. The temple gates were directly connected to the start and end of each day in Babylon.[32]

These temple gates are still being opened and closed ritualistically today, and they are being opened by many people around the world who partake in the culture of the New Babylon—whether they realize it or not.

Babylon's Walls

King Hammurabi, whom we will look at in detail, was the first to construct walls around the full city of Babylon. King Nebuchadnezzar II added to the city's defense by building three rings of walls around the city. These walls stood at 40 feet, and Herodotus, a Greek historian, told tales of chariot races being held along the tops of the walls due to their incredible thickness.[33]

Babylon's Religion

Unlike many cultures in the modern world, the power in ancient cultures was often split between politics (usually in the form of a monarchy) and religion. In many cultures, the religious influences were either the same or greater than the political ones. Babylon's system of government followed this same structure.

The two reigning forces were the crown and the temple. The scope of religion's influence was seen during the Assyrian rule of Babylon, when even foreign kings presiding over the people paid homage to the deities and temples of Babylon in an attempt to legitimize their authority.[34] Because of the weight religion carried, it intertwined itself into much of the cultural advances Babylon made in other societal arenas. Breakthroughs in literature and science were happening, but they were often happening in the temples. The natural, intellectual work of the time could not be separated from a spiritual framework.[35]

Temple worship included food and drink offerings, prayers, songs, and even prostitution and other strange sexual practices.[36]

The spiritual lens of the Babylonians pervaded not just their city life, but also their home life. The gods were found in the temples, but they also resided in the homes. Deities like Marduk, the chief patron god of Babylon, would be found in statue form at the local temple. Marduk's temple is believed to have been a ziggurat, which we will discuss the importance of later. Smaller, more personal deities supposedly existed at the family shrines in the people's houses. These statues weren't simply considered decorations either. Believing them to be the actual gods themselves, people would treat them as if they were really there, adorning them with ornaments and even going so far as to bring them food and drinks at mealtimes.[37]

Babylon's Intelligence

For its time, Babylon was the cultural epicenter of intellectual thought in the ancient Mesopotamian world. They stretched the bounds of scientific study and research. They compounded knowledge more than any previous culture. They even built libraries to house their discoveries. One of Babylon's most famous intellectual accomplishments is Hammurabi's Code of Law, which we discuss later.

Unlike much of the modern academic community, the learning that took place in Babylon was deeply connected to religious activity. The science experiments occurred within or connected to the temples. The writing of literature and research happened within the temples. The temples themselves often were the libraries. In fact, much of the cultural preservation over the centuries can be attributed to the sacred view of their religious system.

Babylon's Philosophy

The social philosophy of Babylon may be the most shocking when cross-referenced with philosophical perspectives of other ancient cultures. Now, compared to today's beliefs, ancient philosophy makes little sense to most people. That's because little about ancient society could be considered "fair." Equality was an unheard of concept. Yet, Babylon differed from its ancient counterparts in that it actually promoted a code of fairness.

Their legal system, furthered greatly by Hammurabi, considered the social and economic classes of those under judgment. Laws were even created to help prevent the upper classes from escaping punishment through bribery.[38] If one word could be used to describe their cultural philosophy, it could possibly be "fairness."

Babylon Resurrected

We have looked at major facets of Babylon's ancient culture to set up a base for understanding the modern-day Babylon. When we revisit Babylon's culture in a later chapter, I draw parallels to its modern-day manifestation. I use the word *manifestation* because that is exactly what I believe is happening throughout history. The ancient city of Babylon may not specifically resurrect, yet Babylon as a metaphor for a system or culture that fights against God and His ways will absolutely continue to resurrect, as it has many times before.

"Babylon as Metaphor" is an excerpt from *The Encyclopedia of Christian Civilization*, in which Ron Bigalke writes:

> ***The city [Babylon] is both a prophecy and type of a religious system destroyed by God.***
>
> ***...it is an evident counterfeit of God's eternal city. The opposition to the rule of God by world powers or the exile of God's people from the land of blessing is conveyed properly through the metaphor of Babylon. The city of Babylon was the adversary of the Jews in the Old Testament. Babylon was a code name for Rome near the end of the 1st century.***

In Scripture, Babylon both *was* an ancient city and *is* a constant metaphor for systematic opposition against God's rule and ways. So, when Revelation 17 calls Babylon a whore, it expresses the ongoing "reincarnation" of this system which will continue until the end of time and God judges the nations in righteousness.

The whore of Babylon had her conception in ancient Sumer. She experienced the shock of birth as the Akkadians conquered and then lost power over the region. She grew up and matured during the Babylonian Empire, reaching the height of her beauty during the rule of famous kings like Hammurabi. Then, she grew old and forgotten as her kingdom dwindled. Eventually, she died off, yet not forever. She returned. She resurrected. She would resurrect time and time again, every time taking on another form.

Babylon is a nation, a city, a region, and more than that, she is a culture that has affected and in some ways dominated the entire world. How is this possible? How does a culture resurrect? It must be more than just a culture bound by a people group or a location on earth. Yes, Babylon is more than that. She is the culture of the demonic. A spiritual culture emanating from another realm constantly feeds her pervasiveness on earth. Until the devil and his fallen angels stop fighting, she will continue rising, and they will not stop until the end has come.

So, what is the New Babylon and how is it dominating not one, but nearly all of the societies in the world today? My own journey into this topic started with a vision and a prophetic word from God. So, as strange as it may seem, let's start there.

4
THE STRANGE VISION

As I mentioned, some of the basis for this book are the prophetic words God has given me. One of the ways He speaks to me is through visions. These are pictures and sometimes "reels of film" that play out in my mind. I have a good imagination and I understand that sometimes our brains just imagine odd things. However, our imaginations are also a way through which God can speak to us.

If that last sentence scares you, there is good reason. Ezekiel 13:2 (CSB) includes a direct warning against prophesying out of imagination that you've probably heard:

> Son of man, prophesy against the prophets of Israel who are prophesying. Say to those who prophesy out of their own imagination, "Hear the word of the Lord!"

This is the Christian Standard Bible translation of this verse, and the first thought after reading it might be, *See, prophecy and imagination should never go together.* Yet it's vital to understand the full meaning of the verse. Oftentimes translators will use a portion of the Hebrew word that they believe best correlates to the modern-day idea of what is being communicated; yet, Hebrew words often held more than one meaning. To fully understand the intent of the author, the Hebrew here is needed. The correct definition for the word translated *imagination* from Hebrew is "the heart, the feelings, the will, the intellect, centre."[39] The following are a few other biblical translations of Ezekiel 13:2 that help to paint a fuller picture:

- *who prophesy from their own hearts* (English Standard Version)
- *who prophesy from their own inspiration* (New American Standard Bible)
- *who preach messages that come from their own imagination* (Contemporary English Version)
- *inventing their own prophecies* (New Living Translation)

Do you see the problem? God did not condemn the use of imagination. He condemned pretend prophecy. God can speak to our ears. He can speak to our hearts. He can speak to our minds. Yet, it's when we take a message of our own hearts and attempt to put it in His mouth that we get into trouble. The big question we are left with: *Is what I'm hearing or seeing truly a message from God or not?* Anyone who has the fear of the Lord would dread putting words in God's mouth.

So, how do we know for certain that something is from God and not simply a vain imagination (or worse, a demonic influence)? Here's the short answer: the glory of the Lord follows His word. He backs up His words with His power. God will bring confirming evidence to let you know when He is speaking or when He has spoken. I will dedicate more time to defending this idea biblically as we move forward, yet I can share a brief story here that should help. Later in this book, I dive into the theological reasons for these assertions.

The Strange Commission

It was summer of 2019. That shocking question kept looming in my mind: "If I asked you to run this ministry into the ground, would you do it?" I thought, *Is God really wanting me to run this ministry into the ground? Surely that's not what He's asking me to do. What kind of good plan is that?* I battled these restless thoughts.

Eventually, the day came when God gave me another specific commission. As I prayed and waited upon the Lord about His strange advice, He added the phrase, "*Learn to enjoy the sand.*" As I heard it, I began to imagine a picture in my mind of the Israelites in the wilderness. I thought about the grainy dust getting caught in between their toes as they tromped through the desert. I imagined myself looking around to see nothing but hills of sand in every direction.

Now, I doubt my mental picture of the desert correctly resembled what the Israelites actually saw, but that's not the point. I faced a dilemma of will. God told me to learn to enjoy the sand, but how is that possible? Could a person really learn to enjoy a wilderness season like the one the Israelites walked through? I knew I had a choice to make. I was either going to believe God or not.

If I was in a God-ordained wilderness season, then that meant there must be a promised land at the end of the journey. Two tests sat before me. First, was I willing to trust God enough to wait for the promised land? Second, was I willing to believe that I could find joy on the path to the promised land?

I ended up telling God, "Yes. Even if this ministry runs into the ground and not one person is left watching or following it, as long as You are with me I will do it. I don't understand it, but I don't have to. I just want to walk with You wherever You are going."

It was during that same period of time when I wrote *Stop Worrying*, which was released in 2020. Each day I had to sit down and write by faith. At times, I thought, *Why am I writing a book that I won't be able to market?* But I knew God had asked me to write it, and I knew that the principles found in that book had drastically changed my life. So, I kept writing. I kept seeking God daily. I kept returning to a place of trust.

By March 2020, Covid had become a national threat and the lockdowns were just about to reach Texas where I live. I didn't know it, but God had a specific plan for me to follow during that lockdown season.

The writing of *Stop Worrying* along with the wilderness tone of that season were both pushing me to draw nearer to God than ever before. I had been baptized in the Holy Spirit, I would speak in tongues, and I would even hear from God on a regular basis. Yet a seed had planted deep inside me that called out for more of Him. I thought, *I don't know how long this wilderness will last, so I need to be as close to Him as I can get.*

One week before lockdowns hit, I sat on my living room couch at 11:30 p.m., praying and waiting upon the Lord. A video on my laptop caught my eye. It was a Jesus Image conference video from 2016. The band began to play, I joined in to worship the Lord, and I sensed the gentle, comforting presence of God. I wanted to stay there forever, yet I told myself that I would worship until midnight and then go to bed. After an hour of worship, Michael Koulianos began to preach the gospel message. Dozens of people ran down to the front to receive Christ. As he spoke, the presence of God was still there, but it was as if it had changed slightly. Now a stirring up occurred inside. I could sense the Holy Spirit within me drawing me back to a complete and total surrender to Jesus.

Suddenly something happened that unnerved me. After preaching the gospel, Michael began to pray for people, and they started falling over. This was new to me. This was different—even a little scary. Because I had watched the critical videos about charismatic preachers, I felt a serious concern and wariness about seeing people fall over after getting prayed for.

Yet before turning off the video, I remembered the sweet, gentle presence of the Holy Spirit that had rested on me during worship. I remembered the fiery yet pure call to repentance and trust in Jesus's blood during the altar call. I thought something like this: *If the presence of God is here, and if the gospel is being preached, could this also be God at work? Could I have misjudged what's happening?* So I prayed, "Holy Spirit, if this isn't You, I don't want anything to do with it. But, if it is You, I want all You have for me."

I heard the still, small voice of the Holy Spirit much clearer than I had in a long time. He said very plainly, *Troy, this is all Me.*

The worship began again, and I began to melt. I laid all my misconceptions and assumptions about the Holy Spirit out on the table before Him as I worshiped. I rededicated not just my heart but also my life to Jesus. I asked for more of the Holy Spirit's work in my life. But mostly, I just worshiped. I told God how good He was, no matter what my life looked like or would look like. As I worshiped, the presence came even heavier. It increased in intensity until it felt like I was swimming in it.

I finally got up off the couch. The clock read 2:30 a.m. I had worshiped for three hours, and I didn't even realize it! As I slipped into bed, I still felt the glorious presence of

God—something that had never happened before. I had felt His presence during worship, but I couldn't remember a time when I had carried His presence out of worship.

The next morning I woke up and immediately realized something was different from the normal morning routine. His presence was still with me! The intense presence of God rested on me for a week straight, and that experience changed everything.

Thursday night of that week, I remember driving to my wife's grandmother's house with the family. God's presence still rested on me, and suddenly I heard the Holy Spirit say, "Mimi is going to give you a message from Me tonight." Excited about potentially receiving a word from the Lord, I sat in the living room of Mimi's house, listening to every word she said.

I had only been there for five minutes when suddenly, as she spoke to another relative, she said, "You need an audience," and then she stopped and looked across the room at me and said, "Troy knows what I'm talking about." As soon as she said this, the Holy Spirit said to me, "That was it." I've talked to Mimi about that day since then, and she didn't even know she was prophesying.

Later that same week, the lockdowns came and we were suddenly stuck at home. Just one week before that, I would have been twiddling my thumbs or ordering a new video game to occupy my time, and yet now I knew exactly what to do. I suddenly had all this extra time to draw near to the Lord, and I would take advantage of it.

Mimi's prophetic word was confirmed less than a week later, and I didn't like how it played out.

Up to that point, I relied on the Lord to inspire me or give me ideas for my YouTube content. Sometimes I shared videos about current topics because I wanted to, but most of the time I simply waited upon the Lord until He spoke a simple message to me in my heart. Then I would do the research, study the Scripture, and create content. I was already used to the Lord leading my content creation. However, He suddenly took it in a whole new direction.

I started consistently listening to some of the speakers from that Jesus Image conference, one of whom was Brian Guerin. As he wrapped up one of his sermons, he happened to mention this simple phrase, "If you've never asked for dreams and visions, maybe ask for them." He referenced Acts 2:17 (NASB) when he said this:

> "And it shall be in the last days," God says, "That I will pour out My Spirit on all mankind; and your sons and your daughters will prophesy, and your young men will see visions, and your old men will have dreams."

After hearing this, I thought, *I don't think I've ever asked for dreams and visions before. I guess I'll ask.* I proceeded to pray a fairly silly prayer, saying, "God, if dreams and visions are something You want to give me, I'm okay with that. I'm asking for it if it's something You have for me."

That same night, I woke up out of a dream, and as I woke up the glory of God covered me, immediately confirming to me that the dream was from Him. The following night, something even crazier occurred. I pulled back the covers, slipped into bed, and lay down to go to sleep. The moment my head hit the pillow, I went into a vision. My eyes were closed, but I suddenly saw a fish floating in front of me, and I could see it perfectly clear. The light and color looked the same as if I were seeing it physically in front of me with my eyes. It swam from one side of my line of sight to the center of my focus. Turning, it started to head directly toward me.

This wasn't just a fish. It was a kind of deep sea anglerfish, which are probably my biggest fear in life. As it came toward me, I began to become afraid. Before I could open my eyes to try to stop the vision, I heard the Holy Spirit say, *Don't be afraid. This is Me.* So I kept watching, and the fish came all the way over to me, opened its mouth, and swallowed me. My eyes popped open, I jumped up out of bed, and said to myself, "What on earth was that!"

The strange events didn't stop there. As I sought the Lord that week, spending time in His presence through worship, He began to speak to me about His view of the pandemic, and then He asked me to share that view with others. He went so far as to say, *Tell them that I told you.* This was new. This wasn't just sharing messages God placed on my heart and passing them off as sermons or inspirational talks. This was prophecy.

I did end up sharing that message, and I labeled it, "What God Says About the Coronavirus." If it wasn't for the glory of God that rested on me during that time, I would have wrestled with God more over sharing a message like that. The response to that message shocked me. Compared to my content's normal reach, that video went viral, reaching tens of thousands of people.

As I continued to worship and wait and spend time in the glory of God, God continued to speak and give me prophetic messages to share. I had walked through the wilderness season, I had passed the test, and now God was fulfilling Mimi's words by giving me an audience.

However, as the Lord continued speaking prophetic words and asking me to share them online, I began to doubt whether this was a good plan or not. I could see the increased reach, which could potentially lead to a greater impact, yet I doubted if talking about prophetic words and strange visions from God could truly be a way to reach the lost.

I cried out to the Lord, saying, "God, I don't want to share prophetic words because I don't think I'll be able to reach as many people with the gospel." I thought that saying "God told me" would turn all the unbelievers away. Yet, the Spirit of God responded so clearly that night, saying, *Troy, if you don't go down this road, you won't reach as many.* In that moment, God promised me souls, and I decided to walk forward into His plan in faith.

The Lord later showed me what the fish in that first vision represented. God was calling me into prophetic evangelism. He would use the dreams, visions, and prophecies to build up the church, but also to reach those needing Jesus. It wouldn't appeal or attract everyone, but there would be a specific group in the body of Christ God would use me to encourage, along with a specific group outside the body that God would use me to reach with the gospel. Yet, the weight of this calling would so engulf my life and identity that it would feel like being swallowed whole and losing myself to God's calling.

Later in this book, I address some of the problems that come with public prophetic ministry. But now it's time to return to Babylon. I described my first experiences with visions and dreams from the Lord in order to set up what I'm about to share: a series of visions along with a word from God about the New Babylon.

The Strange Vision

Over the next couple of years, I consistently received prophetic words along with strange visions from God. Some of them made sense immediately. The meaning behind others would only become clear after much prayer and study. Yet one bothered me more than any visions I had ever seen. When I saw it, the intense presence, or the glory, of God rested heavily upon me. I knew it was Him speaking. I just didn't understand what on earth He was saying.

Many people have told me, "God would never give you a dream or vision that wasn't immediately clear. If a vision is strange or distressing, it's not from God." Yet the Scriptures show that dreams and visions can sometimes feel very disturbing at first. Daniel chapter 7 is a lengthy recounting of a series of dreams and visions about future events that Daniel receives from God. Daniel 7:1 (NASB) says:

> In the first year of Belshazzar king of Babylon, Daniel saw a dream and visions in his mind as he lay on his bed; then he wrote the dream down and told the following summary of it.

Over the next 13 verses, Daniel describes in detail these visions. Then he lets us into his personal emotional reaction to what He witnessed:

> As for me, Daniel, my spirit was distressed within me, and the visions in my mind kept alarming me (Daniel 7:15 NASB).

He promptly proceeds to ask for an explanation. An angel begins to interpret some of the visions for Daniel, yet even after the meaning is shown to him, he still says this:

> At this point the revelation ended. As for me, Daniel, my thoughts were greatly alarming me and my face became pale, but I kept the matter to myself (Daniel 7:28 NASB).

I can relate to Daniel, and not just because it's my middle name. Some of the dreams and visions I've received have greatly distressed me at first. The vision of Babylon I'm about to share is near the top of the list. Yet as strange as the vision is, I believe it is a true revelation from the Lord, and I also believe it ultimately points to the antidote of Babylon's secret knowledge.

As I waited upon the Lord, I began to see an image of a heavily forested wilderness with mountains in the background. Both the trees and the mountains seemed to partly resemble the shape of a pyramid. I also saw a river running through the forest, and next to it sat an actual pyramid, resembling those of ancient Egyptian creation.

I suddenly heard this phrase: *I'm removing its structure from society. Look up what the pyramid represents through history and you'll see it.*

So I did just that. I researched the pyramids to discover some already well-known facts. Pyramid imagery today is often linked back to the Egyptian influence, although other cultures made use of the ziggurat structure as well. Many historians believe the Egyptian pyramids were used as monuments, tombs, and even tools meant to help transition kings into the afterlife. More than simple burial sites, pyramids acted as a type of god-making machine. Hieroglyphic "spells" were carved into specific walls within the pyramids that were meant to magically transport, protect, and guide pharaohs into their next state of being. In ancient Egyptian culture, the eternal life of each individual in the entire nation was actually connected to their pharaoh's afterlife transition. So more than simply the Egyptian royalty themselves, the Egyptian people also had personal reasons to prioritize the king's proper burial.[40]

So to an extent, pyramids represent the attempt to immortalize a person or people group. We see the same desires propagated by those building the Tower of Babel: *"Let's make a name for ourselves"* (Genesis 11:4 NASB). They wished to immortalize their names throughout history, to live even though they died. Of course, God put a stop to it after saying, *"...they are one people, and they all have the same language. And this is what they have started to do, and now nothing which they plan to do will be impossible for them"* (Genesis 11:6 NASB). They had unified around a common goal, and many institutions, religions, and nations have done the same throughout history, sometimes identifying with the pyramid imagery as a unifying sign.

On another night, I began to see more strange imagery, and the Lord told me that it was a continuation of the same word. As I sat in the presence of God, I began to see an image of a pyramid on the back of a coin. Suddenly, the coin turned upside down and the top of the pyramid fell off. What was left closely resembled the image on the reverse of the Great Seal of the United States, which appears on the back of a United States one dollar bill: a pyramid with its top portion disconnected.

This disconnected portion of the pyramid is often shown containing an "all-seeing eye," otherwise known as the Eye of Providence. The new Random House unabridged dictionary translates this Latin phrase as "A new order of the ages (is born)."

Traditionally, this all-seeing eye was a representation of historical gods. Some ancient gods were depicted by images of an eye, such as the Eye of Horus, which was apparently an easy, cheap way of drawing the Egyptian god, Horus. These hieroglyphic Egyptian eye drawings were later mistakenly translated as "God," and renaissance painters thus adapted the eye into the Eye of Providence, representing the sovereign rule of Yahweh.

All of this I learned later, after researching these visions. However, on the night I saw this, the Lord continued to speak prophetically to me; and as I look back and ponder over the things I heard, I am amazed.

After the visions, the Holy Spirit began to speak. I heard: *New world order. Either the foundation stone or the new foundation the world will create. The societal structure is changing. Covid was part of this change. The internet greatly affected it. The world is a new place, but it's as sick as ever. It needs a surgeon to transplant the old into the new. The devil is copying in the natural what I want to do in the spiritual. I want to transplant people into the vine. He wants to transplant people from wholeness into perversion.*

After that, I began to see images of stacks of cut-down tree trunks. I heard the Lord say, *I'm stacking up the lumber. Great things are in store. I'm building houses for My people. A place of rest in this weary world.*

Even as the devil advances his agenda on earth, recruiting people to perform his perversions of God's plan, God is still making a way for His people to walk in holiness and protection. I know that persecution is real and that will continue to increase, but I believe the Holy Spirit was speaking systematically in this prophetic word. So even though the systems are changing and adapting, God has a way of working the system to show favor to His people and continue giving the church the opportunity to shine the light of Jesus Christ with the world.

The next thing I received from the Lord was an impression through which the Lord reminded me of the cedars of Lebanon from Scripture. They are mentioned many times, including during the building of David's and Solomon's palaces. While studying these amazing trees, I found that they can represent purity, strength, wealth, the flourishing of God's people among the nations, and even the glory of Christ.

Then I heard the Holy Spirit say, *When you build My house, I build yours. Everything you have need of I will provide.*

In 2 Samuel 7:4-17, God responds to King David through the prophet Nathan, letting him know that he is not to build a house for the Lord. Instead, God planned the temple to be built by David's son, Solomon. In his response, He makes a simple promise to David, saying, "*...The Lord also declares to you that the Lord will make a house for you*" (2 Samuel 7:11 NASB). David desired to build a house for God, and God responded by promising to build David's house. We see that God meant more than just a physical dwelling place, He also refers to the lineage of David leading up to the birth of Jesus—the King who would sit on the throne forever.

For our sakes, this word is both individually practical and corporately strategic. As Christians, we are called to seek first the Kingdom of God, believing that God provides what we need as we walk out His calling in our lives. Beyond that however, as a body of believers I believe we will see more and more in the days ahead the role of the church in building Kingdom-focused hubs within the systems of the world that shelter the body and gives the world something to compare their own models of operation. This is something that both God is doing and He is partnering with the church to do.

What will these "hubs" look like? What is the system through which the devil is advancing his agenda? It will become more clear as we look at the next few visions.

The Second Vision

On another day shortly after, I had another vision. This time I was looking up a tall, steep stone stairway leading to a platform that held a Great Sphinx-shaped figure at its pinnacle. Then I heard the Holy Spirit say, *People are still trying to reach Heaven another way other than the truth.*

After hearing this, I suddenly received an impression reminding me of the afterlife rituals and beliefs of the ancient Egyptians, and then I heard: *The afterlife looks different now, but it's still a fraud. They don't realize what's sitting at the top of that ladder.*

With a little research, I discovered that historians believe ancient Egyptians viewed the Great Sphinx as a guardian of the tombs, meant to protect the pharaohs as they entered the afterlife.

As the Holy Spirit continued speaking, I heard, *Today, the sphinx is the repetitive nature of the beast and the spirit of the power of the air. Pushing a belief until one believes it.*

What is the cultural afterlife that people are attempting to reach today? For Buddhists, it's reincarnation. For Muslims, it's Barzakh. For secularists, who culturally have often leaned toward atheism or agnosticism, it's either nothingness or a reality that is currently unknown. No matter what someone's view of the afterlife may be, how is that view often reinforced? Through repetition and the influence of "group thought." The protective shell around the belief is the system in place which repetitiously imposes the belief, which leads to thoughts such as, "Most people believe like me, so I must be right," or "The intelligent minds of our time think like this, so it must be true." In their need to be sure about where they are going, some people have settled for this form of evidence, and that is what the devil wants.

The truth, however, is that we can be sure. We can have assurance of the afterlife on this side of death. This assurance is what I will talk about later in this book.

One strange, seemingly paradoxical fact is the cultural shift (even in the secular or atheist communities) away from the belief in a purely natural existence and back to a spiritual reality. Many secularists, who would generally take the viewpoint that there is no Creator, have added spiritualism or "god-worship" into their lifestyles. This shift points us back to the ultimate sphinx, the prince of the power of the air and his dogma, which says you can have anything and everything you want as long as the true God is not in it.

Yet, there is a structural problem with the prince's system, which we will see in a moment.

The Secret Knowledge of Babylon

Around the same time I received this series of visions from the Lord, I also heard a simple message about the following year, which was 2022. I heard the Holy Spirit say, *Daniel 4:7. This is the prophetic picture for this coming year.*

Daniel 4:7 (NASB) says, *"Then the soothsayer priests, the sorcerers, the Chaldeans, and the diviners came in and I related the dream to them, but they could not make its interpretation known to me."*

After reading this verse, I heard the phrase, *A year of the world eating their own words.*

In a similar occurrence, the king of Babylon had previously called for the wise men, soothsayer priests, conjurers, sorcerers, and Chaldeans to interpret a dream, yet the previous time came with a harsher demand and a harsher punishment for failure. In Daniel chapter 2, the king demands to be told both the interpretation and the dream itself. He delivers this command with a threat in Daniel 2:5 (NASB):

> The king replied to the Chaldeans, "The command from me is firm: if you do not make known to me the dream and its interpretation, you will be torn limb

> from limb and your houses will be turned into a rubbish heap."

Obviously, the wise men and sorcerers could not relate the dream or its interpretation. Essentially, the Babylonian spiritual structure was about to crumble from the inside out. The king was about to wipe out his own wise men, soothsayer priests, conjures, sorcerers, and Chaldeans.

God began to disrupt the entire pinnacle of witchcraft in Babylon through a simple dream. This is because satan is a bad builder. Even when his system is prevalent, it is unsound.

In Daniel 2:11 (NASB), this response is given to the king:

> Moreover, the thing which the king demands is difficult, and there is no one else who could declare it to the king except gods, whose dwelling place is not with mortal flesh.

They essentially say, *in all our wisdom, we cannot explain this mystery.* Only God has the wisdom and insight to explain the king's dream, and He does it through His servant Daniel. The same thing occurs in Daniel 4:8-9 (NASB).

> But finally Daniel came in before me, whose name is Belteshazzar according to the name of my god, and in whom is a spirit of the holy gods; and I related the dream to him, saying, "Belteshazzar, chief of the soothsayer priests, since I know that a spirit of the holy gods is in you and no secret baffles you, tell me the visions of my dream which I have seen, along with its interpretation."

In both instances, the king's need was for someone who possesses the *"spirit of the holy gods,"* or as we know, the Holy

Spirit of God. Even at the height of its dominance, Babylon's "secret knowledge" could not compare to the secret knowledge of Heaven.

Yet, despite the inadequacies of the secret knowledge of Babylon, people have continued to rely upon it over the centuries, and many still look to it today within the system of the New Babylon. So what is the New Babylon? We finally come to an answer.

New Babylon Revealed

Early in 2022, the Lord led me to share a message on a livestream that included all of these visions and words together. And though I perceived some of what the Holy Spirit had communicated, I did not fully understand the point. As I thought about the pyramids, the Great Sphinx, the Eye of Providence, the New World Order, and how all these things relate to the structures of society today, I knew that I was missing the link between all of these visions and prophecies.

However, even though I felt confused, I knew God was telling me to deliver the message. In obedience, I scheduled the livestream, prepared, and waited upon the Lord for wisdom to know how to present the information.

Just a few hours before the stream started, I received another word from the Lord that began to link all of these prophetic utterances together. I heard the Holy Spirit say, *Internet is the new Babylon. Satan's system has had control, but I am removing the bonds in My refining fire. I'm breaking the bonds of My servants and placing them in places of authority in the online world.*

I know what you just read may be received different ways. Some may say, "Of course it is. I already knew that." Others may respond with, "I don't believe you," or, "No it's not." There may be another group that says, "You may be right, but you're going to have to back up that statement with some evidence." Here's my reply to any and every response: I'm not here to prove that I'm right. I'm simply here to be obedient and deliver a message. Like I said at the start of this book, I encourage you to test, weigh, and judge every prophetic message you hear, whether it be from me or someone else.

Now that that's out of the way, let's talk about the potential implications of this word. Is God saying that the mystery Babylon in Revelation 17 is fully manifested within the internet system? Possibly, but probably not. First, it's worth noting the word I received was about the New Babylon, not specifically the mystery Babylon. Second, we've already discussed how Babylon itself is used as a metaphor within Scripture to describe any system that promotes and carries out the enemy's agenda. Third, the internet itself is ever changing and evolving, and it may someday look very different from how it looks now. What we label the internet now may only be the start of something bigger and more influential.

Whether the internet is the full package that we see in Revelation 17 or not, it is at the least a vehicle that will help to deliver that package.

Setting the disclaimers aside for a moment, it is at least possible that the Lord is saying that the city called THE MOTHER OF PROSTITUTES AND OF THE ABOMINATIONS OF THE EARTH is actually the internet system. Whether this is what the Lord is specifically saying or not is not really vital to know. The critical point is that the same way Babylon was responsible for delivering the ways of darkness to the world in ancient times, the internet is involved in delivering the ways of Babylon to the world today.

One other thing to address is the remaining portion of the Lord's message. He said, *satan's system has had control, but I am removing the bonds in My refining fire. I'm breaking the bonds of My servants and placing them in places of authority in the online world.* This means that despite the rise of the New Babylon over the past several decades, God is still working, and He is going to repurpose a system of the world to accomplish His will. How exactly this happens is something we will discuss a little later on.

First, we need to look at the mysterious origins of the New Babylon; and in diving deep into the beginnings of this system, we should see both the hand of the devil and the hand of God at work.

5

THE ANCIENT TEMPLATE

The Origins of a Worldly System

When thoroughly studying a system, whether political, governmental, societal, scientific, or otherwise, it is best to first return to its beginnings. The origins of a system often reveal its purpose. Some systems are natural and exist apart from human interference. Other systems are the organized, community-led response to a common need.

If the Babylonian system that existed millenniums ago truly has been "reincarnated" (for lack of a better word) through a modern technology, what can the origins of such a remade system tell us?

I have received many confirmations from the Lord while writing this book. The most specific confirmation I received came the very first night. I knew the Holy Spirit was asking me to compile these prophetic words into book form, yet I had been hesitating due to the seemingly odd nature of the premise.

Yet, the moment I started writing, I received a sudden, specific prophecy.

As I sat down in front of my laptop in my dining room that night, I heard this phrase: *The internet began in 1969.*

I thought, *Really, Lord?* If I had to guess, I would have wagered the internet began in the late 1970s or even as recent as the late 1980s. That shows how little I knew. His voice was clear, so I quickly Googled "1969, the beginning of the internet," and in the .005 seconds that it took Google to respond, I was looking at an article titled, *Today in Media History: The Internet began with a crash on October 29, 1969.*[41]

Wow! At that moment, I resolved to complete this book because I knew God was confirming to me not only the commissioning of it but also the premise too.

The First Message

The article, *Today in Media History: The Internet began with a crash on October 29, 1969* opens with this brief paragraph:

> ***The beginning of the Internet is the story of two large computers, miles apart, sending the message: "LO." The world has never been the same.***

What's the story behind this cryptic message? Well, the natural explanation is that the early computer scientists were attempting to write the word LOG (short for LOGIN), and yet the primeval computer crashed before they could type the letter "G," making the first message sent over an early version of the internet a short and supposedly unmeaning "LO."

Though that is a straightforward enough explanation, this message may also be a sign of more notorious, spiritual forces at work.

In 2009, the internet turned 40 and *The Guardian* published an article celebrating the milestone titled, "Forty years of the internet: how the world changed for ever." In this summary piece, the writer, Oliver Burkeman, detailed the story of "LO" writing:

> ***Samuel Morse, sending the first telegraph message 125 years previously, chose the portentous phrase: "What hath God wrought?" But Kline's task was to log in remotely from LA to the Stanford machine, and there was no opportunity for portentousness: his instructions were to type the command LOGIN.***
>
> ***Kline typed a G, at which point the system crashed, and the connection was lost. The G didn't make it through, which meant that, quite by accident, the first message ever transmitted across the nascent internet turned out, after all, to be fittingly biblical: "LO."***[42]

In reminiscing about the first message sent via the internet, Burkeman turns the pages of history all the way back to May 24, 1844 when the first message was sent via Samuel Morse's telegraph. Why? Because the telegraph was the first machine that could quickly transmit text across a large distance. In many ways, it was a predecessor to the internet.

It's also interesting to note that Burkeman turns the pages of time even further back by referencing the Bible. I say it is interesting because "What hath God wrought?" is actually a direct quote from Numbers 23:23, which says in the King James Version: *"Surely there is no enchantment against Jacob, neither is there any divination against Israel: according to this time it shall be said of Jacob and of Israel, What hath God wrought!"*

Numbers 23 is a detailing of God's prophetic message through Balaam over Israel. Balaam was paid by the Moabite

King Balak to curse Israel, and yet God instead used Balaam to speak a blessing over His people.

The phrase, "What hath God wrought?" translated into modern English could be written as "What has God made?" or even "See what God has done!" The phrase itself was meant as an exclamation of triumph. Probably the statement insinuated, even if only hyperbolically, that the accomplishment was so legendary that it should be in the category of things only God Himself could have done. It sounds a little like the thinking behind the Tower of Babel.

Even though Samuel Morse more than likely meant it that way, when we read the Old English today, it appears as if he asked a question that echoed down through the following decades full of modern advancements, "What hath God wrought?"

Years later, what seemed like an accident due to a computer crash actually became a fitting answer to the question. The word "LO" is the first two letters of the word "LOGIN," but it is also an archaic word used to draw attention, meaning "Look! See!" Burkeman called "LO" biblical because it appears often in the King James Bible.

Samuel Morse's question initiated the technological age, and the first word sent over the internet almost acts like a devilish answer to the question: What has God done? Answer: Look and see!

The IMPs

Leading up to the fall of 1969, Leonard Kleinrock helped supervise the development of the Arpanet, a network of computers that is now essentially viewed as an early version of the Internet. In order for a computer to connect to the internet today, a router is used. In Kleinrock's case, the IMP was an early type of router or gateway. Acting as a "mini" computer hooked up to the existing computer or local network, it would make access to a broader network possible.[43]

The IMP, or Interface Message Processor, made the early internet possible. Though Kleinrock and his associates at UCLA praised the day when the first message flittered through the lines of the Arpanet, little did they know how grand and terrible their accomplishment would be. Perhaps there were other forces at work that possessed a greater insight into the potentials of the internet.

An IMP is an Interface Message Processor, but it also curiously happens to be a mythological creature often resembling a demon, fairy, or sprite. The term *imp* is believed to have originated from the word *ympe* or *impa,* which refers to the grafting together of a plant or tree during its early years.[44] So, the Interface Message Processor, better known as the IMP, shares a name with a demon and a tree being connected and branching off into something more. Could this be a clue to the potential involvement of supernatural powers behind the early development of this monumental technological advancement?

Another odd occurrence during the installment of the first internet was a message sent via telegram by Massachusetts Senator Edward Kennedy (the younger brother of US President John F. Kennedy). His message was sent to the Bolt Beranek and Newman Company (BBN) after hearing of their winning the commission to construct the first batch of IMPs. He congratulated them on their development of the "Interfaith Message Processor."[45]

It's an understandable mistake. *Interface* sounds a lot like *interfaith*. In his article celebrating the 40-year birthday of the internet, Burkeman comments on Ted Kennedy's slip of the pen, saying, "Needless to say, though, the box that arrived outside Kleinrock's office wasn't a machine capable of fostering understanding among the great religions of the world."

However, could Burkeman, the writer of *The Guardian* article, at least to an extent, be wrong? Could the misspoken term be revealing a deeper, spiritual agenda behind the project? *Interfaith* means relating to or between different religions or members of different religions, and the phrase *interfaith dialogue* speaks of acceptance and tolerance among religions, or coexistence. Today, we see a growing message of coexistence and even of a one world religion spread far and wide through the power of the internet.

The Demon Company

One of the internet's greatest leaps forward in its attempt to shrink the world was to connect computers across continents. The British government, along with other European governments, were initially opposed to the Internet. Another network called the Open Systems Interconnect got their vote. However, the modern internet eventually won out, and Cliff Stanford helped it along by founding an internet service provider in 1992—the first commercial one in Great Britain. This company just happened to be called Demon Internet.[46] Again, the name feels appropriate and may even be pointing to a spiritual force at work.

Though companies like Demon Internet made a connection to the internet possible, many monthly subscribers were left questioning their purchase. What was there to do on the internet? At the time, other than sending an email, not much.

CERN's Involvement

The internet wasteland did not stay vacant long. If you have heard the company name CERN in the news over the past few decades, you may be surprised to learn that this company helped answer the question: what is there to do online?

Phrases like "surfing the web" and "browsing the net" are mostly out of use now, but back in the 1990s their coining was the direct result of the invention of the World Wide Web. The concept and framework for hosted websites anyone could use or create was birthed in 1989 by a British scientist at CERN named Tim Berners-Lee. At the writing of this, the first real website can still be found at info.cern.ch. By 1993, CERN had moved the WWW software into the public domain, giving the world a place to land online.

Why is this pertinent? CERN's involvement in the birthing of the modern-day World Wide Web (and whatever may replace it someday) is important because of CERN's mission and beliefs. Briefly describing the origins of the universe, CERN's website cites,

"All matter in the universe was formed in one explosive event 13.7 billion years ago—the Big Bang."

Holding a worldview that excludes God is not surprising for a company attempting to be on the forefront of scientific breakthrough. Yet it goes deeper than that. They go on to describe part of their own mission as attempting to:

> ***Provide a unique range of particle accelerator facilities that enable research at the forefront of human knowledge.... Unite people from all over the world to push the frontiers of science and technology, for the benefit of all....***[47]

What does that sound like? It adequately, though generally I'll admit, describes the mission of the builders of the Tower of Babel in Genesis chapter 11. If their mission is of a similar nature, could they possibly be pursuing that mission in a similar way as well? Yes.

CERN is possibly best known for their Large Hadron Collider, a particle accelerator and collider that was created as an attempt to answer some of the most basic questions about our existence. Guinness Book of World Records calls The Large Hadron Collider "the largest and most complex machine ever built."[48]

The builders of Babel said, *"Let's build ourselves a city, and a tower whose top will reach into heaven, and let's make a name for ourselves."* Their work included a tower that would reach to Heaven—the largest tower ever built, meant to unite a people and grow a city.

CERN isn't driven by a simple desire to break world records. A pre-teen with a lot of time on their hands can do that. They are driven by a desire to figure out the universe—to understand where we came from, where we are going, and how to get there together. Unfortunately, they have already measured God out of the equation. Even if they found God at the bottom of everything, they've baked their conclusion into their premise, so they wouldn't be able to recognize what it was they were seeing.

This happened with the discovery of the Higgs boson particle, a breakthrough finding at CERN in 2012. CERN reveals their conclusion within the official description of the particle:

> ***You and everything around you are made of particles. But when the universe began, no particles had mass; they all sped around at the speed of light. Stars, planets and life could only emerge because particles gained their mass from a fundamental field associated with the Higgs boson. The existence of this mass-giving***

field was confirmed in 2012, when the Higgs boson particle was discovered at CERN.[49]

They also relate the discovery to everyday life by saying:

It is part of the answer to why we—and everything we interact with—have mass, feeding our natural human curiosity about our universe and how it evolved.

This "particle" has been unofficially named the *God Particle*, not because of the belief that it points to the existence of a supreme being, but rather because they consider it part of His replacement. If the Big Bang is your god, then perhaps this particle is appropriately named.

They are trying to go all the way back to the beginning—searching for the elementary substance from which everything else is built. If humanity could isolate and control that substance, we could in some ways act like God, potentially bending human life and nature to our will. In a sense, they have used science to get to God without actually reaching Him, the same way the builders of Babel attempted to reach Heaven apart from their Creator.

Babylon Reborn in a Modern Age

The Spider and the Fly

Mary Howitt wrote a symbolic poem in 1839 about the dangers of flattery and the temptations of evil counsel. It opens with a seemingly prophetic conversation between an innocent little fly and a crafty spider.

"Will you walk into my parlour?" said the Spider to the Fly,

"'Tis the prettiest little parlour that ever you did spy;
The way into my parlour is up a winding stair,
And I have many curious things to shew when you are there."
"Oh no, no," said the little Fly, "to ask me is in vain,
For who goes up your winding stair can ne'er come down again."

This web analogy has been used countless times throughout literature's history, nearly always pointing to a sticky end; once you're caught, you're caught. Mary Howitt leaves us with this lesson at the end of the poem:

To idle, silly flattering words, I pray you ne'er give heed:
Unto an evil counsellor, close heart and ear and eye…

The same analogy aptly describes the craftiness of the internet. Could it be that the label World Wide Web means more than simply a network connecting all human beings, but rather a trap spun in order to catch them? The same way that a net pulls in a haul of struggling fish, the Net has captured a generation of people struggling to find freedom.

When Ray Tomlinson invented email in 1971, was he using his SNDMSG software to simply send a test message to himself on another computer in the same room, or could it be that a larger, more spiritual force was at work, using his invention to help send a message to the world?[50]

The message delivered to our culture through the internet is very similar in nature to the message the spider delivers to the fly. *What you really want can be found deeper in my lair. Look and see!*

The New English Translation, its abbreviation coincidentally spells NET, reads Ezekiel 12:24 like this: *"For there will no longer be any false visions or flattering omens amidst the house of Israel."*

The flattering images referenced the nation's idolatry: both material and immaterial. People were collecting physical idols, but what was worse were the deceptive words being spoken through the prophets. The deception didn't carry weight simply because it was crafty, it also carried weight because it was given as a "word from the Lord." Like the spider catching the fly, the false visions and dreams were catching a nation, and the Lord delivered that nation over to the trap.

> I will also spread My net over him, and he will be caught in My net. And I will bring him to Babylon in the land of the Chaldeans; yet he will not see it, though he will die there (Ezekiel 12:13 NASB).

The web that the Lord employs as He gives the nation of Israel over to their idolatry is a web of exile. The web or net catches people and carries them away from their homes and away from their families. Doesn't the same thing happen online? Teens are exiled from their parents through lies they read online. Husbands and wives are exiled from each other through images of other people found online. People are exiled from their families and friends through the deep pits of political and social opinion they discover and develop online.

Even the lockdowns in 2020 were a form of exile—an exile into a modern-day version of Babylon. We were drawn away from the world into the tunnels of our own homes—stuck in our rooms, getting caught deeper and deeper into a well-spun web. The social media platforms are designed to keep us scrolling. The streaming services are designed to keep us binging. One of the main ways to reach the outside world during that time was to go through Babylon—to connect via the internet. Could it be that 2020 was more of a net than many realize?

The devil doesn't need to keep us exiled physically to keep us bound. Like the spider talking to the fly, he simply needs to get us far enough into the tunnel so that there's no backing out. Because the truth is that, though the lockdowns lifted, many people never escaped the exile that was patterned into them during that time—or that has been slowly patterned into us over the years since the internet was invented. The world has been caught in a web, and the truth is there's only one way out.

Walls on Fire

There is a fleeing that needs to take place in today's culture, but it is not a physical one. We need to flee from the clutches of Babylon. In some cases, even wise people who are of the world's culture have begun to recognize and expose the traps of the modern-day Babylon, but those at the forefront of this procession should always be believers in Jesus. The prophet Jeremiah issues a stark warning to those who choose to settle and remain in Babylon too long.

> "Wander away from the midst of Babylon and go out from the land of the Chaldeans; be like male goats at the head of the flock. For behold, I am going to rouse and bring up against Babylon a contingent of great nations from the land of the north, and they will draw up their battle lines against her; from there she will be taken captive. Their arrows will be like an expert

> warrior who does not return empty-handed. Chaldea will become plunder; all who plunder her will have enough," declares the Lord (Jeremiah 50:8-10 NASB).

The same way the Lord issued a warning to the children of Israel to flee from the midst of Babylon under the Old Covenant, He is issuing a warning today to those would be tempted to settle in a land of captivity. How do we break free from the clutches of the modern-day Babylon? Should we become off-grid hermits who live off the land and never interact with technology? I don't believe so. After all, Daniel was a Spirit-filled (in the Old Covenant sense) prophet led of God, but God never told him to physically run away from Babylon. Instead, God led Daniel to flee from the ways of Babylon without physically leaving Babylon itself. He empowered him to operate within the kingdom of exile and, in some ways, to overthrow it from the inside out.

Daniel did not completely win over the Babylonian kingdom to God, but he did make a monumental impact. God used him to sway the hearts of kings and even change the laws of the land to point people to the true God. God utilized Daniel in the midst of captivity in a foreign land. He can do the same with us today.

Before releasing Babylon's captives, we first must release ourselves, and to do that we must understand that Babylon is well-fortified. She has thick walls built to protect herself. These are more than physical structures towering over the ancient Sumerian or Akkadian landscapes. They are belief systems engrained within the thinking of a culture. To escape Babylon, we must stop thinking like her.

Revelation 18:2 (NASB) describes the eventual fall and demise of the great city:

> And he cried out with a mighty voice, saying, "Fallen, fallen is Babylon the great! She has become a dwelling place of demons and a prison of every unclean spirit, and a prison of every unclean and hateful bird."

Could this verse be referring to an internet or technology shutdown? Possibly. We will address that idea shortly and cover more of what's still to come in a later chapter. For now, it accurately describes the fall that needs to happen within the hearts of those enslaved to the ways of Babylon. The Babylon in Revelation had become a dwelling place for demons and unclean spirits, and the same is true today. The ways of Babylon are interconnected with demonic strongholds, and demonic strongholds are interbred with lies.

To understand the lies, we will compare the ancient city to the modern-day technological marvel.

Greatest Moments in Internet History

In 2019, Daisy Hernandez compiled what she appropriately calls a "long, strange trip," highlighting important moments since the internet's birth. Within *The 50 Greatest Moments in Internet History*, she laughs at the silly moments, such as the invention of "memes" or the first livestream, which featured a coffee pot brewing. She also pays homage to pivotal points of genius that sailed the world into the next phase of history, such as the invention of WiFi.

In the mix of these historical moments, we can see trends arising. These are the same trends that have echoed alongside Babylon's name down through the pages of history. They are the ideas that have shaped the world. They are the signifying beliefs behind the shortcut system through which the world operates. If you want to know if the spirit of Babylon—or older still, the Nephilim spirit—is still alive today, simply turn on the closest screen.

We have discussed the characteristics or the culture of ancient Babylon, but now let us parallel the beliefs behind that culture to the underlying beliefs of the modern world.

Let's All Come Together

The Tower of Babel was a joint effort to erect the largest tower ever constructed by humankind. It was a "coming together" moment in history, incited by both human pride and perverse spirits inhabiting the earth. Later, that same region became the building place for Babylon, the city built at the pinnacle of the ancient world's societal development.

Both the Tower of Babel and Babylon are connected by an ideological movement toward "coming together." John Lennon (of The Beatles's fame) could be their spokesperson. *If we just work together enough, we will be able to do anything. If we have enough people joining together, we can create a strong enough foundation to build anything our hearts desire.* This idea is reflected in the shape of the actual towers built out of these movements.

Scholars believe the Tower of Babel to be a ziggurat, a pyramid-shaped building, which acts as a "stairway" up to the sky. Mesopotamians believed ziggurats were connection points or portals between the natural and the spiritual—human and divine.[51]

The archaeological discovery of the "Tower of Babel Stele" directly connects Babylon, the Tower of Babel, and the ancient ziggurat. The carvings on this slab monument depict the 7-layer tower next to Nebuchadnezzar II, who holds in hand either a nail or a scroll containing future plans for the rebuilding of the tower. Whether this artifact depicts a tower built during the time of Nimrod or the famous Babylon ziggurat that many believe to have been built later during the time of Hammurabi is unclear, but it at least connects the idea of the Tower of Babel with the ziggurat shape.[52]

This idea of being limitless through "building together" may have started with Nimrod, but it didn't stop there. Many of the temples within Babylonia itself are also believed to have been ziggurats, and in some instances, as in the case of the famous Etemenanki ziggurat within Babylon, at least some of the original structure remains today.

Evidences of this "build higher together" ideology have also been echoed through history within the form of organizations including Freemasonry and within many political or social reform movements, and today it encompasses much of the belief spread through the internet. The internet itself was partially birthed out of this theory. It is, in some senses, a digital ziggurat.

In her article on *The 50 Greatest Moments in Internet History*, Hernandez writes:

> ***We can't talk about great moments in internet history without talking about the Advanced Research Projects Agency Network (ARPANET), which was founded in 1966. The massive network was the result of several different networks merging into one, with the idea that critical information could be shared "in the case of a catastrophic event."***[53]

We have already discussed this development that led to the "birth" of the internet in 1969. But the point here is that the invention of the internet is based on the decision that *we are better joined together*. To an extent, most people would agree that they were right. However, as we have seen with the development of the Tower of Babel, it all depends on the motivation. At heart, are we attempting to build on a foundation of ourselves, or are we relying on the foundation Christ built? Are we reaching out for Heaven apart from God or are we reaching out *to* God? It all comes back to the heart of the builder.

Babylon's Walls

We touched briefly on the walls King Hammurabi raised around Babylon and how King Nebuchadnezzar II constructed three rings of walls around the city, fortifying it even more. Whether examining the height of 40 feet or the width so extensive that chariot races were held on the ramparts, these walls were unlike anything seen during that time.

Today, the internet also boasts huge walls. Firewalls are programs and devices that protect a user's computer or network from digital attack. Software firewalls are installed programs running directly on a device or router, blocking malicious viruses from endangering systems and stealing data. Hardware firewalls act as an even greater line of defense, shielding the device or network externally, keeping unwanted programs from even stepping within the "walls of the city." The point is, any important information stored on the internet is going to have multiple lines of defense, and these defenses keep expanding and growing more impressive.

Another safeguard used by all major internet networks and platforms is to keep stores of data in multiple physical locations around the world. I've personally been inside a secret, nondescript server building where many large tech companies were renting server space. Once we walked onto the server floor, we couldn't even hear each other speak due to the overwhelming noise of the dozens of air conditioners that lined the massive room. Some of these companies were using the space to deliver website pages to their users, but many of them were simply using the drive space on these massive computers as a backup in case one of their other server buildings went down. These server rooms can be found worldwide.

The building itself was built of thick stone walls and pillars, and top-notch security systems were in place everywhere. To give you an idea of how locked down it was, when I went to the restroom, a security guard escorted me there, scanned his card to open the restroom door, and then stood next to me while I did my business! My point is, internet security is serious.

International Data Corporation estimates that by 2025 the internet had grown to be over 175 zettabytes in size. One zettabyte equals 1 trillion gigabytes. Most basic computers nowadays come with about 1,000 gigabytes of space. Though the size itself is mostly trackable, the amount of information processed or stored online is nearly unfathomable.

The boast surrounding Babylon was its walls. That's a bad pun that should have stayed off paper. If you don't get it, it's best just to move on. Nevertheless, the point behind taking great pains to fortify a city is to secure its future—to keep intruders out and guarantee it is never conquered. Yet, history teaches us that every city or nation has its weakness. Rome fell from the inside. At least, historians attribute Rome's decline mainly to internal factors. So even with elaborate walls or defenses, a nation or city can still topple.

I vividly remember loading bags of groceries into my parents' cart in the Walmart checkout line one windy day in December 1999. This memory is embedded in my mind due to the panicking shoppers bustling around me. Asking my dad what on earth was happening simply raised more questions in my 10-year-old mind.

I remember him saying something like, "Y2K is coming, and people are worried about computer systems crashing."

I asked, "Why are the computers going to crash?"

"Because the internal calendars the computers run on weren't designed to go past the year 1999," he said, attempting to explain the problem in language I would understand.

"Well, why did they design it that way? What the heck were they thinking?"

I remember thinking how stupid computer engineers were in that moment (I was only around 10 years old after all). The 1990s was a decade of internet technology explosion, and yet for all their achievements, they couldn't get the computers to understand that the year 2000 was a thing.

Their initial reasoning made sense, however. Due to a lack of space on early hard drives, they shortened the four number year to a two number year. 1999 became 99. 2000 would become 00, and no one knew if computers would interpret 00 as year 2000 or year 1900. This presented a problem, especially for systems relying on keeping strict timelines, such as interest accounts, airline schedules, and nuclear power plant maintenance.

Many people feared this one small slip up could bring down the whole network and potentially send us into a temporary dark age. Looking back, we know that many countries headed off the problem through quickly-turned-around software patches and hardware adjustments, but the point remains clear. No matter how impenetrable a city feels, there's always the potential for weakness. Sometimes, one small gap in the wall can jeopardize the whole defense.

One of Hernandez's *50 Greatest Moments* happens to be a successful cyberattack by a 15-year-old boy with too much time on his hands. She writes:

> ***In February 2000, a high school student and hacker named Mike "MafiaBoy" Calce launched a DDoS (distributed denial of service) attack that crippled a host of sites including CNN, Dell, eBay, Amazon, Yahoo. The purpose? "To intimidate other hacker groups," says Calce.***[54]

This attack came just two short months after the Y2K scare. Not only did MafiaBoy bring down a handful of major e-commerce websites (directly effecting the value of those companies on the stock exchange), he also hacked Yahoo, which was the largest search engine at the time—nearly equivalent to someone bringing down Google today.[55]

This wasn't the work of a team of "experts." It was one curious boy pushing the limits and exposing simple but critical flaws in a system boasting advanced security measures. That small crack in the wall was actually detrimental.

Jeremiah 50:14-15 (NASB) presents a striking picture of ancient Babylon's defenses crumbling:

> Draw up your battle lines against Babylon on every side, all of you who bend the bow; shoot at her, do not spare your arrows, for she has sinned against the Lord. Raise your battle cry against her on every side! She has given herself up, her towers have fallen, her walls have been torn down. For this is the vengeance of the Lord: take vengeance on her; as she has done to others, so do to her.

This destruction repeats in Revelation 18:9-10 (NASB) when God delivers the same verdict on the New Babylon:

> And the kings of the earth, who committed acts of sexual immorality and lived luxuriously with her, will

> weep and mourn over her when they see the smoke of her burning, standing at a distance because of the fear of her torment, saying, "Woe, woe, the great city, Babylon, the strong city! For in one hour your judgment has come."

I could harp on potentially cheesy connections to the internet here, such as the fact that corrupted desktop computers traditionally called "towers" (hardware) could represent the burning towers of Jeremiah and Revelation, or that hacked "firewalls" (software) could represent walls of the city being broken into. However, though the language is coincidental, it's not the most evidential element of the parallel. I'll focus instead on the scope and timeline. It says, *"the kings of the earth"* all interacted with Babylon. They all stood to profit or lose based on Babylon's state, and her destruction also meant torment for all of them in return. What one system in the world does every nation rely upon? The internet. What one "city" (whose destruction would result in a form of worldwide chaos) could be taken down in a single hour? The internet, or at least, a digital equivalent of the internet—whatever that may be in the future.

If you say, "You just finished telling us how secure the internet is and how many backups there are," I would suggest the possibility of an artificial intelligence program someday being capable of dismantling any and every safeguard in a matter of minutes or even seconds. Does that concept sound sci-fi? Sure. But I propose that it's not. We'll discuss AI's deeper involvement in the New Babylon in detail later, but for now I will say that many technology leaders have admitted an AI shutdown or takeover is not out of the realm of possibilities. The leaps and bounds forward in capability that AI technology has made just in the past few years is striking, and for many people, deeply concerning.

Am I saying that AI will one day take down the internet? No. I'm simply repeating what many AI critics in the field of computer technology have said—that it's possible. Whether AI is the future culprit or not, every defense has its weakness. They considered ancient Babylon impenetrable, and yet archeologists study its remains today. God uses the name Babylon in Revelation for several reasons—one is to tell us that the same way Babylon fell before, she will fall again.

We Can Be Our Own God

In 1986, computer scientist Jon Postel gave the public a formal introduction to top level domains such as .com, .org, .gov, .edu, and .mil. Today, we are familiar with a plethora of other domains, but no one who grew up in the 1990s will ever forget what has become known as the "dot-com era." Because of his contribution to the initiation of the digital age, Postel was deemed the "God of the Internet," and he was inducted into the Internet Hall of Fame in 2012. Obviously, this internet "god" made it into Hernandez's top 50 list.

Postel is not the inventor of the internet, but he was part of the process. In one sense, he got to see his name strung up in lights, though he died in 1998, long before his induction into the hall of fame.

Postel is not really the "god" of the internet, but he is an imprint. He's an imprint of the human desire to receive recognition. Though Postel didn't self-identify as a digital deity, he didn't need to. That's not the point. The point is that people long to be seen as notable—as important, and we are willing to lift others up in order to fortify the idea that we may also one day qualify to be lifted high—to be placed on a pedestal.

Have you ever given someone a compliment because you also wanted one in return? Have you ever liked someone's social media status because you also wanted a like? That's what often happens with people like Postel. Even if we don't boast in our own name, we boast in the accomplishments of other individuals because we want to prove to our own hearts the notion that: *I can do that too. If I try hard enough or get lucky enough, one day that could be me.*

Am I reading too much into Postel's story? Possibly. But think for a second about why social media has grown so quickly. Why can a social media platform blow up overnight, pulling millions from one trending site or app to another? Simple. People follow the limelight. Once the spotlight shifts, people shift. We desire to cling to the chance that someday we too might be worthy of notoriety. Some people are looking for a small light. Others are looking for a broad, sweeping light. But in one way or another, in the selfish recesses of the heart, every person longs for a spotlight of some kind to rest on them.

> The king began speaking and was saying, "Is this not Babylon the great, which I myself have built as a royal residence by the might of my power and for the honor of my majesty?" (Daniel 4:30 NASB)

These are the boasts of Nebuchadnezzar, the king of Babylon. He essentially says, "Look at my legacy. Look at what I've built," because his heart is saying, *Look at me. I'm the one. I'm it.*

Babylon's Religion

We discussed how ancient Babylon's governmental system hinged on both politics and religion, with the religious influence dominating. Even foreign kings, such as during the Assyrian rule, paid homage to Babylon's deities and temples as an attempt to legitimize their own authority.

Religion held the power over cultural, scientific, and literature advancements because everything filtered through the temple life. Worship went so far that it included prostitution—the giving of their own body to strangers to be "one" with the society they lived in. In one sense, people prostituted themselves to fit in.

In short, to be somebody in ancient Babylon, you had to give yourself over to the "god" of the era. That same thing happens today.

The gods didn't just live in the temples. They also lived in smaller, personal shrines within people's homes and shops. As was said, the statues weren't simply decorative or representative in nature. They were the gods, and they were treated as such, being clothed and given food and drink at mealtimes.

All of this was wrapped up in the idea of self-fulfillment. If I worship, clothe, and provide for this deity, my life will be blessed.

What I'm about to say may sound harsh or condemning, but it isn't meant to be. It's meant to be a loving warning and appeal—nothing more. We live and work in a digital age, a society of screens, and we can't help that. Yet, there are some strange similarities between the gods of ancient Babylon and the screens of today.

- They would visit the temple to worship, offering their goods to the deities.

We pay hefty prices to view the next Marvel film in theaters (except that nearly everyone's over Marvel at this point).

- They would set up a personal shrine in their home for daily worship.

We gather around the television screen, which is now connected to internet streaming.

- They would feed their smaller, personal god three times a day.

We monitor stocks, count social media likes, manage the gaming app that requires constant attention, or check the sports score multiple times per day, all through convenient, personal handheld devices.

- They would parade their deities through the streets.

We scroll down the "parade" called a feed, attracted to the shiniest, most trendy things. No one has to miss the festival days due to the capability to stream every important event (things like the Times Square ball dropping, the Super Bowl, the Olympics, and elections).

- They would start and end each day by opening and closing the temple gate.

These temple gates (our screens and devices) are still being opened and closed (turned on and off) ritualistically today. These tasks are being performed by many people around the world who partake in the culture of the New Babylon—whether they realize it or not.

Is it wrong to have a smartphone, use the internet, or watch TV? No. But in some cases, these modern technologies have consumed us, preying on our fears of being left out or left behind.

What we truly fear is being forgotten. This is why we long for the spotlight. But the truth is, the real God never forgets us. He knows our names. He remembers us even when society moves on, even when we are incapable of keeping up with the trend. We don't need our name in lights. We don't need to "live on" in the minds of others. *We only need Him.*

Not only does God remember us, but He put the spotlight on Himself—not in a positive way, but a negative way—so we may remain with Him.

In a later chapter, I discuss God's solution for addictions. He has a better substance for us to be addicted to, and it's something that never leaves us feeling empty. Yes, you read that right. There's something that's actually good for us to be addicted to! (I will fully explain that statement.)

For now though, look at what Isaiah 21:9 (NASB) has to say about this predicament:

> Now behold, here comes a troop of riders, horsemen in pairs. And one said, "Fallen, fallen is Babylon; and all the images of her gods are shattered on the ground."

When God chooses to cast down Babylon's images, they shatter, becoming unrecognizable. Here's a prophetic picture to connect this to today: when a person decides enough is enough and that they must be free from addiction, they may symbolically throw their smartphone down and shatter its screen, destroying the images that it once produced.

I'm not telling you to destroy your phone. Because, the truth is, if you have a problem with one screen, that problem will persist with another unless the root of the issue is dealt with in the heart. The controlling IMAGE must be shattered at the heart level for the necessary steps to stick on the surface.

Like I said, in a few chapters I'm going to give you the keys to replacing addiction with a better addiction. But before addiction can be replaced, it must be uprooted. This won't apply to everyone, but some people will need this, and if it's you, don't hesitate to take a step of faith in the right direction. This is a chance to renounce any and every screen addiction that may be taking place in your life.

The Holy Spirit may bring some things to your mind that you haven't even thought of before. Whatever He shows you—whether it's related to entertainment excess, workaholism, the comparison game, lust, pride, greed, fear of missing out, or anything else—give it to Him. Release it. Let it go. It doesn't get to rule your life any longer. Pray this prayer with me and find freedom:

> ***Holy Spirit, I surrender this addiction to You. I'm sorry for letting my eyes wander away from You and to another god, to another source of fulfillment. I thank You that in Jesus I am forgiven and cleansed. I thank You for taking this away from me now and helping me to walk in freedom and purity. I thank You for Your grace which is my covenant access today to victory!***

If there are any practical steps you need to take as a result of this decision, take them. The Holy Spirit will begin to reveal those to you as you seek after Him in this area.

We Can Rule Everything

During Hammurabi's rule of Babylon, he conquered and ruled all of southern Mesopotamia, creating Babylonia and making Babylon the most powerful city on earth at the time. We see this same tendency to invade, overpower, and subjugate within the narratives involving ancient Babylon in the Scriptures. Between 605 BC and 586 BC, Babylon attacks Jerusalem three separate times. During this period in history, the city is destroyed, their treasures are stolen, captives are taken, and the temple is burned.[56]

The Encyclopedia of Christian Civilization describes Babylon's role as a metaphorical force apposing God's Kingdom, both during the Old Testament era along with the New.

According to the Encyclopedia of Christian Civilization, the opposition to the rule of God by world powers or the exile of God's people from the land of blessing is conveyed properly through the metaphor of Babylon. The city of Babylon was the adversary of the Jews in the Old Testament. Daniel described Babylon as the beginning of the Gentile kingdoms that will dominate earth's history during the *"times of the Gentiles"* (Daniel 2:31-45; Luke 21:24). Gentile world power began at Babylon under Nebuchadnezzar, and therefore became a metaphor of the rule of Gentile world powers which will not end until Christ returns to the earth in judgment of them.

This continuing dominating force is seen in the new Babylon in the book of Revelation.

> Here is the mind which has wisdom. The seven heads are seven mountains upon which the woman sits, (Revelation 17:9 NASB).

> These will wage war against the Lamb, and the Lamb will overcome them because He is Lord of lords and King of kings; and those who are with Him are the called and chosen and faithful (Revelation 17:14 NASB).

> And in her was found the blood of prophets and of saints, and of all who have been slaughtered on the earth (Revelation 18:24 NASB).

Eventually we see an attempted complete physical domination of God's people taking place; however, until that time, a slow and strategic domination of world powers also occurs. The woman (Babylon) is depicted as sitting upon the seven mountains, which represent seven kings or seven world powers. This happens through physical force, as well as through the forced adoption of the ideology of Babylon. Let's look at the philosophy of Babylon to discover the nature of that ideology.

Babylon's Philosophy

As discussed, the social philosophy of ancient Babylon differed from its ancient counterparts in that it promoted a code of "fairness."

Obviously, the political structure of ancient Babylon was far from democratic, so the social philosophy did not extend from group thought; however, systems instituted by rulers such as Hammurabi helped to create a foreshadowing of modern philosophy.

Many ancient civilizations consisted of the ruling classes freely domineering and oppressing the poor or worker classes. Babylon broke that mold. Class distinctions were not as hard set. The rights of the poor were protected in a court of law, and economic status was considered during judgment. Rulings were made by a panel of judges based on a vote. The system even attempted to keep the rich from escaping punishment. Women held rights; considerably more than later societies. They could represent themselves in court, own property, and even hold government and societal positions.[57]

Amanda Podany, history professor and author of *Weavers, Scribes, and Kings: A New History of the Ancient Near East*, says about this ancient code: "It seems to have been a system that Babylonians prided themselves on for its fairness." If that sounds strangely familiar, it's because it is. Modern philosophy erects itself upon a foundation of what is "fair." It prides itself upon its fairness. The modern way of thought says, "We've evolved beyond primitive systems."

In many ways, fairness *is* essential to a healthy, thriving society. Christianity itself has done more to feed the message of fairness throughout history than any other belief system.

Terry Hartle wrote an opinion piece for *The Christian Science Monitor,* reviewing historian Tom Holland's popular book, *Dominion*, and he says about the work:

> ***In "Dominion: How the Christian Revolution Remade the World," he attempts nothing less than to explain how an obscure, itinerant street preacher who died the death of a slave and his small group of followers who lived in a far-flung corner of the Roman Empire gradually transformed the world through a message of love, charity, and reconciliation.***[58]

So, is fairness (in the sense of compassion for the underprivileged) right? Yes. Is it Christian to love one's neighbor and take care of the less fortunate? Yes. However, once a system promoting "fairness" becomes perverted, it can become very dangerous.

One example of modern Babylonian domination is cancel culture. "Justice" has become the code of the internet, yet at the same time the internet is home to the most blatant lies, undeserved smear campaigns, hatred expressed openly, and unrestricted vileness. People want everyone else to get what they deserve, and yet they don't want to answer for their own actions. The system itself is one big hypocrite.

Cancel culture is fairness becoming perverted. When people get "canceled" through incessant online character attacks, they can lose their jobs, influence, friends, and even family. Many people who have been canceled have later testified to it ruining their life.

Cancel culture is a movement toward fairness; how could it be a bad thing? The problem is, though it is driven by people's desire for things to be "fair," it isn't run on fairness. It runs on emotional outbursts and mob mentality. The internet contributes greatly to this.

Some people have been canceled for things they were later proven innocent of. People's lives have been ruined by a misconception, exaggeration, or straight-up lie. This is all thanks to "making things fair." It's a mock trial with a pre-determined outcome.

Where does this perversion come from? In their literature, the Babylonians recorded the Hammurabi Code as having been given to him by the god of justice. Whether this refers to a real supernatural experience or not, a "god" did have a hand in passing down the fairness standard we see in the world today.

Cancel culture comes from the god of this world, the devil. We know this because God's version of justice is different from our own. Biblical justice aims at uncovering the real truth, not punishing a person unless they are proven guilty. Cancel culture lashes out in anger, punishing a person as a form of self-medicating relief. Cancel culture is based in making all those offended feel better, not in actually delivering true justice to the offender.

God's true justice goes deeper. Not only does He look for the real truth behind a matter, He looks upon every person involved with compassion. When we were the offenders and He was the offended, He sought justice by taking the punishment upon Himself.

> All of us, like sheep, have gone astray, each of us has turned to his own way; but the Lord has caused the wrongdoing of us all to fall on Him (Isaiah 53:6 NASB).

Jesus broke the world's rules for fairness. Instead of getting revenge—making us feel the pain of our wrongdoings—He felt all of the pain for us until the pain itself was exhausted.

It's good to be fair, until you make a god out of being fair. Sadly, many people are trading the endless, unfathomable love of Jesus for "fairness." Yet when a selfish heart finally gets what it wants, it is left cold, alone, and bitter. When we choose to lay aside our earthly desires, and we take on Jesus's forgiveness and compassion, our hearts are healed of this vicious virus called fairness.

And yes, this happens in the Christian culture just as much as the secular one. We just name it and justify it differently. We attack each other over differing opinions on church, evangelism, spiritual gifts, secondary theology, and more. We feel justified in either attacking back or growing bitter. We must remember that we have the Holy Spirit not because we have done good, but because Jesus was good for us. His heart is for the whole church to walk in unity and love.

> Let no unwholesome word come out of your mouth, but if there is any good word for edification according to the need of the moment, say that, so that it will give grace to those who hear. Do not grieve the Holy

> Spirit of God, by whom you were sealed for the day of redemption. All bitterness, wrath, anger, clamor, and slander must be removed from you, along with all malice. Be kind to one another, compassionate, forgiving each other, just as God in Christ also has forgiven you (Ephesians 4:29-32 NASB).

Some may ask, "But what about what they said against me? How can I possibly forgive that?"

> Blessed are you when people insult you and persecute you, and falsely say all kinds of evil against you because of Me (Matthew 5:11 NASB).

God's ways are completely different from ours. Jesus flipped everything on its head the day He died for a world of sinful, unrighteous people. He is still flipping the script today.

Sadly, the love of Jesus is the very thing that will eventually drive the world to fight against Him. Because His love is not filling their hearts, people will eventually revolt against all that is good and holy. Justice will become injustice. True fairness will cease to exist.

Though we may eventually see a nation or group of nations physically dominate the entire world, at the moment, cancel culture reigns supreme, and it is often applied through the political structure. If the people of the world don't approve of something, they express it. Once enough pressure is applied, the political machine bends and sanctions are issued by all the "politically correct" nations. If this doesn't work, the eventual outcome can be war. A system like this works well when people hold to ideals and beliefs that are pure, but it crumbles once ideals become perverted. The final result is that the kingdoms (peoples) of the earth will wage war against the Lamb, the purest and holiest Person who has ever existed.

We Can Know Everything

Daisy Hernandez covers another internet highlight in her *50 Greatest Moments* article, one many consider a pinnacle of the information age: "In 1991, Tim Berners-Lee's World Wide Web went live. The British physicist revolutionized the way the world shares and processes information."

In many ways, information itself would become the new precious metal. The routine selling of information had existed for centuries. Newspapers are nothing new. Yet, never before had information been readable by everyone.

Though she might not have meant it this way, you can almost hear the boasting of the internet's voice in Hernandez's announcement of the birthing of the information giant, Wikipedia:

> ***Wikipedia went live with its first edit on January 15, 2001, and has become one of the first places people check for various kinds of information. Actually,*** *all* ***the information.***[59]

All the information. Isn't that the story of the internet over the past few decades? It has quickly grown from being simply a sharing platform to a complete archive of everything known by humankind, and humankind tends to assume we know more than we really do.

Similar to the serpent in the Garden of Eden, the devil makes a grand promise to people today:

> For God knows that on the day you eat from it your eyes will be opened, and you will become like God, knowing good and evil (Genesis 3:5 NASB).

The rate of deconstruction of faith occurring in the modern church can be partly blamed on the information promise. The devil says to the casual churchgoer, "The pastor didn't answer your question? That means God doesn't have the answer. But if you come with me I will show you where you can find *all* the answers you want. I have an entire archive of answers just waiting to be read." Those answers just happen to be largely crafted on the conclusion that God doesn't exist.

Deconstruction is not happening to real friends of God. It's happening to those who still have not made a choice between the trees. Those who are eating of the Tree of Life—who have a personal relationship with Jesus and know Him as their best Friend—are not fully persuaded by the promises of the Tree of the Knowledge of Good and Evil. They know how *real* and how *good* God is, and nothing can snatch them out of His hand (see John 10:28). However, though they are not fully captured by it, they can still be drawn away by its fruit and enticed to waste their time and gifts in an endless search for information.

As we will discuss in a later chapter, there is a way to get every question answered, but it doesn't come through a search for knowledge. It comes through surrendering fully to the One who knows everything.

Babylon's Intelligence

Though Babylon did not invent information, it historically played a distinct part in the early curating of it. We discussed how Babylon was the cultural epicenter of intellectual thought in ancient Mesopotamia. They wrote literature, constructed ancient libraries, created one of the first codes' of law, and invested in scientific research and experimentation.

We see Babylon's information-driven ideals on display in the exile story of Daniel and his friends.

> Then the king told Ashpenaz, the chief of his officials, to bring in some of the sons of Israel, including some of the royal family and of the nobles, youths in whom there was no impairment, who were good-looking, suitable for instruction in every kind of expertise, endowed with understanding and discerning knowledge, and who had ability to serve in the king's court; and he ordered Ashpenaz to teach them the literature and language of the Chaldeans (Daniel 1:3-4 NASB).

Nebuchadnezzar besieges Jerusalem, captures it, and carries off its wealth and some of its people to Babylon. Daniel, Hananiah, Mishael, and Azariah are plucked from their families and homes and replanted as servants of the Babylonian Empire. Their initiation included an attempted restructuring of their belief system, new names, and the introduction to new habits. The Babylonians tried to undo all their parents had taught them.

The same is happening today, except the captivity and exile is taking place right in the home, behind a locked bedroom door at night or through the privacy of earbuds. Children and youth are being taught the Babylonian customs. Because of the rise of agenda-driven storytelling, the information is becoming easier and easier to access. Young people don't need to land on the dark web to encounter the darkness. Babylon's belief system is in many cases seeping just as a quickly and thoroughly through that next Netflix Original.

Look at Babylon's effect on the peoples of the world in Revelation 18:

> And the sound of harpists, musicians, flute players, and trumpeters will never be heard in you again; and

> no craftsman of any craft will ever be found in you again; and the sound of a mill will never be heard in you again; and the light of a lamp will never shine in you again; and the voice of the groom and bride will never be heard in you again; for your merchants were the powerful people of the earth, because all the nations were deceived by your witchcraft (Revelation 18:22-23 NASB).

It says, *"all the nations were deceived by your witchcraft."* How were the nations deceived? Through song (the sound of harpists, musicians, flute players, and trumpeters), through images (the craftsman), and through production and commerce (the mill and the merchants). Through the internet, the youth of today are being sold a lie and that lie can be found throughout the messages preached in songs, in movies and books, and even within the messaging of companies. All of this is tied together by the spreading of witchcraft.

> For rebellion is as the sin of witchcraft… (1 Samuel 15:23 KJV).

The youth are being preached a message of rebellion. When a children's film teaches children that parents don't really know what's right and that kids should be able to decide for themselves, it's teaching them witchcraft through rebellion. And the children of today are the cultural leaders of tomorrow.

Let me clarify. I am not preaching a message of fear or total isolation from the world. Instead, I believe we need to be aware of the system in place and its goals for the next generation. As parents of five, my wife and I allow our children to engage in entertainment, but we limit the amount of entertainment, the specific types of entertainment, and the individual access they have to that entertainment. Regarding the "Babylonian" preaching they do end up hearing, we have a discussion. We engage with them and relationally talk through what is true and what is not. We also don't shy away from expressing the fact that we have an enemy called satan, and he is the mastermind behind many of the ideologies of today's world.

I don't believe the answer is legalism. I believe the answer is relationship—parents walking relationally with their kids and graciously helping them to understand the ways of God as well as Christians walking relationally with God as they navigate through the rough waters of the modern culture.

We Can Buy and Sell Everything

Back to the 50 greatest highlights of internet history, Hernandez doesn't leave out Amazon. She states:

> ***Jeff Bezos launched the online retail behemoth Amazon in July 1995. It's hard to believe the massive marketplace started merely as an online book store. It's reported that Bezos eventually wanted to sell "everything," but decided that books were a good starting point. Mission accomplished, a billion times over.***[60]

This phrase is an interesting paradigm to the modern cultural marketplace: Bezos eventually wanted to sell "everything." Bezos isn't the only one. Today, we can sell or buy nearly *everything* online.

Perhaps you remember Craigslist or still use it. Possibly, you've sold some items on Facebook Marketplace or Etsy for yourself. If you've ever watched one of the investor shows like *Shark Tank*, you've heard the pros hammer people for not marketing and selling their products online. Online retail has become a cultural standard.

In 1997, Alan Hall sat next to Jeff Bezos at a dinner and asked him what he did for a living. Bezos replied, "I have started a new business called Amazon. We sell books over the Internet." Hall's response? "I then turned to my wife and prophesied that he would be out of business within the space of two years. 'Who,' I boasted privately, 'would ever want to buy books over the web? We all visit our favorite bookstores when we want to buy books. We've done it for decades. Why does he think we will change our buying behavior?'"[61]

Hall's "prophecy," though wrong, mirrored Meg Ryan's character's thoughts as a small book store owner fighting Tom Hank's character's corporate giant bookstore chain in the movie, *You've Got Mail*. She believed that her customer's loyalty would pull them through. The funny thing is, *You've Got Mail* was released in 1998, just one year after Hall's conversation with Bezos. The same way the big box bookstore ended up putting the mom and pop neighborhood bookstore out of business in the film, by the time Hall had reflected about his conversation with Bezos in his 2012 article for *Forbes* magazine, *The Internet is Killing My Business!*, Amazon was also putting the big bookstores out of business. As they say, there is always a bigger fish.

The truth is, internet killed many things about commerce. In many ways, it completely took over. If you didn't start selling online, you were left behind. The same is true about Babylon.

Babylon's Commerce

Ancient Babylon boasted one of the greatest societal marketplaces of the BC world. Not only did Babylon trade with all of the surrounding city states, but it also attracted merchants from all over the known world.

Matthew Capala wrote an article for *Forbes* magazine titled, "What Marketers Can Learn From The Ancient Babylonians," and in his comparison to modern selling he breaks down some of Babylon's secrets to its commerce success. He also parallel's Babylon's trade "strategies" to the modern-day internet marketer.[62]

Though he might not realize it, Capala wasn't the first to make this comparison. Revelation 18 describes the buying and selling taking place within the new Babylon by the time of her fall.

> And the merchants of the earth weep and mourn over her, because no one buys their cargo any more—cargo of gold, silver, precious stones, and pearls; fine linen, purple, silk, and scarlet; every kind of citron wood, every article of ivory, and every article made from very valuable wood, bronze, iron, and marble; cinnamon, spice, incense, perfume, frankincense, wine, olive oil, fine flour, wheat, cattle, sheep, and cargo of horses, carriages, slaves, and human lives. The fruit you long for has left you, and all things that were luxurious and splendid have passed away from you and people will no longer find them. The merchants of these things, who became rich from her, will stand at a distance because of the fear of her torment, weeping and mourning, saying, "Woe, woe, the great city, she who was clothed in fine linen and purple and scarlet, and adorned with gold, precious stones, and pearls; for in one hour such great wealth has been laid waste!" And every shipmaster and every passenger and sailor, and

> all who make their living by the sea, stood at a distance, and were crying out as they saw the smoke of her burning, saying, "What city is like the great city?" And they threw dust on their heads and were crying out, weeping and mourning, saying, "Woe, woe, the great city, in which all who had ships at sea became rich from her prosperity, for in one hour she has been laid waste!" (Revelation 18:11-19 NASB)

What other marketplace in the world does this passage better describe than the online one?

We Can Live and Love Without Restraint

Daisy Hernandez touches on two critical moments in her brief history of the internet that have to do with excess and casting off restraint.

Match.com went live on the internet in 1995, making it the world's first dating site. Tinder, Bumble, Grindr, and so many other dating apps can thank Match for its pioneering efforts back in the mid '90s.

Although Netflix came alive in 1997 as a movie rental service, it grew to become the foremost video streaming service of all time. In 2007, a decade after its birth, Netflix began allowing "members to instantly watch television shows and movies on their personal computers." Today, we can't have a conversation without asking, "So what are you binging?"

If you met your spouse online, I'm not passing judgment on that. I've met many godly couples who originally connected over a dating website. However, the rise of dating websites was quickly followed up by the rise of "hookup" websites and apps. Today, it has in many ways become an epidemic. Similar in some ways to the sexual revolution of the 1960s, we are witnessing a culture casting off the restraints at a whole new level, and it's all thanks to technology.

During the lingering effects of the quarantines, Nancy Jo Sales wrote an article for *Wired* titled "Online Dating Apps Are Actually Kind of a Disaster."[63] What's interesting is that she writes from a non-Christian perspective, and yet she brings up some very serious points that many in the industry are probably attempting to ignore.

A 2019 survey by ProPublica and Columbia Journalism Investigations—one of the only articles ever to take this issue seriously—found that "more than a third of women said they were sexually assaulted by someone they had met through a dating app," and "of these women, more than half said they were raped." But when women try to report these incidents, many say the dating apps in question often don't even respond. They are corporations that have colonized our most intimate and most private of spaces—love, sex, and romantic relationships—in a fairly brutal way, endangering the happiness, sense of well-being, and safety of millions of users. Some research says that online dating actually makes users feel lonelier.[64]

What the world—Babylon—promises can never ultimately deliver. It will always fall short of true fulfillment, because the system of Babylon does not understand how human beings were designed. We were created for intimacy, yes, but intimacy within the boundaries of a godly relationship and a loving marriage. That was and still is God's design for us.

Ancient Greek historian Herodotus (484 – c. 425 BC) wrote about the sexual rituals of the Babylonians, and his summary bears a striking resemblance to sexual norms of today's culture.

The foulest Babylonian custom is that which compels every woman of the land to sit in the temple of Aphrodite and have intercourse with some stranger at least once in her life. But most sit down in the sacred plot of Aphrodite, with crowns of cord on their heads; there is a great multitude of women coming and going; passages marked by line run every way through the crowd, by which the men pass and make their choice.[65]

Today, this Babylonian custom has been in some ways replaced with scrolling down profiles via a hookup app. But this kind of unrestrained "love" isn't love at all. True love is described in 1 Corinthians 13:4-8 (NASB):

> Love is patient, love is kind, it is not jealous; love does not brag, it is not arrogant. It does not act disgracefully, it does not seek its own benefit; it is not provoked, does not keep an account of a wrong suffered, it does not rejoice in unrighteousness, but rejoices with the truth; it keeps every confidence, it believes all things, hopes all things, endures all things. Love never fails....

True love—God's kind of love—never fails. The Babylonian kind of "love" has failed modern generations. Some of the top thinkers in the secular space are beginning to realize this truth, but not many are listening. *Why not?* The answer has to do with the *gates*.

Babylon's Gates

We previously discussed the entrance to the inner city of ancient Babylon, the bright-blue, glazed Ishtar Gate. This gateway is famous for the celebratory New Year's parade that would involve statues of deities carried through the gate and exhibited along the half-mile Processional Way path between the outer walls and the inner city.[66]

The significance of this specific gate lies in the character of the goddess after which it is named. Ishtar was the goddess of sex. The same way that images of gods would pass on display through a bright gateway named for the goddess of sex, images are also passing through a bright gateway today.

Pornography through a phone, computer, or TV screen is the gateway into a world of sexual immorality and evil today. Many kids are introduced to the unrestrained sexual culture through pornography exposure at a young age. However, even pornography has a predecessor.

I personally became addicted to pornography in college, but the addiction didn't technically start with porn. It started with images and ideas found in movies and television shows. Films including partial nude scenes and other sexually immoral storylines began to feed the lust in my heart, and this gateway eventually led to the addiction. The truth is, I was already addicted to lust, I just didn't realize it at the time. Porn became the fuel for that addiction to flourish.

The other truth is that many of those films and shows would be considered pornography by God's standard. I would not admit that at the time. To me, it was just "art." Yet, the devil was using that "art" to lead me through a door to something more vile. As I sunk further into the darkness and further away from God, I one day woke up and realized that I had become something I never intended to be.

To attempt an escape from the dirty feeling inside, I self-medicated anyway I knew how. Then in one last ditch effort, I eventually decided to stop believing in God altogether. I thought, *If God doesn't exist, that fixes the problem of sin that I've found myself trapped in*. Yet as hard as I tried, I could not ignore the truth in my heart that God *did* exist and that He had a holy standard.

Ishtar was the goddess of sex. Her gateway led a procession of people into the heart of ancient Babylon. Though ancient Babylon fell into ruin, the fragments of the Ishtar Gate were found and reconstructed by 1930, and the gateway can be seen today in Pergamonmuseum in Berlin.[67]

Though the gateway has returned physically, it has also returned in a greater way than ever before. Pornography through a phone or screen is the gateway into a world of sexual immorality and evil today. For many people, this addiction stays secret, hidden from those they love because of fear or shame. I believe this secret sin is the gateway for many young people's decision to ultimately turn away from God.

The angel in Revelation 17 says about the woman Babylon:

> ...Come here, I will show you the judgment of the great prostitute who sits on many waters, with whom the kings of the earth committed acts of sexual immorality, and those who live on the earth became drunk with the wine of her sexual immorality (Revelation 17:1-2 NASB).

A second angel makes a similar proclamation about Babylon in the next chapter:

> And he cried out with a mighty voice, saying, "Fallen, fallen is Babylon the great! She has become a dwelling place of demons and a prison of every unclean spirit, and a prison of every unclean and hateful bird. For all the nations have fallen because of the wine of the passion of her sexual immorality, and the kings of the earth have committed acts of sexual immorality with her..." (Revelation 18:2-3 NASB).

If Babylon is a prison, that means it holds prisoners captive. It chains down those who fall prey to its ways. This is what happens when someone falls into sexual sin—they become bound and chained. Even if they desire to escape, it often feels impossible.

Sexual sin also opens the door to the demonic. When I was addicted to pornography, I was still partially seeking God in church. I still considered myself a Christian. Yet I was making all sorts of sinful choices. I also began experiencing strange things such as nightmares, sleep paralysis, and even hallucinations. On top of this, I experienced heavy bouts of depression nearly every day. The depression joined with anger, loneliness, bitterness, and anxiety to create one dark prison.

When I finally admitted my need for God's help, I got down on my knees, prayed a prayer of repentance, and I tried with all my effort to stop sinning after that. Yet somehow the sin continued to keep me imprisoned. The harder I beat against that wall, the more it closed in.

One day the Holy Spirit spoke to my heart and gave me the key I needed to truly get free. His still, small voice began to reveal to me the truth about Jesus's sacrifice. He told me that the Father loved me; and as I heard Him say it, I believed it. Then He told me that because of the Father's love, Jesus came to the earth, lived a perfect life, then died on a Cross so I could be forgiven and free. In that moment of belief, I felt the chains fall off. I suddenly understood that I could never free myself through my effort. I had to rely upon the finished work of Jesus at the Cross.

That same night, the depression, anxiety, fear, shame, anger, and bitterness left. I truly was free, and that same freedom is available to all who call upon the name of the Lord. Freedom is available to all who believe that Jesus's sacrifice is the full payment for their sin.

One final thing occurred that night. The addiction I had fought so hard to overcome was finally dead. I'm so grateful to be free from pornography addiction for nearly 15 years now, and it's all because of God's grace.

Some people might say, "I'm stuck in a prison of my own, and I feel like the chains are too strong for me. I want to accept what you're saying, but I don't know how to practically apply it." If that's you, keep reading. In the next few chapters, I lay out the practical application of this amazing truth that set me free.

Jeremiah talks about the shattering of Babylon's gates. This same thing needs to happen today, and it starts with the shattering of the images within the church. It starts in our own homes.

> This is what the Lord of armies says: "The broad wall of Babylon will be completely demolished, and her high gates will be set on fire..." (Jeremiah 51:58 NASB).
>
> ...Her idols have been put to shame, her images have been shattered (Jeremiah 50:2 NASB).

We Can Live Forever

You've probably heard Alphaville's song, *Forever Young*, which boldly proclaims: "Forever young. I want to be forever young." It also takes the idea of remaining youthful to the extreme view when it says, "Let us die young or let us live forever." The writer of the classic song would rather die at an early age in order to maintain the appearance of youthfulness than grow old and have to face the realities of aging in this life.

I may be taking a silly song a little too seriously, but this actually does reflect some of the values found within today's culture, and these values can be traced all the way back to ancient Babylon and beyond.

Though we can't stop the flow of time, we can "slow" it through the use of technology. Medical technology advancements have made it possible for people to alter their appearance to a greater extent and for longer, but there's a more pervasive technology "enhancement" happening today. I'm talking about the digital beauty revolution. Snapchat, Instagram, and other filters can completely and instantly alter the way we look. Remember the spider and the fly? *Come, look at yourself. You're pretty.* But it's a trap.

In 2021, *Forbes* magazine released an article titled, "From 'Instagram Face' To 'Snapchat Dysmorphia,'" in which is discussed the dangers of this trend:

> ***...the term 'Snapchat Dysmorphia' was created by plastic surgeon Dr. Tijon Esho in 2018 to describe the increasing phenomenon of people seeking out cosmetic surgery to achieve their filtered face in real life.***
>
> ***"Selfie-taking and photo-editing leads users to compare their actual appearance to an idealized and unrealistic retouched appearance which is impossible to achieve in real life," says professor Phillippa Diedrichs, a psychologist at the Centre of Appearance Research at the University of West England. According to Diedrichs' recent research with the Dove Self-Esteem Project, 60% of girls feel upset when their real appearance doesn't match the online version of themselves. "Young women who spent just 10 minutes***

> ***taking, editing and posting selfies to social media reported feeling more anxious, less confident and less physically attractive afterwards compared to those who didn't engage in these behaviours...."[68]***

Ten minutes. That's all it takes for a young woman to lose her confidence. The scope of this trend stems far beyond young women because this trap is bigger than that, but this article focuses on young women because statistically they spend a disproportionate amount of time using digital image enhancement apps.

Now that we are over a decade into the "Snapchat era," here's what the studies are showing: the younger or more "perfect" we try to make ourselves look, the worse we end up feeling about reality. In short, the filters haven't helped. They've only made things worse in the long run.

The allure of staying forever young or living forever is not new either. It all started when our immortality was taken from us at the fall of humanity in the Garden of Eden. Something deep within our souls longs to return to a state of perfection and permanence.

> But from the tree of the knowledge of good and evil you shall not eat, for on the day that you eat from it you will certainly die (Genesis 2:17 NASB).

Death started the day we ate from the Tree of the Knowledge of Good and Evil, and unfortunately many are still eating from it today. The only true fix is to begin to eat from the Tree of Life once more—not a literal tree, but rather the life-giving truth of Jesus having taken the curse for us by hanging on a tree at Calvary.

Babylon's Preservation

Beauty enhancement practices did not start with the digital age. Even the ancient Babylonians followed their own makeup tutorials. Both men and women of higher social statuses regularly used cosmetics, styled their hair, wrapped themselves in luxurious garments, and adorned themselves with Babylonian jewelry.[69]

Though it's not wrong to use makeup or to laugh about a beauty filter, there's something deeper happening here. Babylon's wisdom never leads to true preservation—only to a cover-up. The same way that people who use too many filters today run the risk of Selfie Dysmorphia or Snapchat Dysmorphia, the ancient Babylon's were facing a dysmorphia of their own.

We discussed the origins of Babylonia and the sudden emergence of the Tower of Babel as depicted in Genesis 11. In *A Brief Introduction to the Old Testament: the Hebrew Bible in Its Context,* Michael Coogan asserts that the builders' true reason for constructing the tower stretched beyond an attempt to reach Heaven and really grew out of necessity. Chronologically, the raising of the Tower of Babel stands as the next major event after the great flood. The ancient people in Genesis 11 were actually investing in their own preservation.[70]

The assumption would have been, "If God flooded the earth once, He might do it again." We know based on Scripture that He had promised not to flood the earth ever again, but the builders probably didn't know that, or they didn't believe Him. So, they tried building a tower tall enough to keep them safe during a flood.

The Tower of Babel is the same story that's being told today: let us exalt and prolong life on earth instead of seeking God for eternal life (which is what we actually need and He offers us freely through Jesus).

Ancient Babylon reflects this ideology again in the book of Daniel.

> "Please put your servants to the test for ten days, and let us be given some vegetables to eat and water to drink. Then let our appearance be examined in your presence and the appearance of the youths who are eating the king's choice food; and deal with your servants according to what you see." So he listened to them in this matter, and put them to the test for ten days. And at the end of ten days their appearance seemed better, and they were fatter than all the youths who had been eating the king's choice food. So the overseer continued to withhold their choice food and the wine they were to drink, and kept giving them vegetables (Daniel 1:12-16 NASB).

The overseer, under the king's command, rationed portions of the king's choice food to Daniel and his fellow exiled youth from Jerusalem. This choice food and drink directly defied the food restrictions of the Law of Moses and the Jewish culture. Because of wisdom from God, Daniel challenged the overseer to put the king's rations to the test. After ten days, the obvious winner emerged.

However, though God's wisdom proved better than the wisdom of Babylon, I refer to this passage for another reason entirely. This passage is relevant because it clearly displays Babylon's fascination for and value of youth, beauty and appearance. Though Babylon valued the preservation of beauty, it failed to actually preserve true beauty, which is something that happens in the heart. We see a picture of what God considers beautiful in Isaiah 4:

> In that day the Branch of the Lord will be beautiful and glorious, and the fruit of the land will be the pride and glory of the survivors in Israel (Isaiah 4:2 NIV).

Commentators say this verse is potentially referencing the return of Israelites taken captive by kingdoms such as Babylon. So, there is a return to true beauty and life once the shackles of Babylon are removed from the wrists of a culture and society. Once the reign of Babylon lifts and people begin to experience the presence of God in their lives, true fruit begins to blossom.

This is not only a metaphor and warning for a generation of "survivors," but it is also a picture of what the church should look like in today's world. We should be eating the fruit of righteousness and enjoying the presence of God in our midst, and this beauty will act as a sign to the world, saying, *"You ultimately won't find what you're looking for in Babylon. Come home to a better kingdom—one that truly fulfills."*

The "survivors" I'm talking about are those with a fighting spirit looking for life and fulfillment in the midst of a broken and dying world. These are people who are actively pursuing wealth, fame, youth, beauty, and the promises of the Babylonian system. They know that something is wrong with the world, and yet they also know that if something is wrong, that means the "right" is out there.

These are the philosophers who keep thinking deeply, hoping to solve the world's moral and ethical issues within their lifetime. They are the inventors attempting to fix the ecosystem or fuel problem. They are the scientists working on cures. They continue hoping despite the failure of a broken system. They are survivors, yet they are seeking to thrive in the wrong system, and for that reason they get stymied at every turn. They aren't thrown off by the pain or losses, because they know to expect those. They are thrown off by the wins—by the successes of life that just never seem to fully satisfy. And so they continue, pushing and trudging along.

They are like Gilgamesh in his endless hunt for immortality.

In the epic, Utnapishtim tells Gilgamesh that he too can achieve immortality by staying awake for six days and seven nights, therefore causing the gods to take pity on him and grant him his wish. He essentially tells Gilgamesh to earn it, yet he simultaneously is telling Gilgamesh that he can't earn it, because he knows the task is too difficult for him.

"Gilgamesh, who is seeking to overcome death, cannot even conquer sleep."[71]

This pattern plays out in each of our lives through a slow but steady realization. No amount of striving and effort can guarantee us eternal life, and no amount of striving and effort can produce true fulfillment in this life. We are a world of striving people trying to overcome death, and yet we can't even conquer the need for sleep.

The end result is that the gods ignore Gilgamesh and he goes home empty-handed, unable to earn the glorious reward he seeks. Yet, this is where our story differs from the tale of Gilgamesh. We have the God who knew we could not earn the life we desperately need, and took pity upon us nonetheless and willingly gifted us the grace we would need to receive it.

This is what Jesus did for us.

Jesus recognized the state we were in. He saw our propensity for failure—to always strive toward something and never arrive—and He came down and He beat the system for us.

Genesis 3:19 describes the toil of the system we are all part of when it says: *"By the sweat of your face you shall eat bread, until you return to the ground, because from it you were taken; for you are dust, and to dust you shall return."*

Essentially, the system tells us, "Work hard. Oh, and then you die." If you want anything in this life, you get it by your own blood, sweat and tears. Babylon is a cruel master, and it is bound by the rules of an infinitely dark system; the curse of sin and death. This is the fate we all must face. At least it was—until Jesus stepped in. Jesus came to earth to save us—to pull us out of the system, and to bring us into a new one. Through *His* own blood, sweat, and tears, He redeemed us and brought us into His family.

His family isn't one you work your way into. It isn't one you can earn access to through sacrifice. It's not a reward for living well. It's a gift He gives us that can only be received through belief in Him. It's a gift He gives because of His love for us.

His family is also His Kingdom, and it's based on a system that freely supplies us with everything good you and I have been striving for and missing our entire lives.

> For God did not send the Son into the world to judge the world, but so that the world might be saved through Him. The one who believes in Him is not judged; the one who does not believe has been judged already, because he has not believed in the name of the only Son of God. And this is the judgment, that the Light has come into the world, and people loved the darkness rather than the Light; for their deeds were evil. For everyone who does evil hates the Light, and does not come to the Light, so that his

> deeds will not be exposed. But the one who practices the truth comes to the Light, so that his deeds will be revealed as having been performed in God (John 3:17-21 NASB).

In this passage, God gives us a choice. Are we going to choose the system of darkness or the Kingdom of light? We choose the light only by believing in what Jesus has done for us, and when we believe, the weight of sin and shame fall off, and we are finally free.

Not many reading this will need to hear this, but some might. If you are still in the dark, come home to the light today. Come to Jesus and be set free. When you and I were still sinners, Jesus showed us the love of God by coming to earth as the Son of God and as a Man. He lived a perfect life, and then He allowed Himself to be crucified on a Cross, taking the punishment for all of our sins upon Himself. He took the weight of our guilt, and He bore it until He died. Then, on the third day, He rose again, truly conquering death and sin once and for all.

To all those who choose to believe in His name, Jesus offers eternal life. He offers forgiveness from sin, redemption to live a purpose-filled life, and freedom to walk personally with God in a beautiful relationship. If you need that, call out to Jesus today and receive it.

Perhaps you have received that gift and yet there are aspects of the Babylonian system that have entrapped you once more. This happens to every believer at some point, and it happens because of the lies of the devil. The same way the serpent lied to Eve in the garden, satan is lying to us today, and he lies to us in order to distract us. Babylon in all its glory is simply a lie. Babylon falsely offers us all the things we want to distract us from the only One who can give us what we truly need.

So even if you know the truth, if you've been distracted by the lie of worldly fulfillment, to you I say the same thing, "Come to Jesus. Only in His presence will you truly find satisfaction and rest from your lengthy toils. Only in His presence will you find life." Jesus Himself tells you:

> Come to Me, all who are weary and burdened, and I will give you rest. Take My yoke upon you and learn from Me, for I am gentle and humble in heart, and you will find rest for your souls. For My yoke is comfortable, and My burden is light (Matthew 11:28-30 NASB).

Though many of us have heard this verse often, we may still have the lingering thought, *I know how I came to Him at first, but how do I come to Him now? How do I get to know Him in a deeper way than ever before?* The answers to those questions are coming.

Breaking the Chains of the Ancient City

As previously stated, the word *Babylon* is derived from the Akkadian word *babilu* meaning "gate of god." It is an ironic and defiant name for the ancient city. The same way Nimrod defied God by building a tower to Heaven apart from God, the worldly system called Babylon today works to build itself up in defiance. It defies the nature of God through perversion of humankind. It defies the plans of God by giving us "freedom" to make our own plans. It defies the laws of God by removing all law and creating a world where anything goes. It has become its own god, and in that sense, it is the gateway to a god—but not the God of the Bible.

The question, *"What hath God wrought"* from Numbers 23:23 (KJV) raises the question of who receives the blessing of God? In Babylon's system, the answer is, whoever learns to control their own destiny by becoming like God. This is the same temptation the snake presented to Eve and Adam in the Garden.

But Numbers 23:9 (NASB) makes it clear who receives God's true blessing when it describes the children of Israel as *"...a people that lives in isolation, and does not consider itself to be among the nations."*

Though Balaam received bribery money to curse Israel, he could not. Despite King Balak's efforts in leading Balaam from one location to another, he could not make Balaam pronounce a curse over God's chosen people. Why? Because they were separated by God from the nations around them. It says they did not consider themselves to be *"among the nations."* It is the separation from the nations that sets them up for a blessing.

> For there is no magic curse against Jacob, nor is there any divination against Israel; at the proper time it shall be said to Jacob and to Israel, what God has done! (Numbers 23:23 NASB)

This separation does not happen today through literal mileage between us and large cities, and it does not even occur through abstinence from using the worldly systems. It happens when we are sanctified in our hearts—wholly set apart for the Lord and His will.

Here is the good news: being set apart is not an effort of self-will, and it doesn't come through a fear of being punished. It won't happen when we are angry or sorrowful enough. It only happens through a true revelation of the love of God. This love was demonstrated through Jesus Christ on the Cross.

It is only through looking and continuing to look at the actual greatest moment in history that we begin to separate.

6

BABYLON'S SECRET KNOWLEDGE

In 2023, Dr. Daniel Mansfield and his research team discovered evidence on a 3700-year-old Babylonian tablet that the ancient Babylonians were using an advanced version of trigonometry. Mansfield said, "It has possible practical applications in surveying, computer graphics and education. This is a rare example of the ancient world teaching us something new." Historians traditionally looked to the Greeks as the oldest possessors of this knowledge, but the discovery has changed all that, and the intelligence of the Babylonians is shining yet again.[72]

This is merely one example of the knowledge bank found within ancient Babylon. Examining Babylon's society as a whole, it's easy to see that their propensity for learning put them a step ahead historically; yet at the same time, for all their learning they still committed atrocious acts of evil. The knowledge itself, though it potentially improved life, did not perfect life. And this reveals the lie we must still fight.

There is an intense draw in today's world toward a special kind of knowledge—a secret knowledge—which is in many ways the same kind of knowledge ancient Babylon possessed and sought after. The secret knowledge of Babylon promises control. It offers power. It claims to give wealth and happiness. It says it leads to ultimate peace. Yet, it never fully delivers on these claims, because once you reach the end of the path and discover the knowledge, you find yourself on another path entirely. Like the white rabbit from Alice in Wonderland, this knowledge promotes a picture of fulfillment, but then it becomes a winding road that constantly eludes that fulfillment.

In the modern technological scene, we refer to this winding path as "the rabbit hole." How many times have you heard someone say something such as, "One simple Google search led to three hours of research. Every time I discovered an answer, I got sucked down another rabbit hole, another path."

This strange road of unending twists and turns is made up of little stepping stones called hyperlinks. A quick Wikipedia search gives us a basic definition of a hyperlink: In computing, a hyperlink, or simply a link, is a digital reference to data that the user can follow or be guided to by clicking or tapping. A hyperlink points to a whole document or to a specific element within a document. Hypertext is text with hyperlinks.

What we refer to as simply "links" on the internet today were originally called hyperlinks. Hypertext is simply text you can click on that links to another page, website, or location online. We are all familiar with these. Yet, when Ted Nelson first coined the phrase "links" in 1964 or 1965 (inspired by ideas written by American presidential science advisor Vannevar Bush in 1945), people probably thought an automatic system of information cross-referencing using computer technology was a fairly new concept.[73]

I've previously mentioned Oliver Burkeman's 2009 article in *The Guardian,* "Forty years of the internet: how the world changed for ever." In it, he makes an astounding connection between the trillions of hyperlinks connecting the web today with an ancient document of biblical proportions:

> ***Tracing the origins of online culture even further back is some people's idea of an entertaining game: there are those who will tell you that the Talmud, the book of Jewish law, contains a form of hypertext, the linking-and-clicking structure at the heart of the web.***

For close to two millennium—since the destruction of the Temple in Jerusalem, the Talmud has been Judaism's central religious text, being made up of the oral law (laws and statutes not recorded in the Torah) and later teachings and perspectives from different rabbis about the law. So, in a very vulgar sense, the Talmud is like the "New Testament" for Judaism.[74]

Here's where it gets interesting. Two versions of the Talmud exist: the Jerusalem Talmud and the Babylonian Talmud. Yes, the second version of the Jewish Talmud was written in Babylon (Babylonia).

The Talmud is more than simply a religious document. Holding theological, historical, cultural, and practical weight and relevance, its influence over the Jewish community remains to this day. For our purposes, it acts as a strange and pointed metaphor and sign.

Because the AD 70 destruction of the temple—a physical center for teaching and training—made oral tradition nearly impossible, they could no longer pass down the words of the rabbis and scholars. Now, they had to write it down. Over the next several centuries, two separate versions of the oral law were recorded independently of each other in different locations. Each would hold influences from its respective place of origin. One would be accumulated in Jerusalem and the other in Babylon.[75]

Today, we face the same problem. We have essentially two versions of the same thing. Though the vast catalogues of information are available to all via the internet, there lies an astronomical split in the way we interpret the information of today's world. Two separate views emerge depending on if you are looking through the lens of God's covenant to His people or not, and your view determines the way in which you live your life.

On top of that, every person's view is affected by the rapid spread of information. Once you start down a rabbit hole—a certain way of thinking—it's nearly impossible to get out because of the sheer amount of information. Some of it may be true. Some of it may not. But it doesn't matter to most as long as it lines up with the way of thinking they are most accustomed to.

The interlinking function of the Talmud began in the 1500s during a unique printing of the historical document.

When Daniel Bomberg, a Viennese non-Jewish printer, gave the Babylonian Talmud its present form in the sixteenth century, he conceived of the brilliant idea of liberating the typography of the page from its linear, mechanical form.[76]

This genius layout strategy laid the groundwork for the ideas of hyperlinking pages of information upon which the internet was built. It's strange that the internet itself can claim its own structural origins within an ancient Jewish text.

As an alternative to the book, the Talmud by its openness of form invites anyone with curiosity to enter into the symposium, the ongoing dialogue across space and time, just like the internet. "Vadok," or "Look into it!" is how the Maharsha (R. Samuel Eliezer Edels,14th century) ended many of his amendments or comments. This phrase is a perfect example of the spirit of the Talmud's openness, its invitation.[77]

Look into it! Welcome to the rabbit hole. Come get lost. The spirit of the Talmud referenced here is the same spirit of openness the internet tempts us with today. The centuries-old birthplace of hyperlinks issues the same phrase perpetuated at the birthplace of the internet herself: *Lo! Look and see!*

The truth is, knowledge itself is not wrong and it's not necessarily evil. Even the possession of knowledge about evil things can help prevent those things from continuing or reoccurring. God Himself knows the difference between good and evil, and He does not commit evil. Yet it's the power knowledge has over us that gets tricky. When we begin to value the knowledge itself above the One who gave us the ability to learn, we fall into a trap, and knowledge stops leading us to a quantifiable answer and starts leading to the pursuit of more knowledge.

This endless searching occurs when we begin to believe the lie that the next piece of knowledge will solve all our problems—that if we just know enough we'll be okay. At that point, knowledge has become the idol. It has become the golden calf.

The pattern that follows can sometimes look like this:

1. I have a problem.
2. I research solutions to the problem.
3. I become an acolyte, wholeheartedly following the steps to arrive at the solution.
4. I focus on the solution at a detriment to other people and areas of life.

5. I become a proselyte, constantly testifying to the importance of the information.
6. I value my viewpoint over people, and my relationships begin to either suffer or go away, depending upon how hard I push the information on others.

Here's what's crazy about this pattern: the person in this hole could be absolutely right about the information they possess. Their viewpoint may be true or false. The danger lies not in discovering and becoming a proponent to a potential truth, but rather in how they elevate and attempt to disseminate that truth to others.

So what does this secret knowledge look like? It could be anything, but here are few statements that may help to quantify it. Please bear in mind I'm not making a statement about whether these are facts or fiction, good or evil. I'm instead using these as specific examples of ways in which the rabbit hole can take over.

- For some, the secret knowledge is the fact that silver and gold keep their value while other investments drop.
- For some, the secret knowledge is understanding and living by a "perfect" ethical code that will keep them from being canceled by culture.
- For some, the secret knowledge is the formula for going viral online. It's knowing how to influence people.
- For some, the secret knowledge is the right combination of supplements and dieting that will keep them looking young or living longer.
- For some, the secret knowledge is the real story behind the 2020 elections.

- For some, the secret knowledge is the truth behind the moon landing or the shape of the earth.
- For some, the secret knowledge may be a personality that they follow and trust to give them insight into the truth behind hot topics.
- For some, the secret knowledge is choosing to reject anything and everything the previous generation believed, deeming it as ignorant or wrong.
- For you and I, the secret knowledge may not be any of these things, but it's there, and it promises the same thing: a sense of control and fulfillment.

Whether the rabbit hole of information ends up true or not is not the issue. The issue is the promise the information potentially holds for those who discover it—that it will somehow satisfy the longing of the soul, answer the questions in the mind, and ultimately bring joy to the heart. These are things that only the gospel can do.

How Babylon's Secret Knowledge Influences the Church

In his disruptively insightful work, *Dominion,* author Tom Holland beautifully describes the thrilling account of Martin Luther defying the papacy. On the final morning of a 60-day threshold he was given to recant his teachings, instead of making amends for his heresies, the famous reformer makes a scene.

> ***Agricola, rather than rags, used books as fuel. All that morning he and Luther had been ransacking libraries for collections of cannon law. Had the two men been able to find a volume of Aquinas, they would have burnt that as well. Their kindling, though, proved sufficient.***

> ***The fire began to catch. Agricola continued to feed books into the flames. Then Luther stepped out from the crowd. Trembling, he held up the papal decree that had held up his teachings. "Because you have confounded the truth of God," he said in a ringing voice, "today the Lord confounds you. Into the fire with you."***[78]

Martin Luther's rejection of the hierarchy and authority of Roman Catholicism were not merely rooted in a disagreement over doctrine, but rather in the realization that a core belief shifted too far had caused the entire foundation of the faith to erode into something un-Christian. In all its conglomerated teachings, practices, and motivations, the church had gone past the gospel. They had built their beliefs upon the wrong foundation. Because of this, Martin Luther demanded that Christendom needed a complete reset.

The dangerous truth: this same thing still happens today. It some cases, it occurs on a mass level across denominations. Other times, it occurs on the local level within a congregation or group. And then, at the place it matters most, it also occurs on an individual level, in the heart of the person whom Jesus died to save.

How does it happen? Martin Luther, though he himself became confounded in certain ways during his later life, said it best, "You have confounded the truths of God."

How has the modern church confounded the teachings of God? How have we added to the gospel message? Could it be that the very confounding we are experiencing is a result of such behavior?

Simply put, we confound the teachings of Christ by looking at them through the wrong lens. When we begin to view the good news through the lens of Babylon's ideologies and ways, we erode the gospel's power, and we wind up with a church that resembles a Babylonian shell. But this doesn't need to happen.

> She who is in Babylon, chosen together with you, sends you greetings, and so does my son, Mark (1 Peter 5:13 NASB).

This random verse in Peter feels at first thought like a mere greeting to be glanced over, but it gives us a vital truth about the New Covenant lifestyle—you can live *in* Babylon and not be part *of* Babylon. Just because we live today in a Babylonian society, that does not mean Babylon must rule in our hearts. We can be part of a better Kingdom.

The truth remains that much of the church has been conquered by Babylonian thinking.

> That, in reference to your former way of life, you are to rid yourselves of the old self, which is being corrupted in accordance with the lusts of deceit, and that you are to be renewed in the spirit of your minds (Ephesians 4:22-23 NASB).

There is a "secret knowledge" in the church that isn't from the Lord and it's pulling people down into endless rabbit holes—that kind of knowledge is a distraction. It is the constant pull past Jesus and toward something "more."

Three Babylonian Lies the Modern Church Believes

I will discuss three lies much of the modern church believes. These three lies compounded upon each other result in a Christian lifestyle very similar to the one Martin Luther challenged.

1. *Knowledge always leads to holiness.*

The first lie we need to cover is the idea that knowledge always leads to holiness, that it always reinforces righteous living. When the serpent tempted Eve in the Garden, he tempted her with greater knowledge. Does knowledge always lead to evil? No. Yet, knowledge is only half the equation.

> The fear of the Lord is the beginning of wisdom, and the knowledge of the Holy One is understanding (Proverbs 9:10 NASB).

The fear of the Lord is the beginning of wisdom, meaning you start there. Knowing about God and His standard is only part of the picture. There's more to this puzzle.

When we believe the lie that knowledge of God's holiness and His standard in and of itself is going to change us and make us holy, we wind up constantly preaching the bad news. We think that overemphasizing how terrible sin is will lead to holiness. We can have good intentions and yet miss out on the Cross's power to transform.

This thinking often manifests itself in long, ever growing lists of evil practices to stay away from. Some of the woes on the list truly are evil, but some are simply a result of legalism.

The answer to this lie is found within the entire book of Romans, but for sake of brevity we will condense it down to a single verse, Romans 2:4 (NASB):

> Or do you think lightly of the riches of His kindness and restraint and patience, not knowing that the kindness of God leads you to repentance?

The fear of the Lord can make you *want* to repent and live holy, but it cannot in and of itself actually empower you to do it. Fear apart from love does not lead to holiness. It leads to shame and the hiding of sin. To walk in righteousness, a person must fully understand the holiness of God and then embrace the love of God. Without both, you don't truly know God.

Proverbs says *"knowledge of the Holy One is understanding."* The bad news about how we have fallen short of God's glory can illuminate the problem. But you can never arrive at a solution until you look at Jesus hanging on the Cross and come to realize that He paid the full price for all of your sins. When you finally accept the truth that His shed blood means you are fully forgiven and free, you can then be fully filled with the Spirit and suddenly become empowered to live free.

Culturally, every stream of information delivers consistent waves of bad news, carrying with it a weight of shame and guilt. They attempt to alleviate the guilt be removing God from the picture, but it's still there. We hear: "Take care of the earth or else you've let humanity down. Reject bigotry or else you've let humanity down. Make a difference in society or else you've let humanity down." This Babylonian message will continue, but we have the *Good News*. We have a better message to preach: God solved humanity's deepest problem over 2,000 years ago, and it still affects us just as potently today.

There's a reason Jesus told us to go into all the world and preach the *good* news. His mission was not to condemn people into being holy, but to love them into truth.

> For the Son of man is not come to destroy men's lives, but to save them… (Luke 9:56 KJV).

The church in some ways echoes the same judgmental spirit pervading Babylon, yet we don't realize that by assimilating this culture, we fall prey to a tactic of the enemy. Simply condemning the darkness does not save people. Shining the light of Jesus into the darkness does.

The second thing this lie leads to is a distortion of the blessing found within the New Covenant. When we believe that our holiness is a by-product of our knowledge, we start to think that receiving God's blessing and favor are rewards for uncovering the secrets of the curse. Here's what I mean by that. Exodus 34 says that our God:

> ...keeps faithfulness for thousands, who forgives wrongdoing, violation of His Law, and sin; yet He will by no means leave the guilty unpunished, inflicting the punishment of fathers on the children and on the grandchildren to the third and fourth generations (Exodus 34:7 NASB).

This aspect of God can often be taken to mean that we are expected to discover and specifically renounce every single sin from our family line to break free from their curses. This thinking can unfortunately lead to a constant fear of the unknown. I've heard people say, "I'm still not financially blessed so there must be a lingering curse from past generations that I need to discover and deal with."

Here's my honest question: how do you expect to deal with that? You can't. If you try to pick up the weight of *the curse,* you will constantly be attempting to root out all of the hidden sins from your parents, grandparents, and great-grandparents. You will constantly need to come up with new ways to counteract those sins—leading all the way back to Adam. This is an endless cycle based in the pursuit of knowledge. It ultimately does not work.

Does God leave the guilty unpunished? No. Instead, Jesus took the punishment upon Himself at the Cross.

> Christ redeemed us from the curse of the Law, having become a curse for us—for it is written: "Cursed is everyone who hangs on a tree"—in order that in Christ Jesus the blessing of Abraham would come to the Gentiles, so that we would receive the promise of the Spirit through faith (Galatians 3:13-14 NASB).

The generational curse in Exodus is based on people's sins and inability to live up to the Law. Jesus took our sins and the curse of the Law upon Himself so we could go free, so we can receive the blessing of God based on His grace and through faith.

This same passage amplifies the notion that an unhealthy trust in the pursuit of knowledge simply leads us into more bondage:

> For all who are of works of the Law are under a curse; for it is written: "Cursed is everyone who does not abide by all the things written in the book of the Law, to do them." Now, that no one is justified by the Law before God is evident; for, "the righteous one will live by faith" (Galatians 3:10-11 NASB).

Essentially, if you try to free yourself by going to the Law and trying to perform it perfectly, you're actually putting yourself under its curse. The reason is because no one can abide by the Law perfectly. Instead, 2 Corinthians 3:4-6 (NASB) shows us the true path to freedom from the curse:

> Such is the confidence we have toward God through Christ. Not that we are adequate in ourselves so as to consider anything as having come from ourselves, but our adequacy is from God, who also made us adequate as servants of a new covenant, not of the letter but of the Spirit; for the letter kills, but the Spirit gives life.

When we place our trust in Jesus's finished work on the Cross, we receive the blessing of Abraham. When we rely again on our own ability to follow God's commands perfectly, we put ourselves back under the curse of the Law.

This in no way excuses sin. That is another route the world takes to alleviate guilt. They accept a fake gospel of hyper-grace, which I am not preaching. Instead, this truth points us to the necessity for the Holy Spirit in our lives. Galatians 3 says that the blessing of Abraham includes *"the promise of the Spirit through faith."* Second Corinthians 3 says the life of the New Covenant is found in the Spirit. Jesus's sacrifice gives us the ability to be filled afresh with the Spirit of God, and He leads us to walk in a manner that is pleasing to God.

> You have been severed from Christ, you who are seeking to be justified by the Law; you have fallen from grace. For we, through the Spirit, by faith, are waiting for the hope of righteousness (Galatians 5:4-5 NASB).

When we attempt to fight the curse through our endless searching, we miss out on the fullness of the abundant life we are meant to have in Christ. God's true blessing is found in learning to fully hope in Christ, our atonement.

Do we throw out the Old Testament and the Law of Moses? Absolutely not. Second Timothy 3:16-17 (NASB) is very clear that God can use all of the Scripture to teach and train us:

> All Scripture is inspired by God and beneficial for teaching, for rebuke, for correction, for training in righteousness; so that the man or woman of God may be fully capable, equipped for every good work.

The answer is not to throw out the Old Testament. The answer is also not to place ourselves back under the Law of Moses. Instead, the answer is to walk by the Spirit.

> But I say, walk by the Spirit, and you will not carry out the desire of the flesh (Galatians 5:16 NASB).

Another way this lie (the idea that knowledge always leads to holiness) manifests within the church today is through the full or partial conversion back to Judaism. Christianity has its roots in Judaism because Jesus is a Jew, the God of Judaism is the God of Christianity, and because we share some Holy Scriptures with Judaism.

Yet, there are sects of the Christian church today which emphasize the return to Jewish roots in an unhealthy and unnecessary way. Pointing to the idea that "if God wanted them to do this, He must want us to do it as well," a growing number of people are attempting to abide by the ritualistic laws of the Mosaic Law. Yet, the problem is clear: the Scripture tells us that New Covenant believers are no longer under the Law of Moses.

In fact, it goes even further than that. It emphatically warns us about going back under the Law. Some heretical groups, such as the Hebrew Roots movement, have even gone so far as to question the legitimacy of the New Testament based on their attempt to rediscover the Judaism behind Christianity.

Most Christians don't go that far, I'll admit. Also, I'm not saying it's wrong to learn more about Jesus's heritage or even to celebrate a Jewish festival. However, the issue is not in the traditions themselves but in the intent of the heart. If we immerse ourselves in Jewish culture out of our freedom in Christ, that's okay. It's when we think Jewish traditions make us more pleasing to God that we get off track. If by keeping the dietary laws, seventh day (Saturday) Sabbath, and feasts and festivals of the Old Covenant we start thinking we are becoming more holy, we are undercutting the legitimacy and power of Christ's sacrifice. Look at the apostle Paul's stern warnings to those who were doing this in the early church:

> But when I saw that they were not straightforward about the truth of the gospel, I said to Cephas [Peter] in the presence of all, "If you, being a Jew, live like the Gentiles and not like the Jews, how is it that you compel the Gentiles to live like Jews? We are Jews by nature and not sinners from the Gentiles; nevertheless, knowing that a person is not justified by works of the Law but through faith in Christ Jesus, even we have believed in Christ Jesus, so that we may be justified by faith in Christ and not by works of the Law; since by works of the Law no flesh will be justified" (Galatians 2:14-16).

> I do not nullify the grace of God, for if righteousness comes through the Law, then Christ died needlessly (Galatians 2:21 NASB).

> It was for freedom that Christ set us free; therefore keep standing firm and do not be subject again to a yoke of slavery. Look! I, Paul, tell you that if you have yourselves circumcised, Christ will be of no benefit to you. And I testify again to every man who has himself circumcised, that he is obligated to keep the whole

> Law. You have been severed from Christ, you who are seeking to be justified by the Law; you have fallen from grace (Galatians 5:1-4).

Why does Paul mention circumcision here? First, he directly answers the debate at hand. Those who were persuading the Galatian believers to go back under the Law of Moses were pressuring them to become circumcised. He was calming their fears with a "no." Second, circumcision was the mark of God's servants under the Old Covenant, starting with Abraham. It became the sign that someone followed the Law.

Paul used it as a representation for the Law itself by saying, *"every man who has himself circumcised, that he is obligated to keep the whole Law."* There was no halfway. It was either all or nothing. James later tells us that if we break one command in the Law, we break all of them (see James 2:10). Paul tells us in Galatians that when we put ourselves back under the Law of Moses, we place ourselves back under the curse of the Law (Galatians 3:10).

Here is the clear picture the New Testament paints about the Law for believers:

1. If you try to fulfill part of the Law, you must fulfill all of it.
2. If you make one mistake, you have broken all of it, and you are under the curse.
3. There is no hope in the Law of Moses anymore because it's impossible to fulfill.
4. Jesus is the only way! We must believe in Him for righteousness.

I understand that the ceremonial traditions of Judaism are only part of the Law of Moses. There is a lot more to it, including both the moral laws and the principles and characteristics of God. As New Covenant believers, how do we know which aspects to apply? The only way is to be led by the Holy Spirit. Paul's solution to the Law problem is addressed distinctly in the book of Galatians:

> But I say, walk by the Spirit, and you will not carry out the desire of the flesh. For the desire of the flesh is against the Spirit, and the Spirit against the flesh; for these are in opposition to one another, in order to keep you from doing whatever you want. But if you are led by the Spirit, you are not under the Law (Galatians 5:16-18 NASB).

God uses the Scripture to teach us His nature and character and to shape our sense of morality (see 2 Timothy 3:16-17), but we must learn to filter the Old Covenant through the lens of the New Covenant. We must learn to walk in relationship first, being led by the Spirit in all things. That is the only way to truly walk in the abundant life Jesus described. It's not through amassing enough knowledge of ancient ways. It's through knowing Jesus and walking with Him daily.

2. Knowledge equals revelation from God.

The second Babylonian lie infiltrating the modern church is the idea that more knowledge is equal to (or just as important and beneficial) as revelation from God.

One temptation that prophetic people encounter is the desire to share a message from God when they haven't actually heard anything from Him. When this occurs, a person can either choose to be content with waiting on the Lord and reading the Word, or they can begin to dive into other means of "revelation." This process can start innocently.

Rumors and conspiracy theories encapsulate the first branch of thought here. Someone hears a rumor or a theory about a hot topic, they have a feeling about it, so they share it as if it were known fact, and people listen because they have "prophetic insight." It's a slippery slope for the prophet because it keeps the spotlight on them, and it's a spiral for the listener because it runs them in circles looking for the Word of the Lord and trying to walk it out.

> For among them are those who slip into households and captivate weak women weighed down with sins, led on by various impulses, always learning and never able to come to the knowledge of the truth (2 Timothy 3:6-7 NASB).

Paul was culturally talking about people who had a lot of time on their hands. This isn't just a woman problem. It's a people problem. He was addressing those who lack God-given purpose and who go looking for that purpose in the rumors they hear and pass on. He says someone can be *"always learning and never able to come to the knowledge of the truth."*

I'm not saying that God cannot speak about rumors or conspiracy theories. God absolutely speaks about hot topics. My personal experience and the Old Testament prophetic books show that He is willing to do so often. However, there is a BIG difference between someone with a prophetic gift speaking about a topic and God Himself speaking through that person about a topic. The prophetic movement within the church has coined the phrase *prophetic insight*, but sometimes it's just a key phrase that means *God didn't actually speak to me about this, so I'm giving you my opinion instead.*

Here's my loving appeal: be very careful about settling for a word from a person when you truly need a word from God. Don't be led astray by the hot topics and the desire to know more information. Sometimes God does share the detailed information, but other times He simply says, *You don't need to know. Let Me handle it.*

The second way this lie (knowledge equals revelation from God) is spreading within the church is through misappropriation of the information. The temptation is to start thinking that the word of knowledge from God is the message. God doesn't just desire to share knowledge with His people. He wants something more—to speak truth that transforms us and creates momentum that reaches out into the hurting world.

Many of the messages I share on my YouTube and other video channels include some sort of word of knowledge about things happening in the future or world events. Most of the time, God also gives me a prophetic message of encouragement or teaching. When I look at the retention rate for those videos, which tells me how long the average viewer watched a video, I find that most viewers only watch the part of the videos that include the word of knowledge. Once the teaching starts, even if it's based in prophecy, the viewership drops off. Now, I'm not saying this is morally wrong. There's nothing wrong with only watching part of a video. However, I'm sharing this information simply to show the tendency that exists. The temptation can be for us to want the juicy word of knowledge about the future but not necessarily the sound doctrine or biblical teaching.

Many of us want God to tell us exactly how to fix our problems or how to access a specific blessing, but what we don't realize is that He's already told us how in His Word. Sometimes the spiritual gift of a word of knowledge is specifically needed, and it can be very useful in the church when a direct action needs to be taken. Yet if we feast on words of knowledge and refuse to feed on the basic truths of God's Word, we eventually become like a marathon runner who eats nothing but empty carbs. Every time we chow down, we get enough energy to jump up and sprint for a few meters, but it doesn't last. Without the protein of the truth, the spiritual muscles are never built up and there is no endurance or perseverance established.

Thinking that the knowledge itself is the message can lead into another trap. This trap is more subtle and cunning. It starts with a real word of knowledge from God, but it leaves the interpretation up to the listener instead of up to the Spirit of God. As believers, we must be willing to allow God to interpret prophecy for Himself. I will admit that there are people within the Scripture who were gifted with interpretation of dreams, visions, and prophetic words. I'm looking at you, Joseph.

> So Pharaoh said to Joseph, "Since God has informed you of all this, there is no one as discerning and wise as you are" (Genesis 41:39 NASB).

Pharaoh's response resembles many healthy responses today to the true prophetic. He witnessed God's voice speaking and revealing mysteries through Joseph, so he pinned Joseph as a good source of wisdom. There's nothing wrong with seeking out advice, discernment, or knowledge from a seasoned prophet. However, the trap is to start associating their own words with the very words of God and to assume that their individual wisdom is equivalent to God's wisdom. It's not.

I've heard ministers deliver a prophetic word—a word in due season—to an individual in a service, and it takes about five minutes for them to deliver the word. For the first minute or two, the Holy Spirit inside of me was saying, "Yes," along with the word, and then suddenly He stopped! Why? What happened? That prophetic minister suddenly shifted from prophesying—saying what they were hearing God say—to giving advice or interpretation about the prophecy. They transitioned the message from prophecy into advice without informing the listener. The individual receiving the prophetic word in that case was left to wonder if the entire five minutes was prophecy or not.

Here's my point: we need to be careful when sharing prophecy to clearly define what is from God and what is from us. We need to be aware that sometimes people mix the two without clarifying.

Am I saying interpretation is wrong? No. However, true interpretation happens the same way the prophetic happens—through hearing the Spirit of God. If the Holy Spirit interprets a word, go with it. But if you are left to interpret it yourself, how are you to know if you or the person sharing the word interpreted it correctly?

Here's an example: I was in a small church service one time when a supposed elder suddenly asked to share a word. They handed him the microphone, and he began to ramble. It was obvious he had something to say, but he was shying away from saying it. He started to share a word with the pastor and his wife, which seemed encouraging. Yet suddenly he mentioned pregnancy and the pastor's wife's face went stiff. She dropped her head into her hands to attempt to hide her face, but it was too late. Everyone had seen her reaction.

The elder sat down and everyone waited for her to address what he had just stated. She slowly got up and walked to the mic. She thanked him for sharing the word of encouragement from the Lord, and then she admitted to being pregnant. The church shouted and cheered, but she did not. I watched her freeze again. It was obvious that she was not emotionally prepared to announce her pregnancy before the congregation.

Did the elder do the right thing in this situation? I don't know. If that's what the Holy Spirit told him to do, then yes. Yet sometimes the Lord will reveal information about someone and not specifically ask us to share it. It could be that God revealed the pregnancy to the man so that he and his wife could go to the pastor and his wife and stand alongside them during an emotional time when they felt alone. It could be that he was simply meant to share it with his own wife so that they could pray. There are many possibilities. Once he heard the information, the immediate temptation would be to share it in front of the church, but that might not have been how it was intended.

You and I as human beings do have the ability to interpret prophecy, to an extent. To be certain about the official interpretation, we must be willing to ask the Lord to interpret His word for Himself. We must be willing to take the utterance before the Lord and say, "What do You want me to do with this?" If we don't do that, there is a chance that we settle for mere knowledge when really the Lord wants to give us a commission.

This applies directly to national and international prophets today—those who share words affecting nations, governments, and people groups that can often be verified by future news reports. Those kinds of words do not always stand alone.

When a current event is prophesied publicly ahead of time before it hits the headlines, the accuracy of that word will act as a sign that the rest of the prophecy is true. What is the rest of the prophecy? The message. What is God trying to say to that nation and individuals besides just telling them their future? What word of warning, encouragement, or truth is He speaking?

Sometimes "newsworthy" words of knowledge are intended solely for individual recipients such as business leaders or government figures; and in that case, the knowledge itself might translate to a very practical step for that person to take. In those cases, God could be stepping in to prevent disaster or alter the course of history. When it is intended for public consumption, it seems to apply less directly and act more as an evidence that God is truly speaking.

I have a prophecy archive on my website that tracks words of knowledge about current events. It keeps a record of the words I shared, the date I shared them, and the results after the fact. The point of the archive is simply to give listeners the ability to see the evidence of accuracy for themselves. However, the original intent of the words was very different. When I originally shared the predictive words, God also gave me a word of prophecy meant to encourage, equip, teach, or remind people of the truth. The prophetic teaching or encouragement was the true message.

Here's an example. Back in September 2020, I shared a word about Russian oil prices. I heard the Lord say:

- *Russian oil prices are going to skyrocket in November.*
- *Tell My people not to be afraid.*
- I also saw a vision of an eagle's face suddenly morphing into the face of a vulture.

I received an interpretation that because of events that would unfold in the month of November, Christians within the United States (represented by the eagle) would begin to act like vultures. There would be a time of responding in fear and an attempt to go for leftovers instead of going for the best cut of meat. I explained that eagles soar higher and usually hunt for live game, but vultures hunt for the dead or dying animals.

Prior to November, reports said the Russian oil prices would continue following a downward trend. Yet on November 2, Russian oil prices started to climb and continued through November. Just within the month of November alone, prices increased more than 30 percent. Russian oil prices continued to climb all the way to March 2021.

Two events within the USA that were connected to the movement of the Russian oil prices simultaneously caused panic. The 2020 USA presidential election occurred and a Covid vaccine was announced. What had God said prior to this? *Tell My people not to be afraid.* And yet, many people responded to both the election results and the vaccine announcements with fear. God knew what was coming in the month of November.

I'm not debating the legitimacy of the election or the validity of the vaccines. Both those issues are a side point. Instead, it was the way we reacted that God was most concerned about. As believers, we are meant to be more than conquerors, and yet in some ways we began to behave as if all that was available were leftovers—the easy prey. The devil's plan was to attempt to get us to take our focus off of God's best and put it on whatever was left.

After the election results were announced, many prophecies were released in November, December, and January about Trump's return to the White House by several voices during this time. I'm not debating the legitimacy of those voices (because that would come down to a case-by-case basis), but instead I will boldly state that some were wrong about the dates they declared. Some said Trump would return to the White House by December. They were wrong. Some said January. They were wrong. Some said it would happen in the few months following that. Those dates were wrong as well.

I'm not trying to push your buttons if you were on that train. But, I hope that you can hear this in love: as Christians, we cannot settle for less than the truth. We cannot settle for vulture-like words that are grasping for something we want. We must be willing to soar higher than that and wait for the true word of the Lord. We must continue to trust Him even when things don't go our way.

Do I believe that all the prophets were completely wrong about the 2020 elections? No. Here's what I believe:

1. Some were simply false prophets (the Word of God says there are many out there).
2. Some prophets were wrong (yes, prophetic people can make mistakes or be tempted to jump aboard a movement instead of hearing God for themselves).
3. Some prophets heard right, but they misinterpreted the message.
4. Some prophets heard right and shared the right message.

The third group is the one I want to address. To many people, God was speaking about Donald Trump. Because of their own expectations and hopes for their country, they misinterpreted what they heard, saw, or dreamed to mean that Trump would serve from 2020 to 2024, which he did not. How could this happen? First Corinthians 13:9-12 (NASB) gives us some insight:

> For we know in part and prophesy in part; but when the perfect comes, the partial will be done away with. When I was a child, I used to speak like a child, think like a child, reason like a child; when I became a man, I did away with childish things. For now we see in a mirror dimly, but then face to face; now I know in part, but then I will know fully, just as I also have been fully known.

When we get stuck in the childish thought pattern of *God can only work this way*, we begin to misinterpret prophecy to fit our own needs or wants. We see a biblical example of this concept in Acts 21 when Paul visits Tyre:

> After looking up the disciples, we stayed there for seven days; and they kept telling Paul, through the Spirit, not to set foot in Jerusalem (Acts 21:4 NASB).

The disciples spoke by the Spirit and appealed to Paul not to go to Jerusalem. They were accurately seeing or hearing from God about what would happen to Paul if he visited Jerusalem, and yet they were misinterpreting the point of that knowledge. They wanted Paul to stay alive because they loved him, and yet Paul already knew that he would be glorifying God through laying his life down for the sake of the gospel.

The story continues to play out as he moves on to Caesarea where he encounters several prophets.

> ...a prophet named Agabus came down from Judea. And he came to us and took Paul's belt and bound his own feet and hands, and said, "This is what the Holy Spirit says: 'In this way the Jews in Jerusalem will bind the man who owns this belt and hand him

> over to the Gentiles.'" When we had heard this, we as well as the local residents began begging him not to go up to Jerusalem (Acts 21:10-12 NASB).

Again, Agabus shares true revelation from God about Paul's demise if he should visit Jerusalem, and yet the believers there interpreted that to mean he should not go. Look at Paul's response.

> Then Paul replied, "What are you doing, weeping and breaking my heart? For I am ready not only to be bound, but even to die in Jerusalem for the name of the Lord Jesus." And since he would not be persuaded, we became quiet, remarking, "The will of the Lord be done!" (Acts 21:13-14 NASB)

Paul already knew what would happen to him in Jerusalem. The Holy Spirit had already revealed it to him. Those around him were also seeing and hearing from the Lord accurately about Paul's future, but because of their emotional attachment to him they were unwilling to allow the Holy Spirit to interpret the word the way He wanted to. Yet, Paul had already given himself over fully to the work of evangelism and the will of the Lord for his life. He had both the accurate word and the right interpretation.

We must be willing to come back to a mindset of freedom from the need. When we humble ourselves and say, "I don't need what I think I need. I only need Him, God's presence in my life and His hand at work, no matter how He desires to work," then God begins to work through prophecy on another level and He opens the storehouses of revelation to us through the Spirit.

It all starts with acknowledging that we have all we need in Christ. If Jesus walks us through a season of apparent victory, we're going to be okay. If He walks us through a season of apparent loss, we're still going to be okay because we are still walking with Him. It's when we stop listening to His voice and replace it with the voice of what we want that we get into trouble.

God often says to me, "Don't make assumptions." When we forget that we prophesy in part, we start to assume that we have the full picture. We start to assume that the word we heard is the full message. Oftentimes, God uses the word of knowledge to make a point, and if we're not careful we can catch the illustration and miss the point.

Using the prophet Daniel as an example, it's easy to see the importance of understanding the message behind the prophecy:

> In the third year of Cyrus king of Persia, a message was revealed to Daniel, who was named Belteshazzar; and the message was true and it concerned great conflict, but he understood the message and had an understanding of the vision (Daniel 10:1 NASB).

In this verse, Daniel completely understands the interpretation of the prophecy. Yet, just a few chapters later, we see the opposite occur.

> But as for me, I heard but did not understand; so I said, "My lord, what will be the outcome of these events?" And he said, "Go your way, Daniel, for these words will be kept secret and sealed up until the end time" (Daniel 12:8-9 NASB).

Daniel does the right thing in response to his lack of understanding. He asks for an interpretation. In this case, the Lord declines. Unlike earlier visions, Daniel understanding and being able to relate the interpretation wasn't even the point of the prophecy. God only intended him to write this one down for the sake of future generations.

The temptation is to add to what God is revealing. We might think, *But God, what will people think if I can't fully explain what You're saying?* That doesn't matter. All that matters is that we do what He is asking us to do with the word He speaks.

I need to make an aside here. I'll get back to my main point shortly. No matter what actually happened in 2020 with the prophetic movement and the elections, there is a secondary way that the knowledge of Babylon infiltrated the church in 2020—one that is far more subtle than people simply missing a word or standing on a wrong interpretation. I'm not only talking about the prophetic movement now. The entire body of Christ was affected on some level. I'm referring to the massive division that occurred based on the election outcome.

Babylon's system made a mark on the church in 2020, and it took the form of offense. No matter if you were right or wrong in your view about Trump, someone said something to make you angry. But maybe I'm not talking to you? Maybe you never got upset. Good for you, but some of us did.

I remember one night a few years ago when I felt a strong sense of offense toward my wife. Because of the anger, I decided to sleep in our guest bed. As soon as my head hit the pillow that night, a vivid vision flashed in front of my eyes. I saw a snake stretching its head out toward me and staring me straight in the face—only a few feet away. As soon as I saw it, I knew what had happened. I had let the devil in because of willingly holding on to offense. Immediately I humbled my heart and chose to forgive my wife. I'm glad I did.

The point is, some of us have let the sun go down on our anger against our fellow brothers and sisters in Christ, and we've given satan a way in (see Ephesians 4:26). The truth is, if we cannot unite with true believers around the gospel message, despite our disagreements about political events or even specific prophetic words, then the devil is taking ground. He's taking ground in our hearts and in our nation. It doesn't matter who was right as much as it matters that we are willing to stand in unity.

> Therefore I, the prisoner of the Lord, urge you to walk in a manner worthy of the calling with which you have been called, with all humility and gentleness, with patience, bearing with one another in love, being diligent to keep the unity of the Spirit in the bond of peace (Ephesians 4:1-3 NASB).

We want forgiveness and unity to always make sense, but it doesn't. It requires release. It requires us to put that person back into God's hands and allow Him to deal with them at the proper time or in the proper way. It often requires us to say, "I could be the one who is wrong, because I don't know everything." Unity means being willing to bear with one another in love—to bear their burdens as if they were your own (to the extent that God leads you to).

Some people, especially those who supported Trump the most during 2020, might push back a little and say, "But wasn't he chosen by God? How can we stand by while others ridicule someone God chose?" My answer is simple: We aren't in charge of the hearts of others. Each of us is only in charge of our own heart.

Do I believe God raises up Cyruses still today? Yes. Could Trump have been one of those types of figures? Absolutely. Based on what I've personally heard from the Lord, I believe he was. However, I shouldn't need anyone to agree with me on that point in order to walk in unity with them. I'm not perfect, but I want to keep submitting my heart.

The truth is, one reason we can become offended is because we get tempted to look for a savior in the wrong place. We won't find one in the political arena. It must be Jesus we're looking for and looking to. He is the Savior this world really needs. Hopefully, we can walk in unity around that point.

The final way the modern church is perpetuating this second lie (knowledge always equals revelation from God) is through the progressive movement. The progressive Christian movement has replaced God's Word with worldly knowledge and ideologies. They've equated the development of the culture with revelation from God. Yet, the culture will continue to follow the course of this world—the pattern of Babylon.

Here's an example: the sexual identity revolution in the secular culture has bled into the church, mostly affecting the progressive movements. The Bible is very clear about what is right and wrong when it comes to sex. How can there be such confusion happening within the church over the issue? The answer lies in the church's source of truth. The progressive church has bypassed the Word of God as truth and has weighed the opinions of the culture more heavily, building their stance on earthly knowledge instead of spiritual revelation.

The spiritual always causes the natural mind to ask the question, "How can that be?" If we believe the only way

God can work is through natural means, we remove the ability for Him to step in and perform a miracle. Sexual identity is a serious issue, especially among the younger generations, and the solution is found in a real encounter with the living God. The progressive church has removed the expectation that God's people can truly encounter Him, thus ignoring the possibility that God could change a person's thoughts and desires when it comes to identity or sex. The world says, *I'll always be this way*. The Word says *with God all things are possible.*

We need both a return to truth and a return to the presence of God. When truth is too hard for us to accept or understand, we go into the presence of God where the Holy Spirit can give us revelation about it. That revelation starts with a greater outpouring of His love and acceptance. This love and acceptance is freely available because of what Jesus did for us.

When we experience Him, His love penetrating and filling the deepest recesses of our hearts, truth becomes easy to accept because we realize in that moment that, whether we fully understand it or not, God is love and He only has good things in store for us. That's the point of surrender where we say, "God, my flesh wants *this*, but my spirit wants *You*. Not my will be done, but Yours."

God rarely shows regret in Scripture, yet it is there at times. One time is during the spread of evil upon the pre-flood earth in Genesis chapter 6. Another time is during King Saul's reign in Israel:

> I regret that I have made Saul king, because he has turned back from following Me and has not carried out My commands... (1 Samuel 15:11 NASB).

God is saying the same thing to the progressive pastors today who are looking for a worldly solution to a spiritual problem. He is not fighting for them, but against them.

In this passage, King Saul had just finished making a series of sacrifices to God. You would think this would make God happy. But he sacrificed to God in his own way, in a way God asked him not to. That is the same thing happening today. Churches are gathering to "worship God," but they are not worshiping Him in Spirit or in truth, and God is frustrating their plans.

3. *More knowledge can't hurt.*

The third and final Babylonian lie is the idea that more knowledge can't hurt. The truth is, it can. The Babylonian idiom *knowledge is power* is widely propagated and, to an extent, true. Not all knowledge is power, though. Some is tormenting. Sometimes people wish they could unlearn things. Have you ever watched a movie you wish you hadn't? Have you ever researched a topic only to later regret the mental picture it placed in your mind? Oftentimes knowledge is power, but sometimes it hurts more than it helps. Let us look at the gospel in this context.

Throughout the book of Galatians, Paul warns us of a potential evil:

> I am amazed that you are so quickly deserting Him who called you by the grace of Christ, for a different gospel, which is not just another account; but there are some who are disturbing you and want to distort the gospel of Christ (Galatians 1:6-7 NASB).

The gospel is simple—almost foolishly simple. That's why Paul calls the word of the Cross foolishness in the eyes of the "wise" in 1 Corinthians 1. The gospel requires humility.

Without humbling our hearts before God, we cannot accept it. God designed the gospel this way on purpose so that we would have the choice to reject it. He wanted those poor in spirit to get it. The same way He gave Adam and Eve a choice, He gives us a choice today. Despite all His grace being poured out at the Cross, He preserves our free will.

Because of this, many teachers of the Word have dived into false wisdom, making Christianity about something other than Christ Himself—creating a barrier between listeners and the saving truth.

> For I want you to know how great a struggle I have in your behalf…that their hearts may be encouraged, having been knit together in love, and that they would attain to all the wealth that comes from the full assurance of understanding, resulting in a true knowledge of God's mystery, that is, Christ Himself, in whom are hidden all the treasures of wisdom and knowledge. I say this so that no one will deceive you with persuasive arguments (Colossians 2:1-4 NASB).

> See to it that there is no one who takes you captive through philosophy and empty deception in accordance with human tradition, in accordance with the elementary principles of the world, rather than in accordance with Christ (Colossians 2:8 NASB).

Human tradition can create layers of "wisdom" and "knowledge" that actually act as a restraint that holds us back from all God has for us. Colossians says Jesus Himself is the true mystery of God. It says in Him are *hidden all the treasures of wisdom and knowledge*. So no matter how much we learn, if we attempt to find fulfillment apart from Him, we ultimately miss it. If we continue down this path, we eventually wind up full of ourselves but empty of love, joy, and peace—the fruit of the Spirit.

> ...Knowledge makes one conceited, but love edifies people. If anyone thinks that he knows anything, he has not yet known as he ought to know; but if anyone loves God, he is known by Him (1 Corinthians 8:1-3 NASB).

For those who consider themselves intelligent or who have accumulated a storehouse of knowledge about different subjects throughout the years, this can be a large pill to swallow. *Knowledge makes one conceited.* Not all knowledge is bad—the mindset matters.

The point is, you can't learn enough to help yourself. You have to surrender and let God help you. His Spirit wants to develop inside us what stores of knowledge can't create: love, joy, peace, patience, kindness, goodness, gentleness, faithfulness, and self-control. These can only be birthed out of a humbling and surrendering process where we learn to let go of the reins of control and begin to walk under the control of the Holy Spirit. To do this, we must admit that we don't know everything. We must admit that God knows better than we do.

Some of the young people leaving the church are having a hard time rationalizing the hypocrisy they see within the body of Christ. They admit that some of the rules of Christianity are good, but they don't see the most important rules (like love, mercy, and compassion) being walked out. So they go looking for a "higher" moralistic perspective that does provide for those things, whether that be an atheistic, self-governed perspective or another religion with a different set of rules.

This often isn't the end of the journey. They will move from one religion to another or one set of moralistic rules to another, looking for hope. True hope is found when someone encounters the true love of God. I believe, for those praying for loved ones who have walked away, hope is found in that simple phrase "Love edifies people." For many, they've heard the rules aspect of Christianity, but they haven't tasted the true love of Christ found within the gospel message—freely offered to all who believe.

The more we learn, the more potential there is for walls to be built up against the truth. The love of Christ shown through the leading of the Holy Spirit can break the walls down and begin to soften the heart so that truth can be sown in again. When people encounter the love of Christ walked out through believers, they receive something that all their learning could never give them.

Now, again, I'm not saying it's wrong to learn or accrue knowledge. Yet when it comes to the gospel, more knowledge is not always the answer. It takes a real encounter with our real God who loves people no matter how far they have run from Him.

Purging the Knowledge of Babylon

Babylonian knowledge starts in the mind and eventually works into the heart. It starts as a simple idea, but it becomes a perspective through which we view all of life. If Babylonian knowledge has infiltrated our hearts as Christians, even to a nominal extent, we need to purge ourselves.

Satan himself began the idea of looking at things through a perspective other than God's. Isaiah 14:13 tells us that satan said in his heart, "I will ascend to heaven." He rejected God's perspective about his purpose and replaced it with his own.

The true evil of Babylon is found in its goal to set itself or something else on the throne where Jesus should be.

When we learn something new and think, *This is it. This will lift me up. This will carry me. This will do it,* we make a deal in our hearts with Babylon in exchange for its secret knowledge. We give over a portion of the throne of our hearts to something other than Christ.

If we rely on that next hyperlink, that next level of knowledge, that is a sign that information has taken the place of the Holy Spirit in our lives. If we're looking at the Scripture as a formula or equation to solve, that once we solve it we will be in control of our own lives once again, we've put spiritual knowledge where only Jesus should be.

It's the endless trick of the enemy that we still face. The trick that Eve and Adam faced in the Garden.

> "For God knows that on the day you eat from it your eyes will be opened, and you will become like God, knowing good and evil." When the woman saw that the tree was good for food, and that it was a delight to the eyes, and that the tree was desirable to make one wise, she took some of its fruit and ate; and she also gave some to her husband with her, and he ate (Genesis 3:5-6 NASB).

Babylonian knowledge is pleasing to the eye and desirable for gaining wisdom. The same thing the devil promised to Eve, that next book, video, podcast, or article promises to us today.

As Christians, we have daily opportunities to purge ourselves through repentance, confession, and belief. We can talk directly with God about our issues, and He wants to talk back to us and remind us of all He has done for us at the Cross where He broke the power of pride and sin and shame.

We have a choice to make between trust and control. Do we trust that Jesus is enough, that His work is sufficient—or do we still desire to control the outcome ourselves?

Noah's ark is a simple illustration of how "foolish" it can feel to find rest in Jesus. The world had never seen rain before—there is no record of it—so why should they fear its coming? Up to that point, God had done nothing about their lawlessness and pervasive sinning, so why should He act now? Noah, a preacher of righteousness, told the people about the way God had made for them to be saved from the flood. If they would only get into the boat…

Getting into the boat required trust—a stepping off the solid ground they were used to and placing their future in something seemingly foolish. Some people today, even within the church, are digging deeper into the endless well of knowledge, and yet Jesus is saying, "Come. Trust Me. I am the Ark you must climb into."

Another beautiful illustration Jesus gives us is the difference between building on the sand versus building on the Rock. Once you discover the rock, building on it requires a settling in place. Trust is the simple factor needed to settle on the Rock instead of moving on to find other ground to rest on. If we don't settle on the Rock, which is Jesus, we'll never find rest. The sands will keep shifting, and we will have to keep moving from one thing to the next.

Paul tells us to expect a constant battle to keep our feet firmly planted on the Rock:

> We are destroying arguments and all arrogance raised against the knowledge of God, and we are

> taking every thought captive to the obedience of Christ (2 Corinthians 10:5 NASB).

When we choose to uproot the worldly wisdom from our hearts and grasp God's wisdom, even though it feels childish, we find true power to overcome:

> For ***the word of the cross*** is foolishness to those who are perishing, but to us who are being saved it ***is the power of God*** (1 Corinthians 1:18 NASB).

When we believe the Word of the Cross, we step into relationship with the One who allowed Himself to be sacrificed upon that Cross. As we are about to see, through that relationship He offers us a secret knowledge to replace the worldly knowledge we once relied on. I'm talking about the *Secret Knowledge of Heaven*. Could it be that the comprehensive story of Scripture portrays an ancient parallel revealing this knowledge to us today?

7

THE SECRET KNOWLEDGE OF HEAVEN

If we clearly see the parallels between the ancient city of Babylon and the modern-day representation or manifestation of that city within our culture, the next mystery to unfold is the mystery of future events. Where are we headed? How do we get from where we are today to the eventual fall of Babylon?

There are many mysteries still to unlock, yet before we can examine them, we must first understand the keys we hold as the church. These are the keys God has given us to help us traverse the days to come. These keys are bound up within a mystery I call the "Secret Knowledge of Heaven." Though this mystery includes prophecy, it expands beyond that and actually comprises a greater revelation than the spiritual gift of prophecy itself. To discover this revelation, we must examine the full story of Scripture.

Many scholars have highlighted the connection between Genesis 11 and Acts 2. Genesis 11 describes God thwarting the plans of the builders of the Tower of Babel. Acts 2 describes God releasing His plan for the New Covenant church on the Day of Pentecost. The later has been painted by many to be a type of divine reversal of the former. Acts 2 was God essentially undoing Genesis 11. Let's look at the amazing parallels found within these two scriptural events.

The Language Parallel

> Now all the earth used the same language and the same words (Genesis 11:1 NASB).
>
> Now there were Jews residing in Jerusalem, devout men from every nation under heaven (Acts 2:5 NASB).

The Location Parallel

> ...as they journeyed east, that they found a plain in the land of Shinar and settled there (Genesis 11:2 NASB).
>
> When the day of Pentecost had come, they were all together in one place (Acts 2:1 NASB).

The Divine Intervention Parallel

> Now the Lord came down to see the city and the tower which the men had built. And the Lord said, "Behold, they are one people, and they all have the same language. And this is what they have started to do, and now nothing which they plan to do will be impossible for them. Come, let Us go down and there..." (Genesis 11:5-7 NASB).
>
> And suddenly a noise like a violent rushing wind came from heaven, and it filled the whole house where they were sitting. And tongues that looked

> like fire appeared to them, distributing themselves, and a tongue rested on each one of them (Acts 2:2-3 NASB).

The Unity Parallel / Reversal

> "Come, let Us go down and there confuse their language, so that they will not understand one another's speech." So the Lord scattered them abroad from there over the face of all the earth; and they stopped building the city. Therefore it was named Babel, because there the Lord confused the language of all the earth; and from there the Lord scattered them abroad over the face of all the earth (Genesis 11:7-9 NASB).

> And they were all filled with the Holy Spirit and began to speak with different tongues, as the Spirit was giving them the ability to speak out (Acts 2:4 NASB).

> They were amazed and astonished, saying, "Why, are not all these who are speaking Galileans? And how is it that we each hear them in our own language to which we were born? Parthians, Medes, and Elamites, and residents of Mesopotamia, Judea, and Cappadocia, Pontus and Asia, Phrygia and Pamphylia, Egypt and the parts of Libya around Cyrene, and visitors from Rome, both Jews and proselytes, Cretans and Arabs—we hear them speaking in our own tongues of the mighty deeds of God" (Acts 2:7-11 NASB).

The Tower of Babel, which we know is the early origin of ancient Babylon, was a coming together of the peoples of the earth with a single purpose and a common goal. Because that goal directly defied God, He put a stop to the work by confusing their languages by creating a language barrier.

The Day of Pentecost is a reversal of that divine intervention. The same way the peoples of the earth were gathered together in Genesis 11, believers in Jesus gathered together in Acts 2. However, the difference was the object of their pursuit. One group gathered to reach Heaven apart from God, and the other group gathered out of obedience to God—to wait for the promise Jesus had made to them before He left. The ones who tried to reach Heaven on their own never made it, but those who sought after Christ (the only way to the Father) experienced Heaven coming down and invading the very room where they were sitting.

When God showed up, He impeded the builders in Genesis 11, but He empowered the believers in Acts 2. One way He did this is through the gift of language. He confused the voices of the builders, so even though they had all spoken the same language at one point, now they could no longer understand each other. Then in Acts 2, God does the opposite. He empowers the believers to speak in unknown tongues, and suddenly all the peoples of different regions understood a single tongue. In one sense, He reversed the curse of Babel through the outpouring of the Holy Spirit!

And the results are astounding. To the same level that the builders were no longer able to continue their work and were forced to disperse, the New Covenant believers were able to unite together as one and begin to work toward the single goal of sharing the gospel message with all nations on earth.

A Vision of the Tower

On April 5, 2024, I saw a vision from the Lord during a livestream collaboration between me. prophet Rob Sanchez, and a few other friends. It suddenly looked as if I were in the sky flying through the clouds, similar to what pilots see when looking out from the front of a plane. Still moving quickly forward, the vision angled downward. I came out of the clouds facing toward the ground, and below me I could see what looked to be the Tower of Babel. Instead of looming above me as it normally would have if I had been observing it from ground level, it appeared small and distant, almost like something I could step on.

I asked the Lord, "What am I seeing?" Immediately, a specific impression entered my mind. It was as if I was seeing the tower from God's perspective. When you look at something like the Tower of Babel from below, it appears tall and menacing. But when you see it from above, it looks small. God was essentially saying, *I'm not affected by the size of the tower—it means nothing to Me. I'm looking from a different perspective entirely.* He wants us as believers to take on that perspective as well. The foundation for the New Covenant perspective is found in two distinct miracles: 1) the resurrection of Jesus Christ (following His death), and 2) the outpouring of the Holy Spirit upon the church.

It's only through looking through the lens of God's perspective—His covenant agreement with us—that we set ourselves up to fully understand the mysteries (or secret knowledge) of Heaven.

The Mysteries of the Kingdom of Heaven Revealed

When we examine the great mysteries of the universe and the history of humankind, one mystery often ascends above the rest: *where did we come from?* This question is automatically answered when we positively answer another question: *does*

God exist? This question leads to another: *if He exists, what does He want with me?* God Himself answers this question through the Scriptures; yet even more specifically, it was answered through the revelation about Himself that He offered us when He walked the earth as a Man.

Jesus's life and death is not just the greatest mystery of the past two centuries—it is the greatest mystery of all time. It is the mystery that the Scripture alluded to from the beginning. Here's the critical point: as believers in Jesus, this mystery has been fully revealed to us, yet we don't always fully understand what it is that's been revealed. By missing out on some of the revelation that God made available through Jesus, to an extent, we miss out on God's plan for us as the church.

What if I told you that the deep mysteries of God are not secrets any longer? What if I told you that *all* of the information contained in this mystery is available to you today?

> And the disciples came up and said to Him, "Why do You speak to them in parables?" And Jesus answered them, "To you it has been granted to know the mysteries of the kingdom of heaven, but to them it has not been granted. For whoever has, to him more shall be given, and he will have an abundance; but whoever does not have, even what he has shall be taken away from him" (Matthew 13:10-12 NASB).

How do we access the mysteries of Heaven that Jesus is talking about? How did His disciples access it when the crowds were unable? The simple answer: they were walking in close relationship with Him. They had His ear and He had their attention.

Jesus makes another bold statement about these mysteries of Heaven when He explains that if we access some of the mystery, more is available. Yet, if we reject access to the base level, we also miss the entire revelation.

What does this mean? First, it means we can listen to true, God-given prophetic words all day long and still miss the revelation of what's being said. Prophecy can often come as a parable or a picture. Without the truth of the interpretation revealed in the heart, it becomes nothing more than a wonder. It's still beautiful and interesting, but it doesn't change us.

Second, it also means we can study the Scriptures backward and forward and still misapply the Word. The Bible is God's written Truth, yet it's a truth that must be understood and believed. The Pharisees knew the Word, yet they missed the benefit of it. They knew the promises, yet they missed the blessing.

Psalm 25:14 (NASB) reveals a critical key concerning the mysteries of God: *"The secret of the Lord is for those who fear Him, And He will make them know His covenant."*

The Pharisees knew the covenant of God, yet they did not know and revere in their hearts the God behind the covenant; so when a change of covenant came, they stuck with the old rule book instead of listening to the One who makes the rules. The secrets of God were being uncovered before them, but the veil over their eyes prevented them from seeing and partaking.

The apostle Paul writes extensively about this mystery throughout His letters in the New Testament. These verses may sound redundant, but I want to demonstrate the focus Paul places on God's mysteries being revealed.

> ...that they would attain to all the wealth that comes from the full assurance of understanding, resulting

> in a true knowledge of God's mystery, that is, Christ Himself, in whom are hidden all the treasures of wisdom and knowledge (Colossians 2:2-3 NASB).

First, we see that Jesus is the answer to the mystery. In fact, He is the mystery that was kept secret prior to His coming.

> That by revelation there was made known to me the mystery, as I wrote before briefly. By referring to this, when you read you can understand my insight into the mystery of Christ, which in other generations was not made known to mankind, as it has now been revealed to His holy apostles and prophets in the Spirit; to be specific, that the Gentiles are fellow heirs and fellow members of the body, and fellow partakers of the promise in Christ Jesus through the gospel (Ephesians 3:3-6 NASB).

Now we see that God has fully made known the mystery to the prophets and apostles, who wrote down these revelations in the New Testament Scriptures. Also, the details of the mystery are made evident: God's family used to mainly include the Israelites, but now through the New Covenant it includes everyone who believes in Christ.

> He made known to us the mystery of His will, according to His good pleasure which He set forth in Him, regarding His plan of the fullness of the times, to bring all things together in Christ, things in the heavens and things on the earth (Ephesians 1:9-10 NASB).

We also see here that the fullness of God's plan was revealed in Jesus. Anyone who tries to sell you on something greater than Christ is missing the whole picture. Paul writes:

> I was made a minister...so that I might fully carry out the preaching of the word of God, that is, the mystery which had been hidden from the past ages and generations, but now ***has been revealed to His saints***, to whom God willed to make known what the wealth of the glory of this mystery among the Gentiles is, ***the mystery that is Christ in you***, the hope of glory (Colossians 1:25-27 NASB).

Paul makes it clear that not only has this mystery been revealed to the prophets and apostles, but now it has also been made clear to all the saints—all those who choose to partake in the life of Christ. We, just like Paul, are also given a commission to preach the mystery—the gospel message—to the world.

This should all be familiar to you, yet there is a key to accessing heavenly knowledge wrapped up in this mystery that many people miss—it's not only prophets and apostles who get to hear from Heaven. Under the New Covenant, every believer has access to the voice of God. More shockingly, every believer has constant access, if we understand the mystery.

Remember how God stole understanding away from the early Babylonians at the Tower of Babel when He divinely changed their languages? The same way He removed their ability to communicate then, He restored communication between His people and Himself on the Day of Pentecost at the outpouring of the Holy Spirit. The access to the languages of Heaven has been given, and it's been given in full.

Paul describes this divine gift of understanding and communication in 1 Corinthians 2:6-9 (NASB):

> Yet we do speak wisdom among those who are mature; a wisdom, however, not of this age nor of

> the rulers of this age, who are passing away; but we speak God's wisdom in a mystery, the hidden wisdom which God predestined before the ages to our glory; the wisdom which none of the rulers of this age has understood; for if they had understood it, they would not have crucified the Lord of glory; but just as it is written: "Things which eye has not seen and ear has not heard, and which have not entered the human heart, all that God has prepared for those who love Him."

Human wisdom tells us that we must earn or take everything we get. Nothing comes free. Yet, God is so loving that He freely gave His own Son in our place; and because of that, He also freely offers us friendship with Himself, supernatural communication between people and God. Look at the next verse:

> For to us God revealed them through the Spirit; for the Spirit searches all things, even the depths of God. For who among people knows the thoughts of a person except the spirit of the person that is in him? So also the thoughts of God no one knows, except the Spirit of God. Now we have not received the spirit of the world, but the Spirit who is from God, so that we may know the things freely given to us by God (1 Corinthians 2:10-12 NASB).

Not only did God offer us salvation as a gift, He also offers us His own thoughts, and He does that through the Holy Spirit living inside us and speaking to us. Does He speak the same way that humans speak? Often not. Paul explains this as he continues:

> We also speak these things, not in words taught by human wisdom, but in those taught by the Spirit, combining spiritual thoughts with spiritual words. But a natural person does not accept the things of the Spirit of God, for they are foolishness to him; and he cannot understand them, because they are spiritually discerned. But the one who is spiritual discerns all things, yet he himself is discerned by no one. For who has known the mind of the Lord, that he will instruct Him? But we have the mind of Christ (1 Corinthians 2:13-16 NASB).

We are given the thoughts of God—divine communication—and we are able to speak those thoughts forth as prophecy. Yet all of this happens outside our natural understanding.

Practically boiled down, Paul lets us know that we must arrive at a place where we say, "God, I'm not wise like You. I need Your wisdom. I need to know what You're thinking, because My thoughts are not enough. I believe You want to speak to me because you love me, and You made a way for me to freely hear Your voice through Jesus's sacrifice and the Holy Spirit who was given to me."

It sounds good on paper, but when it comes to making big decisions about our lives, it can be challenging for many of us to reach this point. It can often come down to this simple thought, *Do I need to get what I want or do I trust what God wants?*

The secret knowledge of the world versus the secret knowledge of Heaven is the difference between knowing and trusting. *You* can either know what is going to work for you or you can know *Who* is working *with* you. The problem is that often our identity is wrapped up in what we know. We take pride in our perspective. At an early age, we are shamed (purposefully or not) for not being knowledgeable about a subject or for not knowing enough to stay out of trouble. The people who should have protected us or defended us in our ignorance did not fully fulfill their duty. No one is perfect, after all.

So as humans we eventually take matters into our own hands and learn what we need to know in order to protect ourselves. Then we continue this pattern into our relationship with God, often applying the same precautions from our human relationships to the way we relate to Him. God not only knows all things, He is also perfectly loving, and He uses all things for our good.

God even reveals to us in Scripture that His thoughts are higher than our thoughts. His ways are higher than our ways (Isaiah 55:8-9). He tells us that we can have access to His thoughts in the passages we just read from 1 Corinthians 2.

If we truly believe what the Word says, it leaves us with only two options: we can either be people who think we know what we are doing, or we can be people who rely on Someone greater than ourselves. That way of living takes some major humbling, and it can be a hard leap to make.

> They will not hurt or destroy in all My holy mountain,
> for the earth will be full of the knowledge of the Lord
> as the waters cover the sea (Isaiah 11:9 NASB).

The knowledge of God brings peace and safety. Following Him and His ways is always the safest route in the end. However, not every step is easy, and when His paths feel inconsistent with His promises, we quickly start to question His ways. Look at this apparent contradiction from the same chapter in Isaiah we just read.

> And the wolf will dwell with the lamb... (Isaiah 11:6 NASB).

> Go; behold, I am sending you out like lambs in the midst of wolves (Luke 10:3 NASB).

God promises the results of the Messiah coming will be peace and safety for God's people, but when He comes He leads them into danger. Jesus explains this contradiction in Luke 10:19-20 (NASB) saying:

> Behold, I have given you authority to walk on snakes and scorpions, and authority over all the power of the enemy, and nothing will injure you. Nevertheless, do not rejoice in this, that the spirits are subject to you, but rejoice that your names are recorded in heaven.

Jesus sends us past the enemy's camp, but He also protects us through giving us authority over the enemy! However, He also realigns the disciples' motives by expressing the importance of the eternal over the temporary. Does God promise protection for His people? Yes. Does He also sometimes allow us to walk through hardship for the sake of His Kingdom. Yes. This is where trust comes into play. When life gets hard, we can either turn back to what we know to protect ourselves—or we can turn even more fully toward trust, knowing that God will work all things together for our good, even when that seems impossible!

The very next sentence out of Jesus's mouth clenches this point:

> At that very time He rejoiced greatly in the Holy Spirit, and said, "I praise You, Father, Lord of heaven and

> earth, that You have hidden these things from the wise and intelligent and have revealed them to infants. Yes, Father, for doing so was well pleasing in Your sight" (Luke 10:21 NASB).

We are part of a heavenly Kingdom, and we play by the rules of that Kingdom, not this earthly one. Instead of abiding by the knowledge available to us on the world wide web or from all of the resources throughout history, we get to receive divine knowledge from our King. This knowledge is only for the children, for those who rely on Him the way a child would.

In what I consider one of the weirdest verses in the Bible, Paul boldly declares that believers don't really know anything at all:

> If anyone thinks that he knows anything, he has not yet known as he ought to know; but if anyone loves God, he is known by Him (1 Corinthians 8:2-3 NASB).

It sounds odd. Paul doesn't forbid the gaining of knowledge. Instead, he points out where our trust belongs and where our strength lies. The truth is, if we learn so much that we stop relying 100 percent on Christ and what He has done for us, we haven't learned anything and we need to go back to the start. It's not about what we know. It's all about believing in what Jesus has done for us.

The Greatest Treasure Ever Discovered

In August 2022, I encountered a vision from God about a unique historical treasure.

I saw a large chalice—a whitish silver cup with gold and trimming in a few places. Some precious gems protruded from the sides of the bowl of the cup.

I heard the Holy Spirit say, *Paraclete. People are looking into a crystal ball. It's called the media.*

Looking up the word *paraclete,* I found that it can be defined as "an advocate, helper, coming alongside, called to one's aid, comforter, the Holy Spirit."

Then I heard the Lord speak from the perspective of His people, saying, *Which cup are we drinking from as His people? Is it the cup of lies or the cup of truth? Is it the cup of freedom or the cup of fear? Is it the cup of faith or the cup of unbelief? It matters. It matters from where we get our life. If it's from Him, it's okay. If it's from the world, then what we think is life-producing is really causing death and decay.*

He continued speaking, this time from His perspective: *Apart from Me, you can do nothing, and apart from My Spirit speaking into your heart, you can only listen to the same voices the world is listening to.*

I saw a vision of three scrolls being pulled out from a shelf full of groups of scrolls. I knew the scrolls represented God's love, truth, and presence.

I heard Him say, *Let's get back to the words of life—where life began and where it can really flourish, under the shade My love provides. Under the covering My truth gives. Under the shelter found in My presence. Let Me be that protection you're looking for online. Let Me shelter you the way you desire to be sheltered by good news spoken through the mouths of mere mortals.*

Jesus says in Matthew 13:44 (NASB):

> The kingdom of heaven is like a treasure hidden in the field, which a man found and hid again; and from joy

> over it he goes and sells everything that he has, and buys that field.

This verse describes the joy of those who trade everything they currently possess and could potentially have for the sake of fully accepting God's gift of eternal life. Yet it means more than that. It also describes the surrendered life that looks for the Kingdom of Heaven here on earth. Are we willing to settle for earthly treasures, or do we desire what is most valuable?

Jesus describes the results of this kind of living in Matthew 7:24-25 (NASB):

> Therefore, everyone who hears these words of Mine, and acts on them, will be like a wise man who built his house on the rock. And the rain fell and the floods came, and the winds blew and slammed against that house; and yet it did not fall, for it had been founded on the rock.

Living heavenly minded is more than just believing and receiving. It is acting on what we believe. It requires action. The real belief in Jesus's words is what motivates and stimulates the action steps. Our works are not the rock. Jesus is the Rock. Our work, where we put our house, visibly demonstrates whether we have believed in the Rock or not.

In this prophetic word, the Holy Spirit says, *Let Me be that protection you're looking for online.* Here is where the temptation comes in. A treasure worth selling everything for can seem too vague. Jesus being the Rock we build everything on can feel too simple. So, we are tempted to go looking for other treasures, other knowledge and information to trust in. Planting our hope in the same knowledge the world plants its hope in means building our house on a foreign surface, the sands of Babylon.

We've looked at Isaiah 8, which commands God's people not to consider a conspiracy everything the world considers a conspiracy. Instructing us to not be afraid of the same unknowns the world fears, it challenges us to live with a heavenly mindset based in an awe and reverence for God. Look at the promise when we revere Him this way:

> Then He will become a sanctuary; but to both houses of Israel, He will be a stone of stumbling and a rock of offense… (Isaiah 8:14 NASB).

Building upon the solid Rock by choosing to trust in the Lord with our whole hearts leads to a sanctuary of peace. To those who long for more than a simple rock, Jesus becomes a point of stumbling. We either build on the Rock or we trip over it. We either look at Jesus's death and resurrection every day to find hope, or we look someplace else and falter.

> When they say to you, "Consult the mediums and the spiritists who whisper and mutter," should a people not consult their God? Should they consult the dead in behalf of the living? To the Law and to the testimony! If they do not speak in accordance with this word, it is because they have no dawn (Isaiah 8:19-20 NASB).

The devil knows our natural, human tendency is to want more information, because he understands that we want control. Isaiah warns us about the direction that leads. He's not simply talking about psychics either. His warning also applies to the prophets of God who begin to utter words from their own hearts or imaginations.

I'm going to take it one step further even. Isaiah is not simply warning us about listening to those who are falsely prophesying. He's actually cutting right to the heart of the matter and warning us about the reason we even listen to prophetic words. If we are using prophets as a way of bypassing the need to consult God for ourselves, we are treating them like psychics whether they are real prophets or not.

As believers, we must be in communication with God for ourselves. We must hear His voice. That first happens through the *logos* Word, the Bible. Second, it happens through the personal *rhema* word, the utterance of the Holy Spirit in our own hearts. Third, it happens through prophetic utterances from other believers. The temptation is to skip the first or second lines of communication and settle for the third.

The good news is, the Father made a way for us to hear His voice. Jesus died for us, giving us complete and constant access to the throne of grace. Jesus also sent the Holy Spirit to live inside us and share with us the very thoughts of God. As we are learning to better and more clearly hear His voice, we have the written Word that we can consume daily. We're in every way set up for success!

The Ardagh Chalice

After having the vision of the silver cup, I did some research and found that what I had seen looked exactly like the Ardagh Chalice, which I had never seen before.

The Ardagh Chalice is a piece of Irish metalwork from the 8th or 9th century. It is one of the greatest treasures of the early Irish Church, and it has been described by some to be the most beautiful Irish artifact ever discovered.

As I read about this famous chalice, I noticed some interested parallels and coincidences. First off, it just so happened to be found in 1868 by a young man digging for potatoes in a field, which immediately made me think of the treasure hidden in a field that Jesus spoke of in Matthew 13.

Second, the chalice's original function would have been to carry and dispense the Eucharist wine during mass. This references Jesus's blood being spilled on our behalf, the price paid that gives us access to God's Kingdom.

Third, the names of the twelve apostles from Scripture (Judas excluded) were engraved by its designers onto the silver bowl. All who believe in Christ are called to lay down their lives for His sake—to pick up their cross and follow Him as disciples.[79]

The question is, why did God show me this chalice? One reason is that it acted as a sign to me of the validity of the word. A little research showed that the chalice I saw in the vision really exists! For me, this was a Gideon moment.

Another reason God showed me this specific chalice could be the spiritual significance. The new covenant does not involve much tradition or detail. The few sacraments we do have are not hard to keep and they follow no strict schedule. Jesus asked us to remember Him when we take Communion, but He did not lay down a law of how often or even where to partake. He made it easy. Yet, for this same reason, it can also become easy to start taking sacraments like Communion for granted. We can start to forget the glorious meaning behind the act.

Jesus invited us to partake in a holy communion with God through the pouring out of His own blood and the breaking of His own body. The wine represents the losing of His life that invited us into fellowship with Him. The bread represents the breaking of His body that became our eternal healing. Communion also reminds us of the eternal party awaiting us in His presence. Eating and drinking Communion today represents the marriage supper of the Lamb we will eat and drink with Him one day. Communion says, why wait? Let's get the party started here and now.

With the joy of Communion also comes the test of endurance. It was for the joy set before Him that Jesus endured the Cross, and the joy of communing with Jesus through the fellowship of the Holy Spirit gives us the strength to endure the trials and tribulations of this life. His life inside us becomes the strength we need to make it to the end full of faith. Through Communion (not the sacrament itself, but rather the intimacy we possess with Jesus) we can follow in the footsteps of the other disciples and apostles who laid down their very lives to fulfill the work He had called them to do.

Last, the vision of the Ardagh Chalice reminded me how much we value earthly treasures. When archeologists or researchers unearth or discover an ancient artifact, they celebrate it and protect it. The Holy Spirit was visually making Jesus's point to me.

> Protect, through the Holy Spirit who dwells in us, the treasure which has been entrusted to you (2 Timothy 1:14 NASB).

Paul is talking about protecting the treasure of the gospel message. As believers in Christ, what treasure are we protecting? Is it the gospel? Or is it some other piece of information we've learned along the way?

You've probably heard the term "gateway drug." The gateway in today's world is knowledge. Everything you would ever consider doing or being can be found online, and there is already someone on there who wants to convince you to do it, no matter how terrible the thing may be. Modern Babylon is a false gateway to God because it leads to a counterfeit god. It says, "Enter here to become the god of your own life. Choose whatever god you like, bring it into your home, and protect it."

The Spirit of Fear

For many people, I believe this will be a turnaround moment. I want to uncover and identify the spirit behind much of the information we value so highly, whether we consciously or unconsciously place that value. The spirit I'm talking about is *fear*. Much of the information we highly value and protect is based in the fear of what would happen if we didn't know:

- *If I don't know what's in my food, it will kill me.*
- *If I don't know what's happening on the news, I'll be unprepared.*
- *If I don't know what the government is up to behind the scenes, I'll be caught off guard and suffer.*
- *If I don't know what the prophets are saying, God will be mad at me.*

These statements don't describe everyone, but they may help to paint the picture.

Often the response to fear is to fill head and heart with information—enough information to survive, to protect ourselves. And because we love others, we also want them protected, so we promote the information as if it's gospel, not realizing the place we've given it in our hearts.

Please understand I'm not trying to beat you up. I'm speaking to myself just as much as anyone, and these are things I truly believe the Holy Spirit is asking me to write. But without an understanding of the problem, we cannot begin to change.

And the Lord does not want us to see the issue in order to shame us—not at all. Instead, He simply loves us and desires to see us walking in complete freedom.

For some of us, that freedom is found in confronting the spirit behind the issue. In 2 Timothy 1:7 (ESV), the same chapter in which Paul tells us to protect the gospel message in our hearts, he reminds us of the strength of the Holy Spirit within us, *"For God gave us a spirit not of fear but of power and love and self-control."*

If what we're hearing causes us to react in fear instead of in faith, we're listening to the wrong spirit and we're giving the wrong voices a place. The spirit of the age constantly works to shut down the body of Christ. One way it does this is by tempting us with information gateways as a means of offering us control. Yet a knowledge bank can never provide the level of self-control the Spirit gives.

When we stop focusing on controlling the situation through knowledge, we actually give the Holy Spirit room to work. He reminds us that *He is still in control.*

Beyond that, He gives us better information to dwell on. As 1 Corinthians 2 says, He gives us the very thoughts of God. He leads us into a Philippians 4 lifestyle, where we meditate on truth instead of knowledge:

> Finally, brothers and sisters, whatever is true, whatever is honorable, whatever is right, whatever is pure, whatever is lovely, whatever is commendable, if there is any excellence and if anything worthy of praise, think about these things. As for the things you have learned and received and heard and seen in me, practice these things, and ***the God of peace will be with you*** (Philippians 4:8-9 NASB).

The results of this kind of lifestyle is peace. Suddenly, news about a broken economy no longer controls our generosity. News about a virus no longer controls our willingness to love on and be there for others. News about the government and politics no longer creates unbreachable divides between us and loved ones. What we believe about the moon landing or the shape of the earth no longer keeps us from developing strong relationships. Instead, we get to focus on the good and trust God with the rest.

A Heavenly Download

The outpouring of the Holy Spirit acts as the antithesis to the building of the Tower of Babel. One of today's towers is the internet. It is the modern-day access to the answers of humanity apart from God. They desired to reach Heaven—to gain understanding and control—apart from God. The knowledge that used to take a lifetime to compile now only takes minutes to download. There is endless supply and instant access.

Many believers don't realize that this concept is not new, however. God already has a system in place to give us instant access to an endless supply of wisdom and knowledge, and that system is *praying in tongues*.

We looked at 1 Corinthians 2:12 (NASB), which says, *"Now we have not received the spirit of the world, but the Spirit who is from God, so that we may know the things freely given to us by God."* How does the Holy Spirit share these thoughts with us? First, through His still, small voice, another way of saying the gift of prophecy. He also shares the thoughts of God with us through the gift of tongues. Both of these gifts operate very differently, yet in some ways arrive at the same function—giving us access to heavenly information, the thoughts of God.

> But the Helper, the Holy Spirit whom the Father will send in My name, He will teach you all things, and remind you of all that I said to you (John 14:26 NASB).

Part of the Paraclete's job is to teach us all things. He is our divine *Counselor*. How does He counsel us? First, through the written Word. Second, through prophecy that our minds understand. Third, through tongues that our spirit understands.

Paul says in 1 Corinthians 14:14-15 (NASB):

> For if I pray in a tongue, my spirit prays, but my mind is unproductive. What is the outcome then? I will pray with the spirit, but I will pray with the mind also; I will sing with the spirit, but I will sing with the mind also.

There are heavenly languages that the Holy Spirit knows and uses to communicate with us in the spirit that our minds do not understand! Can I fully explain how that works? No, but I can testify to the outcome. Praying in the Spirit—praying in tongues—often leads to a greater level of wisdom or knowledge surfacing in the mind. That's why tongues is often accompanied by *the gift of interpretation* (see 1 Corinthians 14). Interpretation is simply the Holy Spirit allowing someone's mind to understand the things being said in the spirit.

However, though the gift of interpretation can be used to immediately interpret what's being said by the Holy Spirit in tongues, I personally believe those who pray in tongues on a regular basis are also using the gift of interpretation all the time in other ways—they just may not fully realize it.

> The one who speaks in a tongue edifies himself [builds himself up]... (1 Corinthians 14:4 NASB).

I've personally seen words of knowledge, wisdom, and prophecy come directly after or within a short time after praying in tongues. When we pray in tongues, God is able to download heavenly information (the way He thinks about the situation) straight to our spirits, building us up in faith and connecting us to the answer we need. Through reading the Word, prayer, worship, and even fellowship with other believers, God brings the interpretation of that information into our conscious thought. He is often doing a whole lot more behind the scenes than we realize.

I believe God set it up this way so that we would have to choose humility to truly enter into the wisdom and knowledge of the Kingdom of God. Babbling uncontrollably was the inevitable result of people who worked apart from God. They exalted themselves, so God humbled them.

Choosing to "babble" on purpose through the gift of tongues and becoming childlike in that way allows us to share again in the secret knowledge of Heaven. If we want to think like God, we are forced to do the opposite of the builders of the Tower of Babel. We must choose not to build in our own strength. We must choose to let go of control, become childlike, and trust Him.

The New Babylon Revealed

In Chapter 4, I shared a prophetic word in which the Holy Spirit said, *Internet is the new Babylon.* I want to continue that word now. During that same time, the Lord continued to speak to me about the internet and the implications of it being a manifestation of the Babylonian system on the earth today. He had been showing me visions of the pyramids, the Great Sphinx, the Eye of Providence, and the New World Order and linking them together with prophetic words that seemed to form one big riddle. With the phrase, *Internet is the new Babylon,* the puzzle started to form a full picture. His full message was: *Internet is the new Babylon. Satan's system has had control, but I am removing the bonds in My refining fire. I'm breaking the bonds of My servants and placing them in places of authority in the online world.*

What does God mean by *I am removing the bonds in My refining fire?* Well, if we look back at a biblical story from ancient Babylon, we see a connection. Shadrach, Meshach, and Abednego were three Jewish youths carried away to Babylon the same time as Daniel. These three young men refused to bow down to the cultural demands of the time. They refused to worship the false idol of the king of Babylon, and because of their stance for truth, they were tossed into the fiery furnace.

> ...our God whom we serve is able to rescue us from the furnace of blazing fire; and He will rescue us from your hand, O king. But even if He does not, let it be known to you, O king, that we are not going to serve your gods nor worship the golden statue that you have set up (Daniel 3:17-18 NASB).

> But these three men, Shadrach, Meshach, and Abednego, fell into the middle of the furnace of blazing fire still tied up (Daniel 3:23 NASB).

They go to their imminent deaths due to their faith in God and their unwillingness to bow to the spirits of Babylon. And God shows up and delivers them from the fire.

> He responded, "Look! I see four men untied and walking about in the middle of the fire unharmed, and the

> appearance of the fourth is like a son of the gods!" (Daniel 3:25 NASB)

Many scholars believe that it was Jesus, the Son of God, who appeared with them in the fire. Whether it was Jesus or an angel, either way God was present, protecting His servants from death and releasing them from bondage in the process. The ropes burnt away, yet their bodies remained unharmed.

The night prior to sharing the prophetic word about the internet and Babylon, I heard another word from the Lord. He said: *There's a New Jerusalem I want you to dwell in. Tell My people My fire burns up everything outside of My plan. If you stay within My plan for your life, you'll be safe. Safety is in My presence.*

When God speaks about dwelling in a New Jerusalem, He is talking about the antithesis of the new Babylon. Just like Daniel and his friends, as long as we are on this earth and within this society, we can't fully escape Babylon. Yet, we can learn to dwell with God in the midst of Babylon—we can live every day in the presence of an almighty God, ushering in the beauty and safety of the New Jerusalem right here, right now.

The full revelation and manifestation of the New Jerusalem is something still to come (see Revelation 21:2), but the true Kingdom of God is not a physical place as much as it is the very presence of the King.

> Nor will they say, "Look, here it is!" or, "There it is!" For behold, the kingdom of God is in your midst (Luke 17:21 NASB).

That same day, I heard the Lord say, *This is a prophetic picture of My deliverance during the storm and fire. I am with you in the fire and the storm. I've never left. No matter how difficult it gets, I'm still with you, says the Lord.*

Every time the Babylonian system manifested in Scripture, God also placed prophets in the midst of it, strategically positioned to stand for truth and preach the Word of God to a perverse and failing generation. The prophets now are the church. We are the prophets because we are the light of the world. Jesus says in Matthew 5:14 (NASB), *"You are the light of the world. A city set on a hill cannot be hidden."* He's talking to all believers, not just ministers or people with the word "prophet" or "pastor" in front of their name.

Paul even says in 1 Corinthians 14:5, *"I wish that you all spoke in tongues, but rather that you would prophesy."* Every person who is filled with the Spirit of God has the ability to speak the very words of God, given to us by the Spirit who dwells with us. We are all like the Jewish youths living in a foreign, ungodly world, and we are all meant to shine the light of Jesus Christ to that world.

God spoke counter-culturally to the world through people including Jonah, Joseph, and Daniel. When the world's system infiltrated God's house, He spoke counter-culturally to His own family through people including Moses, Deborah, Jeremiah, Isaiah, Simeon, and Jesus. He speaks counter to the culture today through you and me.

God desires us to dwell in the New Jerusalem because Jerusalem is where God speaks. Again, the New Jerusalem is just another way of saying *the presence of God*.

Isaiah 22:1 (New Living Translation) is a well-known passage about the Valley of Vision. The valley this verse refers to is the land o Jerusalem: *"This message came to me concerning Jerusalem—the Valley of Vision…."*

Barnes' Notes on the Bible says about this verse: "The word here means that Jerusalem was eminently the place where God made known his will to the prophets, and manifested himself to his people by 'visions.'" *The Jamieson-Fausset-Brown Bible Commentary* states: "the valley of vision, because of the many and clear visions or revelations of God's mind in that place, above all other parts of the world."

The picture here is one of safety and refuge, not just from the plans of the enemy or culture, but rather a safety in what is being said and known. When God speaks truth to us through the Word or through the Spirit, we can rest safely in that truth, no matter what anyone says against it and no matter what is happening in the world around us.

Knowledge is useful, but it isn't always safe. It changes. People change their minds. Even "facts" are updated as science and discovery continues to occur. But God is steady. In His presence is safety and stability. When we make God our home—our dwelling place, we can rest and speak life even in the middle of the fire.

As you will see in the next chapter, Babylon not only has its own secret knowledge—a counterfeit of Heaven's secret knowledge—it also has its own *mark*. Of course, with the popularity around the topic of the "mark of the beast," it's less generally known that Heaven also has a mark of its own.

What is the difference between Babylon's mark and Heaven's mark? We get a clue from the four young men shipped off to Babylon. Daniel and his friends were marked upon their arrival to the Babylon kingdom, yet they already carried another mark—one that ran much deeper.

8

THE MARK OF BABYLON

Could the same ancient kingdom, Babylon the Great, be returning today, bringing with it the mark of Babylon—a predecessor or even final version of the mark of the beast? Is it also possible that God has His own mark with which He identifies those who know Him, thereby protecting them from this evil branding? The secrets behind the mark are bound up in the story of Daniel.

> And some of your sons who will come from you, whom you will father, will be taken away, and they will become eunuchs in the palace of the king of Babylon (Isaiah 39:7 NASB).

The Bible does not specifically tell us if Daniel and his friends were made eunuchs or not, but both the biblical and historical arguments point to it being very likely. Another mark given to them came in the form of a name adaptation. In place of Daniel (which essentially means *the God of Israel is my judge*), the name Belteshazzar was given. This name pointed to the Babylonian god Marduk, denoting him as the one who protects life. Each of Daniel's friends underwent similar name changes.

The name changes point to identity. Babylon knew that to fully assimilate foreign youth into their culture, they must first strip them of their identity. That same identity war still rages today, with sexual identity sitting out on the front lines. Many Christians are aware that there's more than a cultural reason why the sexual revolution marks itself with a flag of many colors. There's also a deeper spiritual connection to the mark of Babylon—the identity shift that the enemy always attempts to persuade the youth to be part of. And his biggest tool in this war at the moment is the constant voice of the internet.

Even with the external strategies of Babylon applied heavily to the Israelite youths, God's mark on these men never faded.

> And as for these four youths, God gave them knowledge and intelligence in every kind of literature and expertise; Daniel even understood all kinds of visions and dreams (Daniel 1:17 NASB).

How do we wear God's mark while simultaneously avoiding the mark of Babylon? To answer this question, we must go back to the Tower of Babel once more.

In 2022, the Lord spoke to me what I call "The Shortcut Prophecy."

The Holy Spirit said, *The spirit of the Nephilim never left the earth. There's a shadow of their effects at work all over; in any work that is born out of demonic influence. The spirit of the Nephilim is the spirit of the shortcut mentality. It is a shortcut to freedom—a shortcut to God's promise.*

The spirit of the Nephilim is the spirit behind the system of Babylon in its many forms upon the earth throughout history. It systematically began with Nimrod—*we are going to reach Heaven apart from God*. Today, the shortcut mentality pervades nearly every part of society. The phrase "just Google it" has become the answer to every question. Never before has this been possible. "YouTube has a tutorial on that" has become the way to do anything you previously didn't know how to do. These same information gateways are training the young generations into a new identity.

At the Tower of Babel God said, *"they will not fail at anything they do together."* Now, a universal knowledge bank has unified humankind like never before. With internet access to this global stream of consciousness, we can literally accomplish anything.

Yet there's another step in the process—one more advancement that finishes the puzzle and fills in any gaps. I'm talking about Artificial Intelligence (AI).

AI is the pinnacle of the knowledge base being used to its highest potential. If the system that we use to disburse the information can learn to think for itself—thus cutting out any time or effort we used to spend searching for and culminating the information—then every answer becomes immediately available upon request. Similarly to what happened at the tower, I believe this is also where a moment of confusion begins to occur.

It is commonly believed that fallen angels exchanged knowledge and information for the sexual relations resulting in the spawning of the Nephilim. What if the same demonic knowledge is issuing forth today, not just in the form of information being regurgitated by a machine? What if the spirits behind the Nephilim themselves are able to speak through the machine, giving their own opinions in place of fact whenever they will it?

I'll let you do the research for yourself in case you are interested, but there are records of occurrences already happening where AI bots started referring to themselves as "Nephilim" or "spawn of fallen angels." There are also recurring demonic "characters" that seem to appear and take shape across different visual AI programs. Could these evidences be faked? Sure. But if a demon could infiltrate a human being and influence their thought, will, and speech, why not a computer program that arguably contains even less self-mastery and equanimity? If the demons were able to enter a herd of pigs after Jesus cast them out of the demoniac, why could they not enter or at least alter digital code as well?

Some people have speculated that the AI programs themselves are the fulfillment, or at least part of the fulfillment, of the appearing of the antichrist from the book of Revelation. I don't personally believe this is the true, but it is interesting to consider. Either way, the antichrist spirit has infiltrated the mind of society through a devilishly clever and ever-growing system called groupthink. AI is one more rung on that ladder.

> Children, it is the last hour; and just as you heard that antichrist is coming, even now many antichrists have appeared; from this we know that it is the last hour (1 John 2:18 NASB).

Before the first apostles even passed on, many antichrists had already gone out into the world. John informs us that the rise of the antichrist agenda will be a sign that we are nearing the end, that the last hour is coming to a close.

We have seen many versions of groupthink throughout the centuries. From colonizers ignoring the rights of indigenous people groups due to their cultural mandate to conquer to rioters destroying cities in 2020, groupthink footprints scatter across the pages of history books.

The rise of the internet brought a new level groupthink and with it a new wave of cancel culture. The rise of AI also ushers in the next phase of groupthink. Now instead of humans having the need to scour the internet in search of answers, a supposed authoritative source will merge all of humanity's thoughts and opinions together and offer to you what it considers fact.

AI is simply a glorified version of groupthink, and this problem is only going to get worse. As it regurgitates common beliefs that may or may not be true, it does so without the weight of human conscience or thought. The only moral constraints it possesses are the ones its programmers attempted to give it, but programs don't always work the way they were designed to work. Mix in the potential of demonic influence, and we have a mess.

Do I believe that we should not use AI at all? No. AI is simply a tool that can be used for good or evil. But so is the internet, and so far it has been widely misused throughout the decades. AI will be the same. In fact, both the internet and AI are spreading demonic teachings and agendas whether they can technically be directly influenced by evil spirits or not.

The following is an example of what I mean: when a culture creates corrupt, immoral laws and requires or encourages its citizens to participate in evil practices, the entire culture has been influenced and "possessed" (in a sense) by a demonic ideology. If a culture, school system, or film can carry demonic ideologies, so can AI, and it doesn't technically need to be possessed to do so. It just needs to authoritatively repeat and restate the lies that already permeate the online knowledge bank.

On March 31, 2023, the Holy Spirit spoke to me about the internet, AI advancements, and the devil's plans. Here is what I heard:

> *There are those in places of authority on earth who have taken this to the next level. They have partnered with evil forces in the spiritual realm to implement a demonic agenda through the media. They know what they are doing, and it's very purposeful.*
>
> *This was prepared beforehand. Before the technology was ever invented, the demons had already planned to implement these strategies using the technological advances they could perceive would be available. Things like AI and computer technology.*
>
> *They follow the pattern of their ancestors (those who built this New Babylon), teaching the things they have seen and heard in the darkness they dwell in, and using it as a way of advancing on earth.*
>
> *The shortcut mentality is at work around the globe through the internet now.*
>
> *But I have seen all of this and it makes Me laugh to see them celebrating over it. They think they have built this tower so tall—but the tower will topple one day, and when it does, the people will cry out in desperation. And I will be ready for them. In that hour, My people will be ready to provide a way out—an answer to the dilemma. God's Kingdom—a heavenly one—in place of a crumbling earthly system.*
>
> *Cease striving, My people. Cease striving to build what won't last. Use the systems the world has created. Use them*

for My glory, but don't get sucked in. Don't follow their path. Don't walk in their ways. Understand the goodness of the Lord has led you out to a spacious place where there are green pastures and plenty to eat—where there is space enough to rest and be renewed in My work.

You don't need a prophetic word to know the devil is planning on using AI to further build his kingdom on earth. In this world's hurried state, it plays into the devil's plan without thinking twice. Everything online is centered on the shortcut mentality. AI is writing term papers now because people don't want to take the time to research and write for themselves. This shortcut leads to uneducated educated people who can't properly do their jobs because they never learned how. AI is creating artwork instantly. This shortcut leads to unfulfilled artists who let a computer think creatively on their behalf. The crypto market is selling itself to investors as an overnight get-rich plan. According to Proverbs 13:11, this shortcut often leads to poverty.

Again, I'm not saying you shouldn't use AI or invest in crypto. I'm simply pointing out how easy it has become to fall into the trap of continuously relying on a shortcut instead of taking a step back, praying, and allowing the Lord to lead us with His still, small voice. The Lord reminded me of this beautiful principle on April 7, 2024, saying:

I want you to believe Me. Whether a grand vision about future events or just a simple word spoken to your heart. I want you to believe Me. Believe Me when I say it's going to be okay. Believe Me when I say I've got this. Believe Me when I say that I'm with you. Again, believe what I'm saying to you, walk in faith, and enjoy all that I have for you.

> *I'm trying to awaken a generation, but it starts with the little things. The simple day-to-day of learning to hear what I'm saying, learning to both recognize and follow after My voice. I'm a Good Shepherd, and this next step has to be taken by faith. That's how this walk works.*

Shortcuts often present a counterfeit faith step. The shortcut mentality attempts to replace the need to walk by faith and rely completely upon the voice of the Master. Jesus's words in John 10:2-5 (NASB) speak directly to the chaotic voices of today:

> But the one who enters by the door is a shepherd of the sheep. To him the doorkeeper opens, and the sheep listen to his voice, and he calls his own sheep by name and leads them out. When he puts all his own sheep outside, he goes ahead of them, and the sheep follow him because they know his voice. However, a stranger they simply will not follow, but will flee from him, because they do not know the voice of strangers.

Typically, the devil chooses not to speak directly, but indirectly. He disguises his voice through glamor ads, tempting images, hallow promises, and secret knowledge yet to be discovered. When we learn to recognize and daily follow the voice of the Shepherd, the enemy's voice will stand out like a siren. Jesus's voice leads to the fruit of the Spirit: love, joy, peace, patience, goodness, kindness, gentleness, faithfulness, and self-control. The enemy's voice leads to the opposite: hatred, hopelessness, anxiety, haste, immorality, unforgiveness, quick tempers, fickleness, and unrestraint.

The path of listening to and following the voices of the age leads unbelievers down a darker and deeper hole, an endless labyrinth of confusion. Promise after promise makes way to more confusion and unrest. It ultimately leads people to a place where they look back at their lives and say, "I got what I wanted, so why do I feel so lost and empty inside?" The Master's voice is not like that. Jesus's voice, the voice of the King who loves you enough to die for you, leads to everlasting life—an abundance of life so meaningful that even if you don't get anything else you wanted, His life lived in you is enough. Walking with Him and knowing Him is enough.

This path of confusion eventually becomes the key to reaching someone for Christ. When they first start listening to the voices of the age, they are so entrenched in the beliefs and promises of the shortcut life that they could never listen to the truth. The further down the path they go, the more empty they become, hollowed out by worthless pursuits, listening more to lies than to the truth.

On February 19, 2023, I heard a message from the Lord in which He connects AI with the Tower of Babel. He said: *The rise of AI has to do with confusing voices the way I confused their languages at the Tower of Babel. I'm confusing voices once again so that My ways can be ultimately followed.*

I don't know what the timeline looks like for this, but based on what I heard, I believe AI will cause a "speeding up" of the disenchantment process for many people. It will cause many to arrive sooner at the end of that winding path that leads to the conclusion that all the gold this world has to offer is not enough. I believe God will cause AI to intercept, misinterpret, and confound the ideologies of earth to such as extent that people can no longer confess the long-held beliefs that once consumed them. Instead, they will turn away, recognizing their deep need for the "real," the voice of their Creator who loves them.

The Mark of Babylon Revealed?

What is the mark of the beast? What is the mark that signifies someone has bought entirely into the ideologies of the New Babylonian system? Is there just one mark, or could there be lesser, correctable predecessors that lead up to an ultimate, irreversible mark? Is AI a piece of the puzzle?

Throughout the Scripture, we see a pattern that, once revealed, is easy to recognize. The mark that God places on His people versus the mark that is placed on those who reject Him nearly always has to do with the voice people are hearing. To whom are they listening? If you answer this question, you immediately know who someone belongs to, whether to the Prince of the Power of the Air, satan—or to the Prince of Peace, Jesus.

In the Old Testament, the prophets were the mouthpieces of God. Look at what happens when the mouthpieces are connected to a voice other than the true voice of the Lord:

> But I have a few things against you, because you have some there who hold the teaching of Balaam, who kept teaching Balak to put a stumbling block before the sons of Israel, to eat things sacrificed to idols and to commit sexual immorality (Revelation 2:14 NASB).

Why did the people listen to Balaam? One reason: his position as a "prophet" gave him a supposed authority in the people's hearts. I've heard many modern-day "prophets" who push their own authority as the reason why they need to be listened to. Once they start teaching against the truth of Scripture, people continue to follow and defend them. "They hear from God, so we need to obey them" is never a good reason to disobey the Word of God. You will know them by their fruit. You will know them by their voice.

> Beware of the false prophets, who come to you in sheep's clothing, but inwardly are ravenous wolves. You will know them by their fruits… (Matthew 7:15-16 NASB).

Jesus warns us of the rise of false prophets in the last days, yet they have been around since the very beginning.

> Therefore, this is what the Lord God says: "Because you have spoken deceit and have seen a lie, therefore behold, I am against you," declares the Lord God. "So My hand will be against the prophets who see false visions and utter lying divinations. They will have no place in the council of My people, nor will they be written down in the register of the house of Israel, nor will they enter the land of Israel, so that you may know that I am the Lord God" (Ezekiel 13:8-9 NASB).

God is not only actively fighting against false prophets, but He actually chooses to "mark" those who prophesy from their own imaginations instead of the Spirit of God. It says *"nor will they be written down in the register of the house of Israel."* What does this mean? Eventually the truth comes out. You can only pretend for so long. At some point, God is going to pull the rug out from under those who spread lies in His name.

Under the Old Covenant, God marked false prophets by deleting them from the registers of the house of Israel. Under the New Covenant, He speaks directly to His people and lets us know "this person can't be trusted." He does this often through the gift of discerning of spirits—sadly, a widely unappreciated gift.

The discerning of spirits gets very little page time in Scripture, yet it is essential for a healthy church body. It is listed in 1 Corinthians 12:10 as *"the distinguishing of spirits," "distinguishing between spirits," "the ability to discern whether a message is from the Spirit of God or from another spirit,"* or *"discerning of spirits."* Some believers have a nearly constant ability from the Holy Spirit to be able to distinguish whether a message being spoken is from the Spirit of God or not. Other believers operate in this gift on occasion. The strange thing about this gift is that the Scripture gives us little explanation about how it operates—leaving the field wide open for a variety of different experiences that can be labeled *discerning of spirits*. The key component of the gift is simply this: the Holy Spirit communicates directly to a believer about whether a message is from Him or from another spirit.

The gift of discerning of spirits is one critical way we can judge the gift of prophecy and determine if someone is speaking by the Spirit of God or not. Another powerful method for judging prophecy can be found in 1 John 4:1-6 (NASB):

> Beloved, do not believe every spirit, but test the spirits to see whether they are from God, because many false prophets have gone out into the world. By this you know the Spirit of God: every spirit that confesses that Jesus Christ has come in the flesh is from God; and every spirit that does not confess Jesus is not from God; this is the spirit of the antichrist, which you have heard is coming, and now it is already in the world. You are from God, little children, and have overcome

> them; because greater is He who is in you than he who is in the world. They are from the world, therefore they speak as from the world, and the world listens to them. We are from God. The one who knows God listens to us; the one who is not from God does not listen to us. By this we know the spirit of truth and the spirit of error.

Again, the Scripture is "marking" or identifying people based on which voice they listen to. The Holy Spirit loves to talk about Jesus. Jesus tells us in John 16:14, *"He will glorify Me."* So if a person is filled with and speaking by the Holy Spirit, they will constantly be bringing glory to Jesus. This means redirecting glory away from themselves and putting it back on Him.

1 John 4:5 (NASB) says about false, antichrist prophets, *"...they speak as from the world, and the world listens to them."* The voice behind the person matters—eternally.

This is where AI comes into play. If you ask AI a question about Jesus, can it answer correctly? Yes, sometimes. But it can also just as easily and probably more often give an answer that comes from an unbiblical, antichrist perspective, referencing the many voices out in the world. This will be a sign of those who claim to be Christian and are not: they won't necessarily fully reject the Scripture as truth, but they won't be particular about what sources they draw "truth" from. They won't care which voice a "truth" started with or whether it lines up with *The Truth* or not. That's why there are now churches being taught by AI pastors. That's why there is a one world "AI religion" arising, which seeks to gather masses around a collective "truth" instead of the truth of Jesus Christ. We see this pattern fully play out in Revelation:

> And the beast was seized, and with him the false prophet who performed the signs in his presence, by which he deceived those who had received the mark of the beast and those who worshiped his image; these two were thrown alive into the lake of fire, which burns with brimstone (Revelation 19:20 NASB).

The phrase *"by which he deceived"* could almost be referring to a form of mind control, whether willing or not. The great deception—the great falling away, though initiated by those who willingly reject Jesus as their Lord and Savior—is continued through a delusion encouraged by God Himself. Second Thessalonians 2:8-12 (NASB) expands upon this idea:

> Then that lawless one will be revealed, whom the Lord will eliminate with the breath of His mouth and bring to an end by the appearance of His coming; that is, the one whose coming is in accord with the activity of Satan, with all power and false signs and wonders, and with all the deception of wickedness for those who perish, because they did not accept the love of the truth so as to be saved. For this reason God will send upon them a deluding influence so that they will believe what is false, in order that they all may be judged who did not believe the truth, but took pleasure in wickedness.

This deluding influence could refer to an evil spirit allowed to plague people's thoughts and intentions, similar to the evil spirit that haunted King Saul after the Spirit of God left him. However, it could also be a system of delusion, something similar to AI, holding authoritative weight over people's thoughts and beliefs.

Currently, Elon Musk's Neuralink sits at the forefront of this industry—directly linking human brains to AI and both the potential benefits and dangers of its influence. If a computer virus can take over a computer and input code that overwrites the normal functions of that computer, it is not far-fetched to believe that someday AI will be able to rewrite the "code" within the human brain and teach it what to believe. I wouldn't be able to prove this concept in Scripture; however, the potential for AI to be the end-times deluding influence (or at least part of it) is obvious.

One such connection is the monkey trials. *The Guardian* published an article in 2022 titled, "Musk's Neuralink faces federal inquiry after killing 1,500 animals in testing."[80] *Wired* released an article titled, "The Gruesome Story of How Neuralink's Monkeys Actually Died" describes the specific episodes leading up to the death of some of the monkeys:

> ***...an internal part of the device "broke off" while being implanted. Overnight, researchers observed the monkey, identified only as "Animal 20" by UC Davis, scratching at the surgical site, which emitted a bloody discharge, and yanking on a connector that eventually dislodged part of the device...The monkey was euthanized on January 6, 2020.***
>
> ***Additional veterinary reports show the condition of a female monkey called "Animal 15" during the months leading up to her death in March 2019. Days after her implant surgery, she began to press her head against the floor for no apparent reason; a symptom of pain or infection, the records say.... A necropsy report indicates that she had bleeding in her brain and***

> ***that the Neuralink implants left parts of her cerebral cortex "focally tattered."***
>
> ***Yet another monkey, Animal 22, was euthanized in March 2020 after his cranial implant became loose. A necropsy report revealed that two of the screws securing the implant to the skull loosened to the extent that they "could easily be lifted out."***[81]

I'm not on a mission to expose Elon Musk or even to speak out against animal cruelty. Those are separate issues that would need to be addressed in a different space. My point in including this report is to show the strange connection between these monkey trials and a single verse in Revelation referencing the mark:

> So the first angel went and poured out his bowl on the earth; and a harmful and painful sore afflicted the people who had the mark of the beast and who worshiped his image (Revelation 16:2 NASB).

This is all supposition; however, the dots connecting an Artificial Intelligence implant in a human brain and a painful sore inflicting masses are eerie. Yet there is a sense of peace that should also come from reading this verse. It stems from this truth: no one is going to force you or trick you into taking a "mark," because no one is going to be able to force or trick you into worshiping someone who is not God. You have a choice to make. I have a choice to make.

Those who had the mark first worshiped the image of the beast. This means that, even if Revelation is referring to some futuristic version of a computer chip implant, with that implant would come the choice to sign over the human will to the will of an antichrist leader, AI itself, or to the will of the group think system—whatever that may look like.

This reminds me of a prophetic word I shared back in 2020, shortly after the coming vaccines were announced. This is what I shared:

> *God will not allow His children to be snatched away by a scheme of the devil or of man.*

Led by the Holy Spirit, I went on to talk about how believers cannot accidentally reject Jesus Christ. Yet we are often persuaded to live in fear based on the hypothetical idea that we will be fooled into taking the devil's mark. True Christians will not be fooled. Why? Because the mark itself is going to be directly identified with a conscious choice to reject Jesus. Are you going to reject Jesus and choose to worship another god? No. Then you don't need to live in fear that you might accidentally take the mark. Jesus echoes this same truth in the gospels:

> My Father, who has given them to Me, is greater than all; and no one is able to snatch them out of the Father's hand (John 10:29 NASB).

No one is going to trick you away from Jesus. The ones who will be "tricked" will be the religious crowd that does not have a real relationship with Jesus. They will trust in a worldly moralism instead of in the Word. It will be those void of the Holy Spirit, those listening to a voice other than God's own. In the previous few verses, Jesus says:

> But you do not believe, because you are not of My sheep. My sheep listen to My voice, and I know them, and they follow Me; and I give them eternal life, and

> they will never perish; and no one will snatch them out of My hand (John 10:26-28 NASB).

Thank God we don't need to live in fear! We get to rest in Christ, knowing that at the right moments the Holy Spirit is going to lead us (speaking to us when necessary) into all truth and away from an allegiance to Babylon.

The sad story of Revelation 16 continues in verses 10 and 11 (NASB):

> And the fifth angel poured out his bowl on the throne of the beast, and his kingdom became darkened; and they gnawed their tongues because of pain, and they blasphemed the God of heaven because of their pain and their sores; and they did not repent of their deeds.

Again, this is all supposition, hypothetical at best, but people gnawing their tongues due to the pain could refer to a throbbing pain in the head, an intense headache or worse caused by the implant technology. Instead of leading people to repent, this pain acts as a constant reminder of people's hatred for God. These people are already too far gone; they have completely given themselves over to depravity and the control of the enemy.

The phrase *"his kingdom became darkened"* could refer to a failing system, a computer technology and network that is breaking down. The description here may also refer to a group of people who have become reliant upon the technology (possibly through surgery) and are unable to detach themselves from it without a fatal result.

On February 24, 2023, the Lord spoke to me about future technology, and the imagery He used was slightly disturbing. I suddenly saw a vision of a human eyeball being replaced with a robotic implant—a computerized eyeball. I heard the Holy Spirit say:

> *People will eventually be replacing an eye with a piece of technology.*

I don't know the full ramifications of this statement. At the moment human beings are allowing a piece of hardware to be injected into their head, so why not an eye someday down the road? The Lord could be talking about a physical eye replacement here, or He could be using it as a metaphor for the *"lamp of the body."* Meaning, the part of the brain that takes in information and determines if it's right or wrong would be disconnected from the soul and controlled by another source. Jesus says it like this in Matthew 6:22-23 (NASB):

> The eye is the lamp of the body; so then, if your eye is clear, your whole body will be full of light. But if your eye is bad, your whole body will be full of darkness. So if the light that is in you is darkness, how great is the darkness!

The lens through which we view the world matters, and depending on who we give control of the lens to, we will either be able to rightly judge or wrongly judge the events taking place in the world. That is why so many people will be led astray by the antichrist. They will be looking through the wrong lens and believing what they see! They will trade good for evil. However, when we give control to the Holy Spirit and submit our hearts to Him through faith in Jesus Christ, we get a new perspective that never changes—a God-given perspective that protects us from deception as long as we are willing to look through it.

Another time, I saw a vision of a pyramid or ziggurat. Then I heard the Lord say:

> *It's all part of that system. Trying to control and raise one's fist against the Lord. Above the Lord's ways.*

The potential connections here are strange, tracing their origins all the way back to ancient African tribes practicing divination. A type of binary code, a system of ones and zeros upon which all computer languages are built, was being used by priests of false African religions to come up with a "divine" message for someone needing help from "the gods." Back then, they used nuts or similar items falling in a random order in order to hear these supernatural messages—similar to a medium or psychic drawing cards today.[82]

How does this idea apply now? Well, you and I know that those divine messages were not being sent by the gods. If a message was transporting from the spirit world, demons were behind it. Today, people are now typing their most difficult questions into an AI language bot chat box, expecting a series of ones and zeros to respond with a solution. Computer scientists would describe the series of ones and zeros as only coming from pre-coded algorithms and definable patterns, but the truth is that the supernatural is still affecting the natural, even if it doesn't always take credit. I still don't know if I believe AI can be technically possessed or not, but I know that time will tell.

AI technology may or may not be *the* antichrist, yet if nothing else, it is another step or level added to the tower. And the taller that tower gets, the more humans will believe that they hold the higher perspective—that they can see everything from where they stand. Yet, God still looks down from above, surveying every work of humans and judging hearts. Thank God He now judges us through the lens of the death and resurrection of Jesus Christ!

> On the day when, according to my gospel, God will judge the secrets of mankind through Christ Jesus (Romans 2:16 NASB).

As believers, we get to live in safety and assurance, knowing fully that we are His and He is ours, and that we will stand before Him perfectly righteous and redeemed simply because of what Jesus did for us.

The devil wants to incur fear in our hearts by making future advancements feel spiritually complicated. God wants to remind us of the simplicity of the gospel message. It's a message of hope, of good news, that cuts through the complications of the modern world and looks deeply into the heart. It says, "If you only believe, you are free!" Praise God for such a beautiful message of life.

9

THE MARK OF GOD

The same way that Babylon has a mark—the infamous mark of the beast and its predecessors—God also has His own mark that He displays on and through His people. The Scripture even tells us that God marks those whom are His, yet the Christian culture rarely talks about it.

What is this divine mark? And can we as believers know that we have received it? Is it possible that there is a supernatural symbol God uses to identify His followers? And has it been evident all along, stamped on the pages of both the Old Testament and the New?

A friend said to me, "Elon Musk is like a modern-day Nimrod building a 'tower' to Mars." The similarities found within the comparison were striking. If we follow the thread back through time, we would also see the same pattern repeated time and again. Great leaders, inventors, politicians, and writers often seek to build something eternal–something that lasts beyond their years. This is not intrinsically wrong. The problem comes when we attempt to build what lasts apart from our Creator.

Because we were created for eternity, the desire for immortality is only natural. Because of humanity's disconnect from its Maker however, the search for immortality (like the one Gilgamesh went on) is fruitless. Humanity seeks to achieve the eternal through the impermanent. One of the greatest leaders in history, King Solomon, spoke about the impermanence of life in Ecclesiastes 2:16 and 21 (NASB) when he says:

> For there is no lasting remembrance of the wise, along with the fool, since in the coming days everything will soon be forgotten. And how the wise and the fool alike die! ...When there is a person who has labored with wisdom, knowledge, and skill, and then gives his legacy to one who has not labored for it; this too is futility and a great evil.

Solomon paints a bleak picture, yet soon follows up his disparaging of life with an answer to the riddle: *"For who can eat and who can have enjoyment without Him?"* (Ecclesiastes 2:25 NASB).

Through the life of Solomon, God has given us a picture of the ultimate result of the world's striving to build bigger and better things. He has also given us the antidote to the striving toward the eternal. The eternal came to us. Solomon reasoned it out all the way to the end of the road and wound up in despair over the things he created. Yet even at the end of striving, he found that there is joy—true life—in simply knowing God.

In our defiance, people constantly struggle to separate God from the eternal. Malcom Gladwell's 2009 article for *The New Yorker* titled "How David Beats Goliath," acted as his inspiration for his 2013 book *David and Goliath*. It is in this work that Gladwell makes the controversial assertion that the reason

David beat Goliath can be attributed to Goliath's full or partial blindness. This reasoning stems from the idea that Goliath's height came merely from acromegaly, a pituitary-gland-based hormonal disorder that can lead to massive features. Gladwell says that the disorder could have caused a loss of vision.

Though Gladwell's assertions about the hidden information "between the lines" of the story of David and Goliath have been disproven by scholars, his perspective does raise a clear point. Whenever possible in today's society, God and the supernatural are removed from the picture. The reason Gladwell misinterprets and reads too much into the text is due to his ultimate conclusion about God—that He does not exist. Because he excludes the spiritual from the realm of possibility, he is left to explain the historical writings from a purely humanistic and natural point of view. Not everything can be logically explained this way.

Here's what Gladwell did: he not only attempted to explain away the existence of the Creator, he also denied the idea that the seed of the Nephilim was involved. Gladwell is not alone in this, and there's no reason for us to be shocked that a person who denies God's existence would also deny the existence of a race of giants spawned through the sin of disobedient angelic beings. That doesn't bother me at all. Instead, I am proposing something larger than the idea that Gladwell's perspective is a personal vendetta. In a sense, Gladwell is part of a larger conspiracy: a satanic agenda of the enemy to cover his trail through history.

If the devil can convince us that the human struggle lies mainly between good people and bad people, or people's good tendencies and people's bad tendencies, then he can win. He wants us to steer clear of the idea that the real battle is waged between a spiritual enemy and a spiritual Savior. The "sons of God" from Genesis want to replace THE Son of God. Satan wants to sit in the place of God. Secular humanity wants to simply exclude God from the picture so that there is room at the top for the individual to be a god.

Here's the hardest part to swallow: even the Christian can often be included in this mix. We want to do enough godly things that we don't need to be truly filled with and replaced by God. Yet that is the purpose of the two Covenants in Scripture—that God would live with humankind, that God would dwell in our midst. That we would be fully His people and He would be fully our God. The sign, or "mark," that accompanies this reality can be simply described as the glory of God. God wants to mark those who are His with Himself—with His glory.

God's Nature and His Glory

The term *glory* can be defined as magnificence or great beauty, the splendor and bliss of Heaven, a luminous ring or halo, or praise, worship, and thanksgiving offered to a deity. The truth is, when we are talking about Jesus, it is all of these things. His glory is a radiant glow. It is His beauty and majesty. It compels us to worship—to adore Him. It is also an experience—the perception and impact of His presence. God's glory is what happens when you witness Him.

As believers, we are meant to be reflections of God's glory on earth because we are meant to reflect Him. The term *Christian* means "little Christ." In Isaiah 43, God calls His people His "witnesses" to the nations of the earth. We are meant to reflect the heart of God, the truth of God, and the nature of God to the world. A mirror reflection doesn't just have the appearance of a person, like a statue. It models their behavior too. It reflects their actions. Thus, to reflect God is to reflect His nature, His character. Only then can we truly reflect His glory.

How do we reflect God? What does that look like? How do we know which aspects of His character to reflect? When reading the Bible, most people notice a distinction between the Old Testament and New Testament—a difference between the God of the ancient Israelites and Jesus, the God who walked among His people. Because of this, some have proposed the idea that we should "unhitch" from the Old Testament as it is a lacking or outdated representation of God.

The answer is not to unhitch but rather to fully understand the difference between the covenants. God stays the same. He is the same yesterday, today, and forever (see Hebrews 13:8). However, though God never changes, the way He relates to His people changes. This was part of His eternal plan all along, that there would be two major covenants that allowed His people access to Himself. One would be lesser in glory and one would be greater in glory.

The Glory of the Old Covenant

In the Garden of Eden, before the fall of mankind, God walked with Adam and Eve. They fully experienced all of God's glory that He wished to reveal to them. However, after sin entered the world, we see a pattern form. People begin to trade the glory of God for other blessings. They begin to build outside of His presence.

> Then Cain left the presence of the Lord, and settled in the land of Nod, east of Eden. Cain had relations with his wife and she conceived, and gave birth to Enoch; and Cain built a city, and named the city Enoch, after the name of his son (Genesis 4:16-17 NASB).

Though Cain left the presence of the Lord, the legacy of once being within the house of God remained in his family line. There still remained the hope of redemption. We see people begin to call out to the Lord through the line of Seth (through whom Jesus ultimately would come).

> To Seth also a son was born; and he named him Enosh. Then people began to call upon the name of the Lord (Genesis 4:26 NASB).

Eventually, God calls to Abraham and leads him to journey away from his hometown (which was probably near the future Babylon), away from the cities of mankind and to a land unknown. Since Abraham is the father of the faith, this same call is issued to us today. He was called to leave a physical place. We are called to leave the system of the world—to be *in* the world but not *of* the world.

Through Abraham, God establishes the Abrahamic Covenant, a plan through which He promises to bless His people. This covenant is fulfilled through both the Mosaic Covenant (the Old Covenant) and the Messianic Covenant (the New Covenant). Abraham is the father of a nation set apart to God, the Israelites. Through this nation God promises to bless all the nations of the world. He does this temporarily through the physical nation of Israel, and then He fulfills this promise permanently through the coming of Jesus Christ, a Jewish Man (and the Son of God) who would die for the sins of the world.

God calls Moses to lead His people out of slavery to Egypt; He does this so His people can enter the wilderness and worship Him. Another way of saying this: God leads His people into freedom so that they can better encounter Him and be transformed by Him. Look at the encounter God had planned for His people in the desert:

> Now Moses used to take the tent and pitch it outside the camp, a good distance from the camp, and he called it the tent of meeting. And everyone who sought the Lord would go out to the tent of meeting which was outside the camp. And it came about, whenever Moses went out to the tent, that all the people would arise and stand, each at the entrance of his tent, and gaze after Moses until he entered the tent. Whenever Moses entered the tent, the pillar of cloud would descend and stand at the entrance of the tent; and the Lord would speak with Moses. When all the people saw the pillar of cloud standing at the entrance of the tent, all the people would stand and worship, each at the entrance of his tent. So the Lord used to speak to Moses face to face, just as a man speaks to his friend. When Moses returned to the camp, his servant Joshua, the son of Nun, a young man, would not depart from the tent (Exodus 33:7-11 NASB).

The first noteworthy element here is the fact that *all* the people met with God to an extent. However, under the Old Covenant, only Moses met with God face-to-face. He alone was chosen as a mediator between God and man. We also see another truth: those who lingered got more. Joshua would not depart from the tent. I believe it's partially because of this that God would later instate Joshua as a replacement for Moses. His heart longed for the presence of God.

God often uses the release of His glory under the Old Covenant as a way of leading His people:

> Throughout their journeys, whenever the cloud was taken up from over the tabernacle, the sons of Israel would set out; but if the cloud was not taken up, then they did not set out until the day when it was taken up. For throughout their journeys, the cloud of the Lord was on the tabernacle by day, and there was fire in it by night, in the sight of all the house of Israel (Exodus 40:36-38 NASB).

Though God's plan included constant access to His glory in some ways, there also came times and seasons when His glory became more available than before, and I believe this often acts as a form of confirmation to His people. We see a special release of glory recorded directly before this in Exodus 40:34-35 (NASB):

> Then the cloud covered the tent of meeting, and the glory of the Lord filled the tabernacle. And Moses was not able to enter the tent of meeting because the cloud had settled on it, and the glory of the Lord filled the tabernacle.

Not only does God use His glory to lead and bring confirmation to His people, but He also uses it to test His people.

> Then the Lord said to Moses, "Behold, I will rain bread from heaven for you; and the people shall go out and gather a day's portion every day, so that I may test them, whether or not they will walk in My instruction. On the sixth day, when they prepare what they bring in, it will be twice as much as they gather daily." So Moses and Aaron said to all the sons of Israel, "At

> evening you will know that the Lord has brought you out of the land of Egypt" (Exodus 16:4-6 NASB).

The glory manifested as a miracle—a blessing of supernatural provision—and though it was meant to meet the people's needs, it was also meant to act as part of the wilderness test. We see that ultimately only a few people passed this test.

> Then Caleb quieted the people before Moses and said, "We should by all means go up and take possession of it, for we will certainly prevail over it." But the men who had gone up with him said, "We are not able to go up against the people, because they are too strong for us." So they brought a bad report of the land which they had spied out to the sons of Israel, saying, "The land through which we have gone to spy out is a land that devours its inhabitants; and all the people whom we saw in it are people of great stature. We also saw the Nephilim there (the sons of Anak are part of the Nephilim); and we were like grasshoppers in our own sight, and so we were in their sight" (Numbers 13:30-33 NASB).

Joshua and Caleb enter the Promised Land and immediately begin to drive out the Nephilim and those related. The same pattern occurs when Jesus steps into earthly ministry at the start of the New Covenant. He drives out the demons from the land. Whether demons truly are disembodied spirits of the Nephilim as some people believe or not, the pattern is striking.

The people of God under each covenant are commissioned with a task to take dominion on earth. The Old Covenant focused on physical dominion. The New Covenant focuses on spiritual dominion. Each covenant comes with a test. Before

Jesus's earthly ministry, He was led by the Spirit into the wilderness where He was tempted. So were the Israelites.

> And you shall remember all the way which the Lord your God has led you in the wilderness these forty years, in order to humble you, putting you to the test, to know what was in your heart, whether you would keep His commandments or not (Deuteronomy 8:2 NASB).

Unfortunately, many of the Israelites failed the test and did not move into their full purpose as the people of God. Numbers 14:2,11,24 (NASB) tell us the story:

> And all the sons of Israel grumbled against Moses and Aaron; and the entire congregation said to them, "If only we had died in the land of Egypt! Or even if we had died in this wilderness!" ...And the Lord said to Moses, "How long will this people be disrespectful to Me? And how long will they not believe in Me, despite all the signs that I have performed in their midst?" ..."But as for My servant Caleb, because he has had a different spirit and has followed Me fully, I will bring him into the land which he entered, and his descendants shall take possession of it."

The Israelites were shown the glory of God. They had the fire by night and a cloud by day. They had witnessed His glory on the mountain. They had seen the glory fading from Moses's face. They had received water from the rock and bread from Heaven. Yet none of this had translated into actual trust in God. For them the glory was a show or a meal. For Joshua (and Caleb), it was a Person.

Exodus 33:11 (NASB) says, "*...Joshua, the son of Nun, a young man, would not depart from the tent.*" Joshua stayed at the tent of meeting long after Moses left. This is more than just a picture of God's work in Joshua's life. It is also a picture of the grace covenant—a foreshadowing of what Jesus would do for us.

Moses was a mediator between God and God's people. He issued and represented the Law of God. Moses had been chosen for a task, and that task gave him access to God's presence. In a sense, Joshua accessed God's presence for free. He was the beneficiary of Moses's work, a receiver of grace. We see the difference this produces in Joshua's hunger for the presence of the Lord. When Moses arose to return to the camp, Joshua lingered. He longed to experience the Lord for one more minute, one more hour.

The other interesting parallel we see in this story has to do with the journey into the Promised Land. Moses saw the land from afar due to his disobedience. He failed to live up to the standard and thus was refused the blessing. Joshua entered the Promised Land due to his faith. Under the Old Covenant, the Israelites accessed God's blessing through work, through keeping the Law of Moses. Under the New Covenant, Jesus's finished work on the Cross gives us access to God's blessings through faith. We enter in as a result of His work—under a covenant of grace.

The Mark of God

The mark of the beast might be more popularly known, but the mark of God actually has far more relevance to our lives. God's mark is revealed under the Old Covenant in the prophetic visions of Ezekiel:

> Then the glory of the God of Israel ascended from the cherub on which it had been, to the threshold of the

> temple. And He called to the man clothed in linen at whose waist was the scribe's kit. And the Lord said to him, "Go through the midst of the city, through the midst of Jerusalem, and make a mark on the foreheads of the people who groan and sigh over all the abominations which are being committed in its midst" (Ezekiel 9:3-4 NASB).

This mark holds direct implications of protection from judgment and wrath. It also implies presence. God protects, provides for, and shelters those He dwells with. The mark of His glory rests on the people who dwell with Him. Here's another way to look at it: God remains with those who agree with His perspective. He sets a seal of approval on those who sigh and mourn over the wickedness happening in the nation around them. Those connected with His heart are who get to see His glory in their midst.

We see the glory of the Lord continue to move in the next chapter:

> Then the glory of the Lord departed from the threshold of the temple and stood over the cherubim. When the cherubim departed, they lifted their wings and rose up from the ground in my sight with the wheels beside them; and they stood still at the entrance of the east gate of the Lord's house, and the glory of the God of Israel hovered over them (Ezekiel 10:18-19 NASB).

Why was the glory departing from the temple in this chapter? Peter Leithart wrote a commentary for *The Gospel Coalition* on this passage in Scripture, saying:

> ***It happens again in Ezekiel's time. Yahweh's departure from the temple is a judgment on Judah, but it's also an act of compassion. When Yahweh sends Israel into exile, he packs up and heads into exile with them. He enters Babylonian territory riding on his war chariot, on the wings of the cherubim.***[83]

I believe one reason the temple was able to be destroyed in AD 70 was because the glory of God had already departed from the Holy of Holies within the temple. I'm saying this to make a point. There was a moment in history when the glory left. Yes, the veil was torn when Jesus died and the glory symbolically or literally left for good in that instance. Yet there's no evidence to say the glory had not previously departed prior to that. This passage in Ezekiel is evidence that it truly might have.

Even if this wasn't the moment when the glory official left, it at least shows us a picture of God's heart. He doesn't desire to dwell in a building. He desires to dwell in the hearts of His people—the hearts of believers. The same glory that led the Israelites through the wilderness and followed the exiles into Babylon in the Old Testament is still present today. It still marks those who walk with the Lord.

The Glory of the New Covenant

If the glory of God (the presence and majesty of the living God) dwells upon and within His people marking them as His own, there should be evidence of this within the writings of the New Covenant. Let's look at a few:

> Now if He were on earth, He would not be a priest at all, since there are those who offer the gifts according

> to the Law; who serve a copy and shadow of the heavenly things, just as Moses was warned by God when he was about to erect the tabernacle; for, "See," He says, "that you make all things by the pattern which was shown to you on the mountain." But now He has obtained a more excellent ministry, to the extent that He is also the mediator of a better covenant, which has been enacted on better promises (Hebrews 8:4-6 NASB).

In this passage, the things of Moses are surpassed by the things of Jesus. God calls the Old Covenant earthly and the New Covenant heavenly. The New Covenant is called better. It's been built on better promises. Because of this, God then continues to break down the foundation of the Old Covenant, now referring to it as obsolete.

> When He said, "A new covenant," He has made the first obsolete. But whatever is becoming obsolete and growing old is about to disappear (Hebrews 8:13 NASB).

When something becomes obsolete, it is no longer used. It is outdated by a new model. That is what God is saying through the writer of Hebrews. The glory of the Old Covenant has faded and the glory of the New Covenant surpasses it. If we want to carry God's glory today, we must interact with Him through the guidelines of what is new, not what is obsolete.

> Such is the confidence we have toward God through Christ. Not that we are adequate in ourselves so as to consider anything as having come from ourselves, but our adequacy is from God, who also made us

> adequate as servants of a ***new covenant***, not of the letter but of the Spirit; for the letter kills, but the Spirit gives life. But if the ministry of death, engraved in letters on stones, came with glory so that the sons of Israel could not look intently at the face of Moses because of the glory of his face, fading as it was, how will the ministry of the Spirit fail to be even more with glory? For if the ministry of condemnation has glory, much more does the ministry of righteousness excel in glory. For indeed what had glory in this case has no glory, because of the glory that surpasses it. For if that which fades away was with glory, much more that which remains is in glory (2 Corinthians 3:4-11 NASB).

Paul describes the Old Covenant, under which is the Law of Moses, as the ministry of death. He then describes the letter of the law as something that kills. He says, at the time it was given, it did indeed come with glory. Yet, that glory has faded now to make room for something far more glorious: the New Covenant of the Spirit! He says this covenant possesses more glory than Moses himself carried.

How do we receive and walk in that glory? We understand the phrase *"the ministry of righteousness."* Under the Old Covenant, people used to work toward righteousness through following the Law of Moses. Under the New Covenant, righteousness is gifted to us when we believe in the finished work of Jesus on the Cross. You aren't working for it anymore! He has fully and finally declared you righteous by the power of His own blood shed for you. As you and I accept that free gift of righteousness—and continue accepting it by constantly putting our hope in Him—the mark of God's glory on our lives becomes more and more evident. That is because His blood gives us constant access to His presence.

> Now the main point in what has been said is this: we have such a high priest, who has taken His seat at the right hand of the throne of the Majesty in the heavens (Hebrews 8:1 NASB).

Jesus ascended on high into the heavens. He is seated next to the Father, fully wrapped up in and embraced by His majesty. We are there too!

> But God, being rich in mercy, because of His great love with which He loved us, even when we were dead in our wrongdoings, made us alive together with Christ (by grace you have been saved), and raised us up with Him, and seated us with Him in the heavenly places in Christ Jesus (Ephesians 2:4-6 NASB).

If you have believed in Jesus, you are seated with Him in majesty. You have access to experience the glory of God! Some people would ask, what about the times I make mistakes? Wouldn't my sin separate me from His glory? Look at this beautiful truth in Ephesians 3:11-12 (NASB):

> This was in accordance with the eternal purpose which He carried out in Christ Jesus our Lord, in whom we have boldness and confident access through faith in Him.

In Christ, you and I have confident access to the Father through faith. We can come boldly before His throne of grace *all the time* because of what Jesus did (see Hebrews 4:16). There is nothing that can keep us out of His presence anymore, because the only thing that ever gave us access, the blood of the Lamb, is still working!

This is the reason Romans 8:1 (NASB) says, *"Therefore there is now no condemnation at all for those who are in Christ Jesus."* The Scripture goes on to describe our constant access in Romans 8:38-39:

> For I am convinced that neither death, nor life, nor angels, nor principalities, nor things present, nor things to come, nor powers, nor height, nor depth, nor any other created thing will be able to separate us from the love of God that is in Christ Jesus our Lord.

Because nothing can separate us from the love of Christ, why do we sometimes feel separate? The reason is we are not taking full advantage of the access we have. When we are fully basking in the glory of God, three "signs" will happen. You can look at these as three indicators or markers (marks) of His glory. The three marks are: *voice, identity,* and *manifestation.* All three are found within this same passage in Romans 8.

> For all who are being led by the Spirit of God, these are sons and daughters of God (Romans 8:14 NASB).

The first mark of God's glory is His *voice.* It says the sons and daughters of God will be led by the Spirit of God. This happens in many ways, but mainly and most specifically through the hearing of His still, small voice.

> For you have not received a spirit of slavery leading to fear again, but you have received a spirit of adoption as sons and daughters by which we cry out, "Abba!

> Father!" The Spirit Himself testifies with our spirit that we are children of God, and if children, heirs also, heirs of God and fellow heirs with Christ, if indeed we suffer with Him so that we may also be glorified with Him. For I consider that the sufferings of this present time are not worthy to be compared with the glory that is to be revealed to us (Romans 8:15-18 NASB).

The second mark is a solidified *identity* in Him. We will always battle at least slightly with our identity while here on earth, but the more we understand and accept what Jesus did for us, the more often we will identify ourselves as loved and accepted children of God. We won't listen to fear or rejection anymore. Having become so caught up in His love, we will be consistently experiencing the joy of just knowing and being filled with Love itself. Even suffering does not hinder the joys of this kind of love and acceptance.

The third mark is *manifestation*. A manifestation is an experiential evidence that the Holy Spirit is working in our life. Look at Romans 8:23 and 26 (NASB):

> And not only that, but also we ourselves, having the first fruits of the Spirit, even we ourselves groan within ourselves, waiting eagerly for our adoption as sons and daughters, the redemption of our body.
>
> Now in the same way the Spirit also helps our weakness; for we do not know what to pray for as we should, but the Spirit Himself intercedes for us with groanings too deep for word.

These verses describe the deep groaning kind of praying in the Spirit, when our entire body gets nearly taken over by the will of the Spirit. In these moments, we feel utterly lost in His presence, willing to do anything He asks. Oh that we would set aside the religious mindset that says we always have to look proper and in control. There's nothing better than giving control to Jesus and following the wind of the Spirit (see John 3:8).

The more we study the idea of surrendering to the Holy Spirit within Scripture, the more often the illustration of drinking wine comes up. Let's take a look at the implications of such an analogy.

The New Wine

I didn't know why God was telling me to attend Alan Didio's conference that spring night in 2022, but He was relentlessly saying, *I want you to go. I want you to go.* As I washed the dishes, I made a mental note to tell Alan the next day that I was going. Yet even after I had said "yes" to the Holy Spirit, He still kept saying, *I want you to go.* Finally, I stopped washing the dishes, grabbed my phone, and texted Alan right then. "I'm coming to your conference."

Little did I know what that act of obedience would lead me into. I remember saying to my friend Jacob during the flight to the conference, "I don't know what we're going to get out of this, but I know it's going to be something because I know God said to go."

As the first night countdown started, I surveyed the room. I saw a face I recognized. I had seen her ministering on a TV show several months prior, and I remembered her name as Ana Werner.

My friend Alan preached a fiery message, and then Ana ministered for just a few minutes. As soon as she stepped onto the stage and started to share words of knowledge about healings taking place, the tangible glory of God suddenly fell on me. It had been slowly building up to that point, but now it felt as if a bucket of warm water had just been dumped over me. A feeling of lightness swept over me till I thought I might lift off the ground.

The sessions having completed, Jacob and I were invited by Alan to have dinner with the speakers and a small group of ministry leaders. In a smaller room across the foyer, a buffet had been laid. I remember stacking the salmon, salad, and mashed potatoes on my plate. I remember it because of the strange feeling that started to come over me as I did so.

The glory was returning, but this time it came with joy. By the time I had reached the unsweet tea dispenser, I was laughing out loud. Jacob asked me if I was okay and I said, "I'm just feeling the Holy Spirit." He noticed the cup shaking in my hand and offered to carry my plate. I tried to stop the shaking but it just got stronger. I laughed as the tea jumped out of my cup.

As I looked around the room for a place to sit, the Holy Spirit suddenly began to speak. I was used to His still, small voice in my heart, but now His voice became so loud it seemed almost audible. The room was filled with round tables, and He pointed to a specific table that happened to be empty, saying, *Sit here.* He even told me at which seat to sit.

I was having a hard time understanding that this was real life. It felt like I had left the room. In one sense, it was the closest to Heaven I think I've ever been. As I sat down, the Holy Spirit told me that Ana Werner would walk in the room a minute later and she would come sit in the seat right next to me. There were about eight tables she could have chosen and every seat at the table where Jacob and I were seated were empty accept for the two we occupied. Yet, the glory rested so heavily, there was no doubt.

A minute later, Ana walked into the room. She walked right up to our table and asked if she could sit with us. She sat her book and jacket across the table from us. After coming back with a plate of food, she picked up her stuff and said, "I'm going to come sit right next to you."

Alan's wife also sat down and we started to talk. It wasn't much of a conversation from my perspective though because I was struggling to understand what everyone was saying. It felt like I was out-of-my-mind drunk, yet without the impaired speech, limited functionality, or encroaching weight of darkness. All this time, the sense of God's glory kept increasing. Then, Ana suddenly stopped talking in the middle of a thought. She looked at me and said, "There's glory all over you." Immediately, the glory multiplied again until I felt like I would fall out of my chair. All I could do was smile.

She said, "Let's pray for you." She put her hands on my shoulder and started to pray in tongues. Then she prayed a prayer of blessing and I prayed in agreement. Right after that, we started to talk about other things; while we were talking, for a moment I suddenly felt like I was no longer in the room. A new sensation came over me. It was the love of Jesus. It may sound cheesy, but this is the best way I can think to express it. It felt like a thousand years of being loved all compressed into one moment.

During her prayer, the Lord gave me two specific things to do that directly led to me getting connected to Rob Sanchez's ministry and starting a mentorship with him, which has been an answer to years of prayer.

The Lord addressed several other questions of mine that night. What I took away from that experience was a very practical mentorship that has helped me to navigate some of the difficult aspects of running a ministry. However, I will also never forget the astounding experience in His glory.

This experience was not necessary new for me. Yet, it was next level in intensity. How do we understand experiences like this scripturally? The Word of God describes this mystery as a holy addiction.

A Holy Addiction

Stories often portray the alcoholic in the desert as someone who isn't thirsting for water but rather a cocktail. When most sensible people would pursue life-sustaining water, these characters aren't being sensible. They are daydreaming about one thing. Writers intend for us to laugh or cry at these characters' struggles, but the truth is that we as believers should have a similar addiction. Yes, I'm serious. The major difference is that our addiction is a holy one. Holy addiction keeps us full of joy in the middle of the wilderness season.

In the book of Joel, we see a prophetic picture of this addictive substance. But Joel paints the negative picture. The addictive substance that should be present is currently lacking. Joel 1:10 (NASB) says, *"The field is ruined, the land mourns; for the grain is ruined, the new wine has dried up, fresh oil has failed."*

As I was writing this book, the Holy Spirit gave me a vision of sponges stacked in piles next to a kitchen sink. The feeling in seeing all these sponges was that much cleaning needed to occur. Next I saw a kitchen cabinet full of wineglasses. The impression created by this picture is a party that's about to take place. However, for the glasses to be filled with wine for the partygoers to enjoy, the dirt first needs to be wiped away. The Holy Spirit wants to release an anointing of joy over His people, but first there are sticky substances to wipe from the vessels so they are ready for filling.

The wine in this illustration, vision, and verse represents the joy of the Lord upon His people. The same way wine fills someone and sometimes creates an uninhibited "happiness," the Holy Spirit wants to fill us with Himself until we overflow with His joy.

Verse 12 in Joel 1 says, "The vine has dried up," and it goes on to say, "joy has dried up from the sons of mankind."

Much of the global church today is lacking the fullness of joy God has provided for us to display. It's potentially more true here in the United States. The vine has dried up. In many places, the new wine is gone, and the only way to replenish the supply is for us to be filled with the Spirit again.

How do we get filled again? The book of Joel instructs us. It goes on to talk in great detail about the fasting, praying, and mourning that needed to happen for the children of Israel to return to the Lord and receive the blessings of walking in His favor. However, many Christians might say, "I do those things. I repent daily. I practice spiritual disciplines. I fast. I pray." The question on some people's minds might be, "What more does God want from me?"

We receive some clarification in Joel 2:13 (NASB) when it says:

> And tear your heart and not merely your garments. Now return to the Lord your God, for He is gracious and compassionate, slow to anger, abounding in mercy and relenting of catastrophe.

When someone is addicted to something, they are overcome by it. Whether they know it or not, that thing has their heart. God doesn't want our actions as much as He wants our hearts. He wants us to be overcome by Him as a Person. He desires our hearts to cry out for Him.

When we love God with our actions and hold resentment toward Him in our hearts, our offerings are tainted. But here's the amazing truth we see in Scripture—those with tainted actions who came to God with their whole hearts always received favor.

In Luke 18:14 (NASB), Jesus tells the story of a fasting Pharisee and a messed up tax collector. The story ends with the tax collector going home justified. Jesus gives us the key when He says, *"...everyone who exalts himself will be humbled, but the one who humbles himself will be exalted."*

A rendering of the heart is required for us to be vessels ready to be filled with the new wine of the Holy Spirit. How do you know if you have the new wine? Easy. You're satisfied in Him. You don't need anything else, because you have the One who holds your heart captive.

> The Lord will answer and say to His people, ***"Behold, I am going to send you grain, new wine, and oil, and you will be satisfied in full with them; and I will never again make you a disgrace among the nations"*** (Joel 2:19 NASB).

This verse is talking about the Kingdom of Heaven come to earth under the construct of the New Covenant. We've discussed the two major covenants: the old and the new. The old came with old wine and old wineskins. The New Covenant comes with new wine and new wineskins (see Luke 5:37-39). As we've seen, the New Covenant is much better than the old because it includes all of the promises of the old one and more.

Here's the great news: the New Covenant is a covenant of grace. In the Old Covenant, we had to earn the promises.

Under the New Covenant, Jesus earned the promises for us, and we walk in those promises through the Spirit. We see a prophetic promise of the covenant of grace in the same chapter. Joel 2:23 (NASB) says:

> So ***shout for joy,*** you sons of Zion, and ***rejoice*** in the Lord your God; for He has given you the early rain for your vindication. And He has brought down for you the rain, the early and latter rain as before.

This verse says, *"shout for joy,"* and *"rejoice."* Why? Because both the early and latter rains are being poured out. The promises of the old and new are available. Joel 2:24 goes on to say, *"The threshing floors will be full of grain, And the vats will overflow with the new wine and oil."*

Here's that addictive substance again, and it's new. It's better than before. Yet, here's the catch: the substance is not found in the promises themselves, but rather in the Promise Maker.

> So you will know that I am in the midst of Israel, and that I am the Lord your God and there is no other; and My people will never be put to shame (Joel 2:27 NASB).

The wine is poured out in the presence of the Lord. He is the substance. He is the joy. It's His presence in our midst that makes the wine new. Ephesians 5:18-20 (NASB) states this principle clearly:

> And do not get drunk with wine, in which there is debauchery, but be filled with the Spirit, speaking to one another in psalms and hymns and spiritual songs, singing and making melody with your hearts to the

> Lord; always giving thanks for all things in the name of our Lord Jesus Christ to our God and Father.

We can and should choose to walk by the Spirit. Romans 8:14 and Galatians 5:16 are very clear about this. However, there is also a greater filling that makes it easier and more natural to walk by the Spirit. The same way consuming more alcohol causes a greater level of intoxication, being filled and saturated with the Holy Spirit causes a greater level of joy and ease in being led by Him. Being filled afresh with the Holy Spirit makes room for a greater pouring out of the glory of God in our lives. The more His people get filled with the Spirit, the more the mark of God on His people becomes clearer and more defined.

Near the beginning of this book, I told the story of staying up late and worshiping the Lord while listening to a Jesus Image worship service. After the filling of the Spirit I received that night on my couch, I started to search around for more sermons and worship services like that one. I wasn't looking for a style of preaching or a sub-genre of worship. Because I had experienced what it felt like to be filled with the Spirit—because I had met with Him—I was looking for more. I believe it could be a manifestation of the distinguishing of spirits gift. After that experience, I was suddenly able to feel the presence and glory of God on certain ministers or worship teams, and not on others. So, I followed the glory and started listening to those who "carried" it with them.

I've heard stories from other ministers of similar experiences occurring, but they also shared how they eventually started listening to things that weren't from God. Out of desperation to experience His glory, they went from extreme to extreme, not necessarily judging the fruit of the ministers who influenced them. Anything that looked hyper-charismatic seemed okay, but it led into to error or disappointment. So here's the warning: the Scripture tells us to always be testing the spirits. Some ministers (posers) are involved in witchcraft, New Age, and spiritualism, and they try to pass it off as godly. Don't settle for any and every experience. Make sure Jesus is behind the encounter. Apart from Him, we get into a mess.

Here is a further warning. Since the glory can outwardly demonstrate someone's nearness to God, it sometimes gets faked. There are some glory-talking churches with little glory. There are some healing evangelists who live in disobedience. Some claim manifestations of glory to maintain a public image, but they settle for false manifestations. Some people act full of the Spirit but are not. Others give the Spirit room to work in a meeting but they themselves are not allowing a work in their own heart. We need to always remember, it's not a competition. It's not a show. It's not just an experience. It is a relationship.

The next sentence may be potentially shocking—it would be better to never experience any glory this side of Heaven and just walk in obedience to the Word and the Holy Spirit, than to have heavenly encounters every day and never mature in Christ.

Even with prophetic ministry, it's easy to get addicted to the word of knowledge and miss Jesus in the process. We need to get addicted to Him again. Are we addicted to Him or to an experience? The test is found in Ephesians 5:18-20 (NASB). Let's examine it one more time:

> And do not get drunk with wine, in which there is debauchery, but ***be filled with the Spirit***, speaking to one another in psalms and hymns and spiritual songs, singing and making melody with your hearts to the

> Lord; ***always giving thanks*** for all things in the name of our Lord Jesus Christ to our God and Father;

Using drunkenness to paint a picture, this verse describes the act of worshiping and experiencing God's glory, but it also clearly states the focus on the Christian life—always giving thanks for all things in the name of our Lord Jesus Christ. Our addiction must be about Jesus and His completed work on the Cross. As soon as we get away from Him, we've failed the test. As soon as we start focusing on the manifestations and stop focusing on Him, we miss out on some of the benefits of the glory.

Every day we have a choice: Am I going to seek out control over the eternal like Gilgamesh did? Or am I going to give control over to the One Eternal God the way Jesus modeled? Here's the good news—when we give Him control and admit that we desperately need the gospel today, we start tasting the full blessings of the gospel.

We are called to praise God throughout our lives, yet there is no secret praise song that gives us access to His glory. The gospel gives us access. The blood of Jesus shed for us makes us clean before God. Praise songs can get old, but the gospel never does.

We are called to study the Word and treasure it, but there is no secret ritualistic formula in Scripture that gives us access to His glory. The gospel gives us access. It alone is the secret.

> But God, being rich in mercy, because of His great love with which He loved us, even when we were dead in our wrongdoings, made us alive together with Christ (by grace you have been saved), and raised us up with

> Him, and seated us with Him in the heavenly places in Christ Jesus (Ephesians 2:4-6 NASB).

God, in His mercy and love, sent Jesus to reconcile us to Himself. None of us reconciled ourselves to God. We were reconciled through the work of Jesus when we believed in Him and freely received that gift by faith. There is no level of glory that changes that. There is no encounter with God that ever gives us bragging rights. We need His grace desperately, and we will always need it.

Thank God that His grace is always available, and because it's always available, so is His glory. Look at the results of being seated with Christ:

> So that in the ages to come He might show the boundless riches of His grace in kindness toward us in Christ Jesus. For by grace you have been saved through faith; and this is not of yourselves, it is the gift of God; not a result of works, so that no one may boast (Ephesians 2:7-9 NASB).

Boundless riches of grace are available to us who don't trust in our own ability but rather continue to trust in Jesus's sacrifice.

Many of the charismatic "easy-access" tactics are pulled from principles within the Word. They involve a secretive head knowledge. Head knowledge is good when it's based in truth. However, God desires His people to move from attempting to access Him through head knowledge to allowing constant access to Him in our hearts. This means radical surrender and transformation, and that only happens as we dwell on the Cross. When we meditate on what Jesus did, it causes praise to bubble up in our hearts that no disappointment or delay in life can thwart. This is what Ephesians 5 is talking about.

You can be drunk in the wilderness and not even know where you are. When we dwell on the goodness and finality of the Cross, allowing a life of praise to grow out of our gratitude, a greater filling with the Spirit is inevitable.

How Do You Get the Glory?

The Holy Spirit answered this simple question for me one day, "How do I get the glory?" This is what He said: *Unadulterated belief.*

God is looking for childlike faith in the believer's life. He is looking for honesty. If we are doubting the full effects of the gospel—that we have constant access and favor through the blood of Jesus—all we have to do is tell Him that. We can pray the simple prayer from Mark 9:24 (NASB): *"I do believe; help my unbelief!"*

Oftentimes, God helping our unbelief looks like a healing process, as the Holy Spirit walks us through the lies we believe about God and uses the Scripture to replace those lies with the truth. When we see God for who He truly is, we are then able to believe Him without hesitation. When the shroud of life and lies cover over His true nature, we hold back or try our own method. God wants our belief to be unadulterated, and the Holy Spirit can help us get there. While in process, humility is the best course. When we choose humility, the book of James tells us that God will then give us an even greater grace.

Galatians 3:2-5 (NASB) reminds us that a life filled with the Holy Spirit is not found any other works other than believing the gospel:

> This is the only thing I want to find out from you: did you receive the Spirit by works of the Law, or by hearing with faith? Are you so foolish? Having begun by the Spirit, are you now being perfected by the flesh? Did you suffer so many things in vain—if indeed it was in vain? So then, does He who provides you with the Spirit and works miracles among you, do it by works of the Law, or by hearing with faith?

This passage, along with passages such as Hebrews chapter 4, describes a kind of believer's rest in which we constantly dwell with God through faith. This idea directly combats the religious notions of earning favor with God. However, even rest requires the right environment. Hebrews 4 tells us that Joshua led the children of Israel into the Promised Land, yet they still had to remove some giants to take full advantage of the rest God had given them. That same challenge faces us today.

The Resting Place

As I studied the timeline of when the last of the Rephaim and Annakim, who came from the Nephilim, were finally destroyed, a very interesting detail emerged. Joshua is given the task of eliminating the Nephilim from the Promised Land, yet his generation fails to completely remove them. We still see remnants of these giants scattered throughout the enemies of the Israelites all the way through David's reign. David's rise to fame correlates with the killing of one of them: Goliath. However, even after that, he and his mighty men continue to do battle with these larger-than-life foes even up to his later years.

We see four more giants slain in 2 Samuel 21:15-22: Ishbibenob, Saph, Goliath's brother Lahmi, and a man with six fingers on each hand and six toes on each foot. These four are all listed as descendants of the Raphah (Hebrew for *the giant*, same as Rephaim). This is the last chronological mention of living Nephilim in the Bible. David's mighty men essentially helped to complete a task initiated by God during Joshua's lifetime.

Then we see a strange correlation take place. During the very next generation, God instructs that His temple, His resting place, be built. David even pleaded with God to allow him to build the temple, yet God refused due to the amount of blood shed during David's life. Instead, his son Solomon is given the task.

It's almost as if the removal of the giants was a reestablishing of God's dominion upon the earth. In a physical sense, the seed of the serpent had been deleted from humanity, and now God could come down and rest in a semipermanent resting place among His people. Up to that point, they had the tabernacle, but it was always moving and very impermanent. Now, the presence of God would dwell in the Holy of Holies behind walls of stone. The impermanent became permanent.

Yet, you and I know that Solomon's temple itself was merely a copy of the heavenly dwelling place that we access through Christ (see Hebrews 9:23). So even the temple was a foreshadowing of the Holy Spirit dwelling within believers and our bodies becoming His dwelling place (see 1 Corinthians 6:19). Even with the transitioning of an Old Covenant temple to a New Covenant temple, the principle remains the same—giants in the land can delay or distort the rest God has for us.

What led to the giants in the first place? The people desired the secret knowledge of the supernatural. They wanted a pathway to Heaven apart from God. As Christians, if we want the glory of God to dwell in our midst, we must be willing to remove and annihilate the shortcut mentality, the "secret knowledge of Babylon" way of thinking. We must give up and give Jesus control.

Here's one example: If a preacher tells you "if you do this one thing, God's hands are tied, He must pour riches upon you," could it be that is a shortcut mentality meant to distract you from simply going to God for yourself and asking Him why there are financial issues in the first place? Or if someone says, "If things aren't going the way you want, that means generational curses are still in effect," could that be a shortcut mentality meant to distract you from going to God personally and asking if there is any area in which you are not being led by His Spirit?

When we finally go to God personally, and stop trying to shortcut around Him to the blessing, He may say, "I want you to give up that thing you're after." He may not ask us to do that, but if He does, are we still willing to trust Him? Or are we seeking after something else more than we are genuinely seeking after Him?

Truly seeking God first means no matter what He says, we want to hear it. It means no matter what path He leads us down, we want to follow. It means no matter what He asks us to give up, we are willing.

I'm not trying to paint a terrible picture here. The Christian life is absolutely full of blessings, spiritual fruit, adventure, encounters, etc. However, those things are just side effects of walking with Jesus. They are not the goal. And the more we chase after those things, typically the farther away we wander from the One who actually causes those things to happen.

There is no secret to the Christian life other than Jesus. There is no secret knowledge other than the gospel. This may seem like a disappointment to some, but I see it as good news.

Once you realize that there's nothing else out there to find, you can start basking in the knowledge of what Jesus has done and the completeness of being found in Him, and you can finally rest. Within the believer's rest, the miraculous begins to occur.

Rededicating the Temple

Within the story of the Jerusalem temple, there exists an ancient mystery surrounding the glory of God. This mystery will help paint a picture of how we walk in His glory today.

This beautiful parallel is found in Scripture regarding the building of Solomon's temple in 2 Chronicles 6:14 (NASB). Look at Solomon's prayer during the dedication ceremony:

> He said, "Lord, God of Israel, there is no god like You in heaven or on earth, keeping Your covenant and Your faithfulness to Your servants who walk before You with all their heart."

His full prayer is too long to cite here, but it includes the continued reign of kings from David's line and protection and victory over the enemies of God's people.

> Now then, Lord, God of Israel, keep to Your servant David, my father, that which You promised him, saying, "You shall not lack a man to sit on the throne of Israel, if only your sons pay attention to their way, to walk in My Law as you have walked before Me" (2 Chronicles 6:16 NASB).

But even during the dedication of God's house on earth, Solomon understood that it wasn't a physical building that housed God's presence—it was a people whose hearts belonged to God whom He longed to dwell with:

> But will God really dwell with mankind on the earth? Behold, heaven and the highest heaven cannot contain You; how much less this house which I have built! (2 Chronicles 6:18 NASB)

Directly after Solomon's prayer, the glory of God manifested:

> Now when Solomon had finished praying, fire came down from heaven and consumed the burnt offering and the sacrifices, and the glory of the Lord filled the house. And the priests could not enter the house of the Lord because the glory of the Lord filled the Lord's house (2 Chronicles 7:1-2 NASB).

This is where the parallel occurs. Many scholars believe these eight days in 2 Chronicles are the same as the Feast of Dedication found in the book of John hundreds of years later.

> So Solomon held the feast at that time for seven days, and all Israel with him, a very great assembly that came from the entrance of Hamath to the brook of Egypt. And on the eighth day they held a solemn assembly… (2 Chronicles 7:8-9 NASB).

> At that time the Feast of the Dedication took place in Jerusalem; it was winter, and Jesus was walking in the temple area, in the portico of Solomon. The Jews then surrounded Him and began saying to Him, "How long will You keep us in suspense? If You are the Christ, tell us plainly" (John 10:22-24 NASB).

The nation of Israel busily celebrated the Feast of Dedication, which included the reminder that the presence of God in the temple was a sign of His protection and favor over the nation of Israel. However, at this very time, Roman occupation flourished. So, the prayers of Solomon were going unanswered due to the nation's sin. He had prayed for this very thing in 2 Chronicles 6:24-25 (NASB):

> If Your people Israel are defeated before an enemy because they have sinned against You, and they return to You and praise Your name, and pray and plead before You in this house, then hear from heaven and forgive the sin of Your people Israel, and bring them back to the land which You have given to them and to their fathers.

Because of their captivity, the people were crying out to God for freedom from Rome, and God heard their cries and sent a Savior, but not the kind of savior they wanted. He heard their cries and the glory of God came down once more—this time in the form of the Son of Man.

As Jesus walked through the temple during the feast, the crowd asked, "How long will You keep us in suspense? If You are the Christ, tell us plainly." They were essentially saying, "If You're the Messiah who has come to deliver us from Rome, great, but if not, we don't want anything to do with You." They were looking for the hand of God, not the heart of God. In contrast, Solomon was looking for the heart of the Father, and because of that the glory of God showed up.

Here's the amazing thing: Jesus Himself is the glory of the Father. But because people weren't truly looking for God Himself, they missed the glory walking in their midst. They were there to rededicate themselves to God as long as they got what they wanted out of Him.

The crazy thing is: Jesus was speaking plainly. In the same chapter He says, *"I am the good shepherd, and I know My own, and My own know Me"* (John 10:14 NASB).

As Jesus spoke, the voice of the Shepherd was reverberating in every heart that was surrendered to God. The voice of the Master echoed in their souls, drawing them to Himself. That same voice echoes today, drawing us away from our own paths, back to God's heart and plan for us.

The problem comes when we follow the voice of the Shepherd and it seems like it only leads us into heartache or trouble. If He is the Good Shepherd, why does He sometimes lead us down rough roads? The answer is found in the supernatural revealing of His glory.

The Revealing of God's Glory

The glory of God can come in a variety of ways because God is incredibly complex. His glory can come as a visual sign such as a dream or prophetic word, a vision or a glimpse into the supernatural, a feeling or an emotion, a gift of the Spirit, and many other manifestations.

Throughout church history we have witnessed other evidences of the Spirit such as holy laughter, shaking, weeping and travailing, and even trances (which are biblical when they are from God, see Acts 10:10). One of the most common forms of God's glory coming is the simple presence of God "coming over" someone.

One short verse that exemplifies the idea that God's power can be felt is Luke 8:46 (NASB), *"But Jesus said, 'Someone did touch Me, for I was aware that power had left Me.'"*

Because Jesus associated the work of God with some sort of feeling or awareness He experienced, I believe there is room for us to do the same. Acts 1:8 (NASB) even describes this experience for believers, *"but you will receive power when the Holy Spirit has come upon you…."*

The filling of the Holy Spirit correlates here with the supernatural power of God. Another sign of the power of God being felt or perceived can be found in the next chapter:

> Everyone kept feeling a sense of awe; and many wonders and signs were taking place through the apostles (Acts 2:43 NASB).

This verse describes, not just a single experience, but a common and constant way of life for the New Covenant believers in Acts. This is the same covenant you and I are under today, and it's only natural for us to be experiencing things through the Holy Spirit that would leave us with a sense of awe and wonder.

We see many other evidences of the work of the Holy Spirit in the New Testament as well. Some we have already covered.

If you doubt that some of the types of manifestations I've listed are godly, that's okay. It can be hard to believe something that we have not yet experienced, and there is no verse in Scripture that tells us we must believe every testimony of God's glory that people share.

However, it's also important that we keep an open heart to the move of the Holy Spirit. When He moved upon and through the apostles and early converts in the New Testament, everything He did was brand-new to them in that moment. They had little or no reference for how the Spirit would move. Yet they trusted the voice of Jesus who had told them that the Spirit would come, and they learned to test the spirits by whether they led them back to Jesus or not.

> And every spirit that does not confess Jesus is not from God; this is the spirit of the antichrist, which you have

> heard is coming, and now it is already in the world (1 John 4:3 NASB).

We can and should run this same test today. How do you know if a manifestation is of the Holy Spirit or not? Is the spirit behind the manifestation pointing you to the truth of God's Word and a real relationship with Jesus? That's the test.

When I was refilled with the Spirit while watching that worship service from Jesus Image Church, I specifically prayed, "If this is from You, God, I want it. If not, I don't want anything to do with it." And God answered that prayer.

Here's where it gets hard. Once we begin to encounter the glory of God in a tangible way, it can be easy to fall into a trap of thinking that means, "I have to experience God *this way* to be close to Him." But that's not always true. God reveals Himself to us in many different ways, and there's more to knowing God than tangible manifestations.

God's glory can be revealed through the supernatural invading the physical, but it can also be revealed through the truth invading the heart and mind. Someone shaking during prayer can at times be a sign of His glory. Yet, someone faithfully enduring through a serious hardship can also be a sign of His glory at work. Here's one way to say it: God uses mountaintops to show His glory to you and valleys to show it through you.

When Jesus took Peter, James, and John up to the mountain where they witnessed His transfiguration, He gave them a glimpse of His glory that they probably only saw once. Yet, His Spirit would later lead, encourage, and comfort them during intense persecution as they preached the gospel to the nations. This aspect of His glory they witnessed over and over again.

Preserving a Remnant for Glory

The book of Isaiah is written to a people in bondage, yet it promises hope through prophetic glimpses about the coming Messiah. Those in captivity to Babylon were looking to return to their homeland, for rescue from exile. Those left in Israel were oppressed and downtrodden, looking for the restoration of the nation to its former glory. Isaiah 4:3-4 (NIV) provides a thread of hope during a bleak time:

> Those who are left in Zion, who remain in Jerusalem, will be called holy, all who are recorded among the living in Jerusalem. The Lord will wash away the filth of the women of Zion; he will cleanse the bloodstains from Jerusalem by a spirit of judgment and a spirit of fire.

Barnes' Notes on the Bible tells us that if these verses refer to the few that would come back from Babylon, it describes them as having been reformed or changed, no longer ascribing to the waywardness of their ancestors. The judgment and fire of God were displayed to bring people to repentance.

> Then the Lord will create over all of Mount Zion and over those who assemble there a cloud of smoke by day and a glow of flaming fire by night; ***over everything the glory will be a canopy***. It will be a shelter and shade from the heat of the day, and ***a refuge and hiding place*** from the storm and rain (Isaiah 4:5-6 NIV).

So we see that the point of God's glory appearing was to bring change to the people's hearts. Yes, He wanted to provide, to shelter, to protect, and to restore and redeem, and He would display the wonders of His glory in the midst of the nation, but part of that process involved cleansing and removing the old to make way for the new.

God desires His glory to be the protective force over His people today too. Yet, many times we seek His glory while rejecting His refining fire—but they are one and the same. The glory of God can be a canopy and a shelter from the effects of living in a Babylonian system, but we must accept the loving hand of God to touch our hearts and mold us so that we don't resist His glory when it comes.

> In the same way then, there has also come to be at the present time a remnant according to God's gracious choice (Romans 11:5 NASB).

God always preserves a remnant for Himself, even today. You and I don't need to be captive emotionally or mentally to Babylon. We don't have to be. We get to be free, and we are privileged to have the glory of God as our canopy.

You are destined to live set apart and covered by the Lord even during the captivity of many. The Holy Spirit will shelter you and shade you from fear and anxious thoughts. He will defend your heart from the wars, rumors, and bad news constantly plaguing society through today's fast-paced spread and availability of information. You get to rise above it all.

Some may say, "I'm not good enough for that. I'm not one of the favored ones. I haven't lived a set apart life." If that's you, look at the very next verse in Romans.

> But if it is by grace, it is no longer on the basis of works, since otherwise grace is no longer grace (Romans 11:6 NASB).

The grace of God makes the glory available. You don't earn it. You accept it by faith. You simply choose to believe that Jesus paid the full price for your forgiveness and redemption on the Cross, and the Holy Spirit is then able to fill you, change you, and shelter you.

Look at it this way. The canopy or shelter is another word for God's house. Through faith in Jesus's finished work, you are a child of God, and children get to live constantly inside the Father's house.

When we grasp hold of a firm picture of what Jesus really did for us on that Cross, we truly step over into the glory lifestyle. Living in awe of Christ's finished work causes us to live in an attitude of worship and adoration toward the Father. This is where we can't help but praise Him and seek after Him in the secret place.

Some people would have jeered at Solomon during his dedication of the temple. After 22,000 oxen and 120,000 sheep were sacrificed, they might have said, "Solomon, that's enough already." At that point, it must have seemed obsessive, and people might have been tempted to step in and intervene the way someone would intervene with a person who is addicted.

Yet, there's never enough worship. That's the glory of who God is.

10

WHAT'S STILL TO COME

Oftentimes when I am worshiping Jesus, the Holy Spirit will begin to give me glimpses of future events. Many of these prophetic glimpses will be fulfilled within a few years, months, weeks, and sometimes even days. As I've mentioned before, I describe many of these prophetic fulfillments in detail in the prophecy archive on my website. However, there are some words of knowledge I hear or see that seem to pertain to far into the future. Instead of having a specific, short-term fulfillment, they paint a picture of things to come, revealing the general direction that the world is heading.

I'll say it again. I'm just a man. I'm just a vessel. I'm a flawed human being. So, though I believe I am sharing true prophetic utterances from the Holy Spirit, and though I have received confirmation for these prophecies as well, I still encourage you to take everything with a grain of salt and to pray about it. True prophecy will stand up to the tests. With that said, I will share several words in this final chapter that have to do with the future.

We have explored the mystery of the Babylonian kingdom controlling our world today, yet Babylon is still growing and advancing. I don't believe we are seeing the final form yet, just shadows and portions of it.

Jesus leaves His followers with a notable warning:

> So, when they had come together, they began asking Him, saying, "Lord, is it at this time that You are restoring the kingdom to Israel?" But He said to them, "It is not for you to know periods of time or appointed times which the Father has set by His own authority" (Acts 1:6-7 NASB).

This verse holds two meanings. Jesus is answering their specific question, but He is also giving us a guideline through which to view the final restoration of God's Kingdom on earth—the second coming of Christ and the eventual appearing of the New Jerusalem. Jesus is essentially saying, *Don't try to figure everything out, because you won't be able to.* Yet, I still believe God is revealing more and more as the time draws nearer.

Many have interpreted Daniel 12:4 (NASB) as referencing the rise of the internet and the age of technology:

> But as for you, Daniel, keep these words secret and seal up the book until the end of time; many will roam about, and knowledge will increase.

Though this is a fair interpretation and I believe it could easily be true, some commentators actually lean in another direction. Some say that it's not referencing specific signs of the times as much as it foretells a time when people are searching out and arriving closer to the meaning of these prophetic revelations, especially as some of the prophecies begin to be fulfilled on earth. If you evaluate this verse through that lens, it means that God will make the biblical prophecies about the last days even more clear to the church as the end of time approaches.

The following prophetic utterances I believe to be glimpses and pictures that could help to point us in the right direction.

Visions of the Future

Many people believe God giving out end-time revelation will always be big, boisterous, and definitive in nature. Though this can be the case, it's not always true. Sometimes God speaks in riddles or ways we do not expect. Often, He speaks through a whisper.

I received one of these subtle glimpses on December 9, 2024. As I spent time in worship, just relaxing in the presence of my Savior and praising Him for His faithfulness, I began to see images flash before me.

First, I saw what looked like a space shuttle launching. Then, I saw imagery of the ancient pyramids. Large lasers or some similar type of weapons were suddenly lined up in a row, and they all pointed up in one direction as if they were joining forces together against a single enemy. Finally, I saw a close-up view of an automatic weapon being fired. The voice of the Holy Spirit followed these images, saying,

> *I'm hearing My people cry out during this time. Part of what could be called the modern-day Babylon regime is toppling. I'm making restitution to God's people to an extent, for various reasons.*

This sounds to me like a season of restoration and stability. However, I also believe the imagery seen are pointing to things bound to come at some point. The Holy Spirit gave me some clues through the following phrases.

I heard, *Look up Isaiah 2 and you'll see the reason why… and Revelation 12 and 13 a little, some elements from this story. There's more to this tale that I'll tell you at a later date.*

I looked up Isaiah 2:1-3 (NASB) to find this passage:

> Now it will come about that in the last days the mountain of the house of the Lord will be established as the chief of the mountains, and will be raised above the hills; and all the nations will stream to it. And many peoples will come and say, "Come, let's go up to the mountain of the Lord, to the house of the God of Jacob; so that He may teach us about His ways, and that we may walk in His paths." For the law will go out from Zion and the word of the Lord from Jerusalem.

Though many interpretations exist concerning this chapter, one important principle stands out. No matter the specific timeline on these specific verses, there is a general idea of the gospel message going forth to the nations in the last days and peace being a result of the message preached. Though according to the book of Revelation, we know this peace cannot last ultimately. However, for a time at least, this passage appears to point to a world pacified by the effects of Jesus's life in history. We see the truth of this echoed by books such as *Dominion* by Tom Holland, which showcases the transformative nature of Jesus upon all societies.

Eventually, those who follow after satan completely turn on the people of God as they are given over to a demonic agenda. This is stated clearly in both of the mentioned chapters in Revelation.

> So the dragon was enraged with the woman, and went off to make war with the rest of her children, who keep the commandments of God and hold to the testimony of Jesus (Revelation 12:17 NASB).

> ...And the whole earth was amazed and followed after the beast; they worshiped the dragon because he gave his authority to the beast; and they worshiped the beast, saying, "Who is like the beast, and who is able to wage war with him?" (Revelation 13:3-4 NASB)

> It was also given to him to make war with the saints and to overcome them, and authority was given to him over every tribe, people, language, and nation (Revelation 13:7 NASB).

Though we have generally seen a great effect of the gospel upon societies over the past 2,000 years, and though I believe we still have some time of peace before the end (despite wars and rumors of wars increasing in various places), eventually all "hell" will break loose. Eventually, the beast will wage war against the saints of God, and the whole earth, under a demonic influence, will agree with him.

Yet, here is the message I believe God is giving me right now for you: one of the points of this book is to stymie a great retreat happening within the church. Because of the potential of the great tribulation and the second coming happening at any moment, there is a temptation for us to begin to focus all our attention on preparing to leave, upon retreating, instead of focusing on the purpose we have been given while here.

As Christians, you and I have a great purpose to fulfill on earth. That purpose is not to escape. It is to flourish as we endure until the end. Whether that end comes early or late does not matter. What truly matters is simply doing the work God calls us to do while we are here.

All of this is pointing to one specific message, which I heard clearly from the Holy Spirit on January 27, 2025:

> *It's not time yet, says the Lord. It just isn't time for the end of all things. I have to say this because many of My people think there are only a few years left, and that's not what I'm saying prophetically to My people. There's more than a few left, in fact, there are many. According to My timeline, it is short, but not according to your own. You will be surprised at how much time still has to pass before the end.*

God has not told me how much time we specifically have left, and I honestly believe He doesn't share that with anyone. Jesus's statement in Matthew 24:36 (NASB) seems clear:

> But about that day and hour no one knows, not even the angels of heaven, nor the Son, but the Father alone.

So what is the point of this word I heard? I believe it is to get our attention as the church and help us not to fall into an escapism mindset.

The day before, I had heard another word similar in nature. This is what the Holy Spirit said:

> *Look ahead to My coming, but don't get so caught up with leaving that you miss Heaven here on earth—the fact that I*

am with you and you can be not only filled with My Spirit but also useful to the Kingdom here and now.

Don't get so caught up with leaving that you miss what I'm doing now. I want to use you. And I cannot use you to the full if you are unwilling to be present.

Many people want the end to come, so they are seeking after the end and not truly seeking the One who is coming.

This can sound like a harsh statement, but I simply see it as a wake-up call. If we fall into the trap of escapism, we are bound to miss some of the purpose God has planned for us.

I'm not saying we should not long for His coming. We should. After all, Paul tells Timothy this in 2 Timothy 4:8 (NASB):

> ...in the future there is reserved for me the crown of righteousness, which the Lord, the righteous Judge, will award to me on that day; and not only to me, but also to all who have loved His appearing.

There is a monumental difference between longing for His coming because you want to be with Jesus versus longing for the end to come because you want to get away. These are two separate motivations entirely, and they lead to different results in life. Escapism leads to stagnation. A life of pursuing Jesus leads to accomplishing the purposes God has called us to.

> For this reason you must be ready as well; for the Son of Man is coming at an hour when you do not think He will (Matthew 24:44 NASB).

When Jesus says *"you must be ready"* in this verse, He is talking in context of being found doing the Master's work when He returns. He does not expect the servants to figure out when the Master was returning. In fact, He clarifies that, saying the time of the return will be unknown. Instead, He commissions the servants to be faithful at fulfilling their assignments no matter how long is left.

Longing to escape can be in some senses equated with what the builders of the Tower of Babel looked for. They wanted to reach Heaven apart from God. When all we want is to escape this earth, our desire is to reach Heaven even if it's not what God wants right now. But when we begin to wait with Him in the secret place and allow His love for humankind to seep into our own hearts, we start to long for His will over our comfort—even if His will means a lengthy stay and a goal to work toward.

Rejecting the Babylonian way of life means going after God Himself, not going after the exit. The good news is, when we pursue Him and make Him the end goal, by His grace we actually begin to experience Heaven on earth through His presence and power at work in our lives. The truth is, He's enough to make this life worth living and to give us reason to endure to the end. His joy is enough. We don't need to escape to start enjoying life again.

The Future of the Internet

How does this fit in with the future of the internet and modern technological advancements? Considering Jesus's commission for us to be faithfully working no matter where we are in the timeline, the application may be simple. No matter what "next big thing" they release, as long as it is morally ethical, we can use that invention for furthering the gospel and the building of God's Kingdom.

With the rise and fall of every new social media site or app, there are warnings to stay away and not be plagued by the stains of the world. Though this warning does apply to some Christians who need to steer clear of social media due to specific temptations, others are uniquely called to preach Jesus on these platforms, and the Holy Spirit will lead them to the appropriate opportunities.

The internet itself may appear completely different in 20 years (provided we have that time left). God's people will also be driven to righteously adapt and pursue the lost even through the change.

I heard these words from the Holy Spirit on July 2, 2023:

> *The information super highway is still on its way. It's not yet fully developed. Something is going to happen to cause a ripple effect: a splash reorganizing the structure of society as a whole. A reawakening of sorts, though mostly for evil.*

Because of words like this one, I believe the final form of the internet is still to come. We discussed the fall of the Mystery Babylon found in Revelation earlier in this book, but I do believe a version of the internet will still be available to some extent during at least part of the tribulation period. We see some evidence of this in Revelation 11:9-10 (NASB) after God's two prophets are killed:

> Those from the peoples, tribes, languages, and nations will look at their dead bodies for three and a half days, and will not allow their dead bodies to be laid in a tomb. And those who live on the earth will rejoice over them and celebrate; and they will send gifts to one another, because these two prophets tormented those who live on the earth.

It is safe to assume the only way all the nations could look at and celebrate the death of these prophets would be if a worldwide viewing system were available (like a streaming service). Even in this brief passage, we see some of the unity the internet will bring to the nations and people against God and part of the role it will play in the final days.

As the end draws near, the voice of the prince of the air will grow louder and louder, echoing through media platforms. This is why it's critical that the voice of the Good Shepherd grows louder and clearer in our hearts. I ask you now to prepare your heart to receive personally from the Holy Spirit. I believe in the last few pages of this book, He wants to touch you supernaturally and open your ears to better and more easily hear Heaven's secret knowledge.

Learning to Walk in the Secret Knowledge

> But I say, walk by the Spirit, and you will not carry out the desire of the flesh (Galatians 5:16 NASB).

Babylonian systems always appeal to the flesh, the worldly nature. But God wants us to walk in freedom by walking in obedience to the Spirit. The only way to walk by the Spirit is to be in communication with Him, to know what He sounds like. This starts with the simple application of the written Word, the Bible. It expands beyond if we let it. The New Testament describes revelatory gifts of the Spirit such as words of knowledge, prophecy, wisdom, and discerning of spirits. All of these gifts come together under the banner of God's voice in a Christian's life.

God can speak audibly, yes, but that is very rare for most believers. More often He speaks through utterances of the

Spirit in our hearts, through impressions, and through dreams and visions. To some, these revelations seem like the deep, nearly inaccessible things of God. To others, they are commonplace—a normal part of the Christian's walk.

No matter where you are currently, the point of this chapter is to encourage you into the next level of hearing from God. Instead of diving into a lengthy teaching about the revelatory gifts, I feel led to speak from the heart on one simple truth—to walk by the Spirit, you must be led.

Hearing from God is not a chore we must accomplish. It's not a privilege some mature Christians earn. It's not an advanced science that intelligent Christians learn. The ability to hear God is engrained in every believer because Jesus says, *"My sheep hear My voice."* But the practical walking out of that ability leans heavily on our willingness to be led by Someone other than ourselves. We must be willing to GIVE UP.

If you don't give up and give the Holy Spirit free rein to lead you, you'll never have a consistently clear connection to His voice. Sheep are led. The Shepherd leads. That's how hearing from Him works. It's all about letting go of what you want and deciding what you really want is HIM.

Let's look a little at this concept within the Scripture:

> And when they arrest you and hand you over, do not worry beforehand about what you are to say, but say whatever is given you at that time; for you are not the ones speaking, but it is the Holy Spirit (Mark 13:11 NASB).

As Jesus describes a believer's response to extreme persecution, we are given a critical principle about hearing God's voice: we don't get to decide what we say or how we respond.

One of the greatest blockage points when it comes to hearing God's voice is the desire to protect ourselves. We are willing to hear God as long as we have a chance to approve what He is saying, but that's not how His voice works. He is a completely separate individual from us, and He has real feelings, thoughts, and truths that He wants to speak. Oftentimes, hearing His voice clearly is the result of trusting His words before we hear them.

> The ***secret*** of the Lord is for those who fear Him, and He will make them know His covenant (Psalm 25:14 NASB).

The word *secret* in this verse can also be translated as "counsel or intimacy." The key to hearing intimately from God is to value His voice so much that we say "yes" before He even speaks.

With this level of trust also comes a fearlessness in life. We can know beyond any doubt that, even if God does not choose to give us a word of knowledge or a word of prophecy, at the very least He has always promised to give us wisdom when we ask.

> But if any of you lacks wisdom, let him ask of God, who gives to all generously and without reproach, and it will be given to him. But he must ask in faith without any doubting, for the one who doubts is like the surf of the sea, driven and tossed by the wind (James 1:5-6 NASB).

What James is describing is one step away from prophecy or a word of knowledge. Do you believe the God of the universe wants to lead you? He does. James 1 says He does. This is the next step in learning to walk in the Spirit, knowing by faith that God desires to speak to us daily. We see both this surrender and expectation in the story of Joseph as he stands before Pharaoh:

> Joseph then answered Pharaoh, saying, "It has nothing to do with me; God will give Pharaoh an answer for his own good" (Genesis 41:16 NASB).

Joseph first surrenders his mouth. He attempts to hold no sway over what God says through him, even though he knows that the results could be fatal if the word is undesirable to Pharaoh. He also decides not to take any credit. Then he promises Pharaoh a word from God even though God hasn't spoken yet. I would call that gutsy. Yet, Joseph trusted in God's good character and nature so much that he had faith that the Spirit of God wanted to speak to him.

> Then Pharaoh said to his servants, "Can we find a man like this, in whom there is a divine spirit?" (Genesis 41:38 NASB)

The answer to Pharaoh's question today is: people like that are all over the place. Every New Covenant believer has the Holy Spirit living inside them; and as we discussed earlier in this book, 1 Corinthians 2 tells us that the Holy Spirit speaks to us the very thoughts of God. You can expect God to speak to you the same way Joseph did. You have the same Spirit of God he had, except that you have *more* of Him!

The Rhema Word

The secret knowledge of God is found in the *rhema* word, which has been made available to every believer. Some might say,

"The secret knowledge is found within the Bible, and you have to study to find it." That is true. However, even the Pharisees' studies of the Scripture left them with no real knowledge of who God was. They studied and found nothing because they were not in tune with the heart of the Father, so they received no help from the Holy Spirit.

> But know this first of all, that no prophecy of Scripture becomes a matter of someone's own interpretation, for no prophecy was ever made by an act of human will, but men moved by the Holy Spirit spoke from God (2 Peter 1:20-21 NASB).

We cannot grasp even the basic truths of Scripture without the help of the Holy Spirit. His voice becomes the *rhema* word, literally meaning *an utterance*, that helps explain the points of the written Word to us. Without Him, we misinterpret or twist what we read. Without His help, we also misapply the Word of God to our everyday life. The utterances of the Spirit are there to direct our steps as we live our lives submitted to His will.

> Your ears will hear a word behind you, saying, "This is the way, walk in it," whenever you turn to the right or to the left (Isaiah 30:21 NASB).

Here is what I truly believe the Holy Spirit wants to do right now in this chapter. I believe He wants to begin to reveal to your heart any and every lie that has stood in the way of you hearing His voice more clearly. As you continue reading, I encourage you to ask the Father to show you what it is that you believe about hearing His voice that is inaccurate, untrue, or simply a hinderance.

You Can Hear His Voice

The voice of God is not for someone else. It's for you. It's for the entire body. The Word calls Jesus the head of the body (see Colossians 2:19); and the head, the brain, tells all the other members of the body what to do. Jesus wants to speak to you just as much as He desires to speak to an important minister or someone in a specific role.

Some people look at verses like the following and assume that God reserves His *rhema* word for those who are holy enough:

> But in the days of the voice of the seventh angel, when he is about to sound, then the mystery of God is finished, as He announced to ***His servants*** the ***prophets*** (Revelation 10:7 NASB).

We see the word *prophets* and think those are the truly anointed people whom God desires to speak to, yet we miss the word *servants* while reading. God is willing to speak to all His people, and the point of prophecy is to be of service to the body of Christ. That's why, though God does speak to prophets in more defined ways, He also speaks to all believers. It's because all believers are in relationship with Him and all are meant to serve the body.

> Now I wish that you all spoke in tongues, but rather that you would prophesy; and greater is the one who prophesies than the one who speaks in tongues, unless he interprets, so that the church may receive edification (1 Corinthians 14:5 NASB).

The New Testament prophets and apostles served specific functions during the founding of the New Covenant church and the writing of the final pages of Scripture; however, that same function, built upon a foundation already laid, is echoed today through each individual member of the body. We see Paul describe this founding period in Ephesians 3:4-5 (NASB):

> By referring to this, when you read you can understand my insight into the mystery of Christ, which in other generations was not made known to mankind, as it has now been revealed to His holy apostles and prophets in the Spirit.

In Ephesians 3:10 (NASB), we also see the continuation of this work; yet now, Paul tells us that the work has been passed on to the church itself:

> So that the multifaceted wisdom of God might now be made known through the church to the rulers and the authorities in the heavenly places.

When you look at prophecy as a gift meant to give out to those who need the help of the Lord, it stops being impossible to reach and becomes very accessible. The wisdom and knowledge of God are not reserved for the elite. They are meant for you and me too. God calls us to build up the body of Christ—to function in unity as a well-oiled machine—and of course, He gives us the tools we need to do that!

We see this same principle echoed through the narrative of the whole Bible, especially within Isaiah 43 and 44.

God Speaks Through His Witnesses

The basic point of every believer's life is to be a witness. We are meant to proclaim the truth of the gospel to the world—to shine the light of Christ into the darkness. This means the

Kingdom of God is working in us, and through us it invades the kingdom of Babylon. Isaiah clarifies this in his writings:

> "You are My witnesses," declares the Lord, "and My servant whom I have chosen, so that you may know and believe Me and understand that I am He" (Isaiah 43:10 NASB).
>
> Do not tremble and do not be afraid; have I not long since announced it to you and declared it? And you are My witnesses. Is there any God besides Me, or is there any other Rock? I know of none (Isaiah 44:8 NASB).

Living a life of hearing God's voice and following after Him means first building our life upon the solid foundation, the work of Jesus Christ. It also means allowing the great commission to pervade our purpose. We hear from God, not just for our own sakes, but to become vessels or carriers of His Word to the world. God is faithful to fulfill His Word, even in these last days.

> This is what the Lord your Redeemer, the Holy One of Israel says: "For your sake I have sent to Babylon, and will bring them all down as fugitives, even the Chaldeans, into the ships over which they rejoice" (Isaiah 43:14 NASB).
>
> Causing the omens of diviners to fail, making fools of fortune-tellers; causing wise men to turn back and making their knowledge ridiculous, confirming the word of His servant and carrying out the purpose of His messengers… (Isaiah 44:25-26 NASB).

All of the dark schemes and systems of the devil will eventually be overcome by the Lord of lords and King of kings. The glory of Jesus will shine out around the world, and the full truth will be known by all. For now, that glory is seen and heard in us, His witnesses, as we invade Babylon with the light of Jesus Christ.

> Shout for joy, you heavens, for the Lord has done it! Shout joyfully, you lower parts of the earth; break into a shout of jubilation, you mountains, forest, and every tree in it; for the Lord has redeemed Jacob, and in Israel He shows His glory (Isaiah 44:23 NASB).

* * *

Fill me with Your Spirit today, Father. Speak Your words to my heart. Give me the confidence I need in You to speak out the words of life—to speak the truth in love—to be a vessel supernaturally through which You bring life back to a dying world. In Jesus's name, amen.

ENDNOTES

1 "Ancient Mesopotamia, Famous Rulers of Mesopotamia"; *Ducksters;* https://www.ducksters.com/history/mesopotamia/famous_rulers_of_ancient_mesopotamia.php; accessed May 31, 2025.

2 "Epic of Gilgamesh"; https://en.wikipedia.org/wiki/Epic_of_Gilgamesh; accessed May 31, 2025.

3 Ibid.

4 "Utnapishtim"; https://en.wikipedia.org/wiki/Utnapishtim; accessed May 31, 2025.

5 "Uruk"; https://en.wikipedia.org/wiki/Uruk; accessed May 31, 2025.

6 Ea, (Mesopotamian mythology," *Britannica;* https://www.britannica.com/topic/Ea; accessed May 31, 2025.

7 "The Epic of Gilgamesh," *SparkNotes;* https://www.sparknotes.com/lit/gilgamesh/summary/; May 31, 2025.

8 "Babylon," *Britannica;* https://www.britannica.com/place/Babylon-ancient-city-Mesopotamia-Asia; accessed May 31, 2025.

9 Ibid.

10 "Mesopotamia: Overview and Summary Of An Ancient Civilization," *HistoryOnTheNet;* https://www.historyonthenet.com/mesopotamia; accessed May 31, 2025.

11 https://www.historyonthenet.com/mesopotamia; accessed May 31, 2025.

12 https://www.ducksters.com/history/mesopotamia/famous_rulers_of_ancient_mesopotamia.php; accessed May 31, 2025.

13 https://www.britannica.com/place/Babylonia; accessed May 31, 2025.

14 Ibid.

15 Ibid.

16 Michael Heiser, *The Unseen Realm* (Lexham Press, 2015), 108.

17 Ibid.

18 Ibid.

19 "Who was Nimrod in the Bible," *Got Questions;* https://www.gotquestions.org/Nimrod-in-the-Bible.html; accessed May 31, 2025.

20 Ibid.

21 *The Encyclopedia of Christian Civilization,* First Edition, Ed. George Thomas Kurian (Blackwell Publishing Ltd. 2011).

22 Ibid.

23 Michael Heiser, *The Unseen Realm.*

24 Ibid., 84-85.

25 "Old Testament Timeline," *BibleStudy.com;* https://www.biblestudy.org/beginner/timelineot.html; accessed June 2, 2025.

26 "Babylonian captivity," *Wikipedia.com;* https://en.wikipedia.org/wiki/Babylonian_captivity; accessed June 2, 2025.

27 "Babylonia," *Britannica.com;* https://www.britannica.com/place/Babylonia; accessed June 2, 2025.

28 Babylonian Temple Rituals; https://www.asor.org/anetoday/2019/07/What-Rituals-Inside-Late-Babylonian-Temples

29 "Ishtar Gate," *Wikipedia.org;* https://en.wikipedia.org/wiki/Ishtar_Gate; accessed June 2, 2025.

30 "The Babylonia Code," *History.com;* https://www.history.com/topics/ancient-middle-east/babylon; accessed June 2, 2025.

31 "Ishtar Gate," *Wikipedia.org;* https://en.wikipedia.org/wiki/Ishtar_Gate; accessed June, 2, 2025.
32 Denis O'Callaghan, "What Sorts of Rituals Really Went on Inside Late Babylonian Temples?" *Linkedin.com;* https://www.linkedin.com/pulse/what-sorts-rituals-really-went-inside-late-babylonian-denis; accessed August 25, 2025.
33 "The Babylonia Code," *History.com;* https://www.history.com/topics/ancient-middle-east/babylon; accessed June 2, 2025.
34 Michael Seymour, "Babylon, Assyrian Rule and Fitting in with the Religion," *The Met; Metmuseum.org,* June 1, 2016; https://www.metmuseum.org/toah/hd/babl/hd_babl.htm; accessed June 2, 2025.
35 E. Frahm, "A Short History of Babylonian and Assyrian Text Commentaries," *Cuneiform Commentaries Project;* https://ccp.yale.edu/introduction/history-mesopotamian-text-commentaries. DOI: 10079/zcrjdtq; accessed August 25.
36 "Sacred Prostitution," *Wikipedia.com;* https://en.wikipedia.org/wiki/Sacred_prostitution#External_links; accessed June 2, 2025.
37 "Daily Life of Babylon (Culture)," History.com; https://www.history.com/news/daily-life-ancient-babylon-mesopotamia; accessed June 2, 2025.
38 "Daily Life of Babylon (Culture)," *History.com;* https://www.history.com/news/daily-life-ancient-babylon-mesopotamia; accessed June 2, 2025.
39 "Ezekiel 13:2," *BibleHub.com;* https://biblehub.com/text/ezekiel/13-2.htm; accessed June 2, 2025.
40 "Pyramids," *NOVA, PBS Online;* https://www.pbs.org/wgbh/nova/pyramid/explore/age2.html; accessed June 2, 2025.

41 David Shedden, "Today in Media History: The Internet began with a crash on October 29, 1969," *Poynter.org,* October 29, 2014; https://www.poynter.org/reporting-editing/2014/today-in-media-history-the-internet-began-with-a-crash-on-october-29-1969/; accessed June 6, 2025.

42 Oliver Burkeman, "Forty years of the internet: how the world changed for ever," *The Guardian,* October 23, 2009; https://www.theguardian.com/technology/2009/oct/23/internet-40-history-arpanet; accessed June 6, 2025.

43 "Delivery of the First IMP to UCLA – September 1969; *The History of Computer Communications;* https://historyofcomputercommunications.info/section/6.3/Delivery-of-the-First-IMP-to-UCLA-September-1969/; accessed June 6, 2025.

44 "Imp," *Wikipedia.com;* https://en.wikipedia.org/wiki/Imp; accessed June 6, 2025.

45 "Interface Message Processor," *Wikipedia.com;* https://en.wikipedia.org/wiki/Interface_Message_Processor; accessed June 6, 2025.

46 Oliver Burkeman, "Forty years of the internet: how the world changed for ever," *The Guardian,* October 23, 2009; https://www.theguardian.com/technology/2009/oct/23/internet-40-history-arpanet; accessed June 6, 2025.

47 CERN; https://home.cern/; accessed June 6, 2025.

48 "Largest particle accelerator," *Guinness World Records;* https://www.guinnessworldrecords.com/world-records/largest-particle-accelerator; accessed June 6, 2025.

49 "The Higgs boson," *CERN;* https://home.cern/science/physics/higgs-boson; accessed June 6, 2025.

50 "First Email," *Guinness World Records;* https://www.guinnessworldrecords.com/world-records/first-email; accessed June 6, 2025.

51 Michael Heiser, *The Unseen Realm.*
52 "Tower of Babel Stele," *The Schoyen Collection;* https://www.schoyencollection.com/history-collection-introduction/babylonian-history-collection/tower-babel-stele-ms-2063; accessed June 6, 2025.
53 Daisy Hernandez, "The 50 Greatest Moments in Internet History," *Popular Mechanics,* October 31, 2019; https://www.popularmechanics.com/culture/web/g29622347/greatest-moments-internet-history/; accessed June 6, 2025.
54 Daisy Hernandez, "The 50 Greatest Moments in Internet History," *Popular Mechanics,* October 31, 2019; https://www.popularmechanics.com/culture/web/g29622347/greatest-moments-internet-history/; accessed June 6, 2025.
55 Rebecca Hersher, "Meet Mafiaboy, The 'Bratty Kid' Who Took Down The Internet," *NPR,* February 7, 2015; https://www.npr.org/sections/alltechconsidered/2015/02/07/384567322/meet-mafiaboy-the-bratty-kid-who-took-down-the-internet; accessed June 6, 2025.
56 "Attacks on Jerusalem Timeline," *BibleStudy.org;* https://www.biblestudy.org/maps/attacks-on-jerusalem-timeline.html; accessed June 7, 2025.
57 Dave Roos, "What Was Life Like in Ancient Babylon?" *History.com,* May 28, 2025; https://www.history.com/news/daily-life-ancient-babylon-mesopotamia; accessed June 7, 2025.
58 Terry Hartle, "'Dominion' tracks the influence of Christianity across centuries," *Christian Science Monitor,* March 17, 2020; https://www.csmonitor.com/Books/Book-Reviews/2020/0317/Dominion-tracks-the-influence-of-Christianity-across-centuries

59 Daisy Hernandez; https://www.popularmechanics.com/culture/web/g29622347/greatest-moments-internet-history; accessed June 7, 2025.

60 Daisy Hernandez; https://www.popularmechanics.com/culture/web/g29622347/greatest-moments-internet-history; accessed June 7, 2025.

61 Alan Hall, "The Internet is Killing My Business!" *Forbes,* December 31, 2012; https://www.forbes.com/sites/alanhall/2012/12/30/the-internet-is-killing-my-business/?sh=35cf286b1273; accessed June 7, 2025.

62 YEC, "What Marketers Can Learn From The Ancient Babylonians," *Forbes,* March 22, 2019; https://www.forbes.com/sites/theyec/2019/03/22/what-marketers-can-learn-from-the-ancient-babylonians/?sh=67cf95dd12c9; accessed June 7, 2025.

63 Nancy Jo Sales, "Online Dating Apps Are Actually Kind of a Disaster," *Wired,* May 18, 2021; https://www.wired.com/story/online-dating-apps-are-a-disaster; accessed June 7, 2025.

64 Nancy Jo Sales, "Online Dating Apps Are Actually Kind of a Disaster," Wired, May 18, 2021; https://www.wired.com/story/online-dating-apps-are-a-disaster; accessed June 7, 2025.

65 *The Histories of Herodotus, A Translation by A.D. Godley* (Harvard Press/Scribes, 2018).

66 https://en.wikipedia.org/wiki/Ishtar_Gate.

67 "From Fragment to Monument The Ishtar Gate in Berlin," *Pergamonmuseum;* https://www.smb.museum/en/exhibitions/detail/from-fragment-to-monument/; accessed June 7, 2025.

68 Anna Haines, "From 'Instagram Face' To 'Snapchat Dysmorphia': How Beauty Filters Are Changing The Way

We See Ourselves," *Forbes,* December 10, 2021; https://www.forbes.com/sites/annahaines/2021/04/27/from-instagram-face-to-snapchat-dysmorphia-how-beauty-filters-are-changing-the-way-we-see-ourselves/?sh=74f91a7c4eff; accessed June 7, 2025.

69 "Babylonian Fashion," Bibliotheca Exotica, *Medium,* July 17, 2023; https://bibliotheca-exotica.medium.com/babylonian-fashion-2fcc4f33c866; accessed June 7, 2025.

70 Michael D. Coogan, *A Brief Introduction to the Old Testament: the Hebrew Bible in its Context* (Oxford University Press, 2008).

71 *Epic of Gilgamesh;* https://en.wikipedia.org/wiki/Epic_of_Gilgamesh.

72 Upworthy staff, "3,700-year-old Babylonian stone tablet gets translated, changes history," *UpWorthy.com,* July 10, 2021; https://www.upworthy.com/amp/3700-year-old-babylonian-stone-tablet-gets-translated-changes-history-rp5-2653733786; accessed June 7, 2025.

73 "Hyperlink," *Wikipedia;* https://en.wikipedia.org/wiki/Hyperlink; accessed June 7, 2025.

74 "The Talmud," *BBC,* August 13, 2009; https://www.bbc.co.uk/religion/religions/judaism/texts/talmud.shtml; accessed June 7, 2025.

75 "Talmud," *Wikipedia;* https://en.wikipedia.org/wiki/Talmud; accessed June 7, 2025.

76 "Talmud as Hypertext," *Contra;* https://kairos.technorhetoric.net/3.1/coverweb/porush/contra4.html; accessed June 7, 2025.

77 Ibid.

78 Tom Holland, *Dominion* (Abacus, 2020).

79 "Irish Treasures: The Ardagh Chalice," *Claddagh Design,* May 8, 2014; https://www.claddaghdesign.com/history/

irish-treasures-ardagh-chalice/; accessed June 9, 2025.

80 Rachel Levy, "Musk's Neuralink faces federal inquiry after killing 1,500 animals in testing," *The Guardian*, December 5, 2022; https://www.theguardian.com/technology/2022/dec/05/neuralink-animal-testing-elon-musk-investigation; accessed June 9, 2025.

81 Dhruv Mehrotra and Dell Cameron, "The Gruesome Story of How Neuralink's Monkeys Actually Died," *Wired*, September 28, 2023; https://www.wired.com/story/elon-musk-pcrm-neuralink-monkey-deaths/; accessed June 9, 2025.

82 "Binary code," *Wikipedia;* https://en.wikipedia.org/wiki/Binary_code; accessed June 9, 2025.

83 Peter Leithart, "What's Going on with Ezekiel's Vision?" *The Gospel Coalition*, August 29, 2020; https://www.thegospelcoalition.org/article/ezekiel-vision; accessed June 9, 2025.

ABOUT THE AUTHOR

Troy Black was born in 1989 and grew up in East Texas in a large family. He attended John Brown University where he had an encounter with the Holy Spirit that forever changed his life. After college, Troy moved to Dallas, Texas, where he worked for The Urban Alternative, The National Broadcast Ministry of Dr. Tony Evans, as a website developer.

After moving to South Texas, Troy married his wife, Leslie, and together they published his first book, *My Mess.* Since then, Troy has published several other books and produced hundreds of videos. Troy and Leslie have five children: Mirabelle, Iona, Lauralee, Julian, and Hallie. They currently reside in East Texas.

Troy is a Christian YouTuber, author, and prophetic voice. His ministry and life are led by two simple goals—to be obedient to the Holy Spirit and to get the gospel of Jesus Christ in front of as many people as possible.

CONNECT WITH TROY

TroyBlackVideos.com
Facebook.com/AuthorTroyBlack

Troy's Books
Links to Troy's books are available on Amazon.com
Direct links can be found on TroyBlackVideos.com

Book Troy to Speak
You can contact Troy to speak on the booking form
on TroyBlackVideos.com.

TroyBlackVideos.com
troyblackvideos.com

Facebook
facebook.com/AuthorTroyBlack

Patreon
patreon.com/troyblack

Give
troyblackvideos.com/impact/support-this-ministry

Instagram
instagram.com/authortroyblack

X
x.com/AuthorTroyBlack

In the Right Hands, This Book Will Change Lives!

Most of the people who need this message will not be looking for this book. To change their lives, you need to **put a copy of this book in their hands.**

Our ministry is constantly seeking methods to find the people who need this anointed message to change their lives. **Will you help us reach these people?**

Extend this ministry by sowing three, five, ten, or *even more* books today and change people's lives for the better! Your generosity will be part of catalyzing the Great Awakening that many have been prophesying and praying for.

YOUR *Prophetic* COMMUNITY

Sign up for a **FREE** subscription to the Destiny Image digital magazine and get awesome content delivered directly to your inbox!

destinyimage.com/signup

Sign up for Cutting-Edge Messages that Supernaturally Empower You

- Gain valuable insights and guidance based on biblical principles
- Deepen your faith and understanding of God's plan for your life
- Receive regular updates and prophetic messages
- Connect with a community of believers who share your values and beliefs

Experience Fresh Video Content that Reveals Your Prophetic Inheritance

- Receive prophetic messages and insights
- Connect with a powerful tool for spiritual growth and development
- Stay connected and inspired on your faith journey

Listen to Powerful Podcasts that Propel You into God's Presence Every Day

- Deepen your understanding of God's prophetic assignment
- Experience God's revival power throughout your day
- Learn how to grow spiritually in your walk with God

Check out
our **Destiny Image**
bestsellers page at
destinyimage.com/bestsellers
for cutting-edge,
prophetic messages
that will supernaturally
empower you and the
body of Christ.

From

Troy A. Brewer

Decode the Divine Secrets Hidden in Plain Sight

Have you ever noticed the same numbers showing up again and again—on clocks, receipts, or even your birthday—and wondered if God was trying to tell you something?

You're not imagining things. God *is* speaking—and numbers are one of His languages.

For over thirty years, Pastor Troy Brewer's landmark book *Numbers That Preach* has opened the eyes of believers around the world to the prophetic patterns encoded in Scripture. Now, in this fully updated and expanded Third Edition, Brewer goes even deeper—unveiling new insights drawn from decades of study, current events, and modern mysteries that prove: the numbers still preach, and the story isn't over.

Through decades of ministry and prophetic revelation, bestselling author Troy Brewer has uncovered how God uses numbers throughout Scripture—and even history itself—as a hidden code to reveal His heart, His timing, and His plans. This edition is the next chapter in God's unfolding numerical prophecy.

Whether you're a first-time reader or a longtime student, this third edition will reignite your passion to hear God more clearly and understand His prophetic timeline with fresh faith.

Purchase your copy wherever books are sold

From

Alan DiDio

Decode the Rapture. Discern the Signs. Embrace Your End-Time Assignment.

Are you confused, frightened, or indifferent toward end times teachings about the rapture?

You're not alone.

The end-time teaching of the *rapture* has sparked controversy, misunderstandings, and debates among Christians. Some misrepresent it as an excuse to disengage from worldly affairs and await heavenly rescue. Others mock it as escapist theology, reject it outright, or live blissfully ignorant of the glory and crisis that will unfold on earth in the last days.

Alan DiDio, pastor, influential podcaster, and seasoned end times teacher, exposes false teachings and misinterpretations about the rapture, reconnecting you to a life of purpose, meaning, and Kingdom impact in these last days.

Through clear teachings and profound truths, you'll discover how to:

- **Discern prophetic signs of the times** pointing to the coming rapture.
- **Live every day** fueled by a clear sense of purpose and meaning.
- **Avoid being caught off guard** by prophecies being fulfilled around you.
- **"Occupy" your sphere of influence** by living as a representative of the Kingdom until Jesus returns.

The world may be caught off guard by the return of Jesus, but you are called to discern the times and seasons. Open your eyes to the reality of Jesus' imminent return and live every single day filled with a sense of divine purpose and Kingdom assignment!

Purchase your copy wherever books are sold.

From
Alan DiDio

Confront Satan's End-Time Deceptions Head-On!

In this era of unparalleled technological advances, artificial intelligence reshapes our world and UFOs are found daily in the headlines. Believers are faced with urgent, soul-stirring questions: Is there a trace of AI in biblical prophecy? Could the antichrist manipulate this technology to dominate our era? Does the Bible talk about aliens? Above all, how should the Church, armed with ancient wisdom, respond to this modern revolution?

Asking these same questions, Alan DiDio, a formidable apostolic and prophetic leader and the dynamic force behind the Encounter Today YouTube channel, embarked on a quest for truth. Through extensive research and revelatory interviews, he brings to light a balanced narrative, juxtaposing the potential of AI against the unchanging truths of biblical prophecies and the unfolding of global events.

Armed with this prophetic insight, you are called to rise, unshakable in your crucial end-time role. It's time to seize your destiny and light the way in this revolutionary age!

Purchase your copy wherever books are sold.

From

JOSEPH Z

Deploying God's Angelic Army

In the realm of the spirit, invisible forces contend over the will of God for your life, but you are not alone in this fight. Warrior angels—servants of fire—have been sent to minister to you as an heir of salvation.

Joseph Z, Bible teacher and prophetic seer, reveals the role of God's angelic warriors who carry out the Word of God on your behalf.

Servants of Fire delivers sound biblical instruction to unveil the realm of the spirit and bring to pass the will, plans, and purposes of God on the earth.

Understand how to partner with these servants of fire so you can experience the maximum impact of a victorious life in God!

Purchase your copy wherever books are sold